CCEA A2
DIGITAL TECHNOLOGY

COLOURPOINT EDUCATIONAL

© 2024 Patrick G Daniels and Colourpoint Creative Ltd

Print ISBN: 978 1 78073 390 6
eBook ISBN: 978 1 78073 391 3

First Edition
First Impression 2024

Layout and design: April Sky Design

Note: The author availed of AI while carrying out research for this book.

All rights reserved. No part of this publication may be reproduced, stored in a retrieval system or transmitted in any form or by any means, electronic, mechanical, photocopying, scanning, recording or otherwise, without the prior written permission of the copyright owners and publisher of this book.

Copyright

Copyright has been acknowledged to the best of our ability. If there are any inadvertent errors or omissions, we shall be happy to correct them in any future editions.

All diagrams are ©Colourpoint Creative Ltd. Front cover image and all internal photographs not listed below are ©iStockphoto.

Pages 6, 7	©Wesley Johnston
Page 72	Public domain
Page 80	©Actron
Page 94	©NASA

Screenshots contain proprietary software from Microsoft and Parallels.

Colourpoint Educational

An imprint of Colourpoint Creative Ltd
Colourpoint House
Jubilee Business Park
Jubilee Road
Newtownards
County Down
Northern Ireland
BT23 4YH

Tel: 028 9182 6339
E-mail: sales@colourpoint.co.uk
Website: www.colourpoint.co.uk

The Author

Patrick G Daniels has a degree in Software Engineering and a PhD in computer science, specialising in visual programming languages. He currently lives in Belfast with his wife and children.

Publisher's Note: This book has been through a rigorous quality assurance process by an independent person experienced in the CCEA specification prior to publication. It has been written to help students preparing for the A2 Digital Technology specification from CCEA. While Colourpoint Educational, the authors and the quality assurance person have taken every care in its production, we are not able to guarantee that the book is completely error-free. Additionally, while the book has been written to address the CCEA specification, it is the responsibility of each candidate to satisfy themselves that they have fully met the requirements of the CCEA specification prior to sitting an exam set by that body. For this reason, and because specifications and CCEA advice change with time, we strongly advise every candidate to avail of a qualified teacher and to check the contents of the most recent specification for themselves prior to the exam. Colourpoint Creative Ltd therefore cannot be held responsible for any errors or omissions in this book or any consequences thereof.

The answers to the questions in this book are available online in PDF format. Visit www.colourpointeducational.com, and search for this book. On the page for the book you will find details of how to download the answers. If you have any problems, please contact Colourpoint.

CONTENTS

UNIT A2 1
Information Systems

1 Networks 5
2 Protocols 17
3 Transmission Media 29
4 Error Correction and Detection 35
5 Relational Databases 39
6 Optimising Databases 48
7 Using Databases 59
8 Artificial Intelligence 69
9 Expert Systems 75
10 Natural Language and Voice Recognition 83
11 Robotics 90
12 Mobile Technologies 98
13 Data Mining 104
14 Cloud Computing 112
15 Legislation 120
16 Ethical Considerations 127

UNIT A2 1
Information Systems

CHAPTER 1
Networks

> **By the end of this chapter students should be able to:**
> - describe networks by their scope: local area network (LAN), metropolitan area network (MAN) and wide area network (WAN);
> - describe the purpose of the network resources: network card, server, switched hub, repeater, wireless access point, media converter, IP address and media access control (MAC) address;
> - define the purpose of an IP address and a MAC address;
> - describe the features of a peer-to-peer (P2P) and server-based networks;
> - evaluate the bus, star and ring network topologies.

1.1 Introduction

In the modern world, virtually all computer systems utilise computer **networks**. Computer networks are the foundation of modern communications. Similar to a network of roads connecting cities, computer networks establish pathways between different devices for a huge range of reasons, for example data transmission between devices, facilitating internet access, media streaming and global communication.

In this chapter we will first consider computer networks by their scope – from **local area networks** (LANs) that operate on a small scale to **wide area networks** (WANs) spanning extensive geographic distances. We will then consider the purpose of each type of network and how each facilitates efficient communication and resource sharing.

A wide range of resources are shared within computer networks, from printers and files to databases and devices that provide internet connectivity. Each of these resources will be considered in turn and their purpose explained.

Accurate data transmission in a network requires accurate device identification. The chapter will explore unique identifiers called IP and MAC addresses. The purpose and advantage of both types of addresses is considered.

There are two prominent network models – **peer-to-peer** and **server-based** – which shape communication and resource sharing. Peer-to-peer networks enable direct device interaction without relying on a central server, while server-based networks centralise resources for efficient management. The benefits and applications of each model will be examined.

Finally, the chapter will consider network topologies, the physical and logical arrangements of devices within a network. We will look at three topologies – bus, star and ring – and the pros and cons of each.

1.2 Scope of Networks

The term **scope** refers to the size, or geographical extent, of something.

For example, a road network can be considered in a range of scopes, depending on what purpose it has to serve.

The road network within the grounds of a hospital, such as Altnagelvin, has a relatively small scope, as it is designed to facilitate the movement of patients and staff within the confines of the site.

The road network of a city such as Belfast has a larger scope and is intended to facilitate transport of people and goods throughout an entire metropolitan area.

The road network of the island of Ireland, by contrast, has a large scope covering tens of thousands of square kilometres. It is intended to form the backbone of the economy of the island, carrying people and goods over long geographical distances.

In a similar way, computer networks have a range of scopes, depending on their different needs. For example, a computer network intended to allow everyone in an office to use a single printer has a very different scope from one designed to connect a series of seismometers around the Pacific Ocean to an earthquake warning centre.

Understanding the scope of a network is crucial in determining not only functionality and use; it also allows a systems developer to determine the most appropriate solution for a given problem. In this section, we will look at the distinct characteristics of **local area networks** (LANs), **metropolitan area networks** (MANs) and **wide area networks** (WANs).

Local area network

A local area network, or LAN, is a network that spans a limited geographical area, typically confined to a single building, office or campus. LANs are commonly deployed within homes, schools, businesses and small organisations. Their primary purpose is to facilitate efficient communication and resource sharing among devices that are in close proximity. Key characteristics of LANs are:

- **Small scope**: LANs cover a relatively small area, such as a home, office floor or building. They typically span distances measured in metres, but never more than a few kilometres, ensuring localised connectivity.
- **High speeds**: LANs generally have high-speed data transmission rates, because they can utilise Ethernet cables, fibre-optic cables or wireless technologies like Wi-Fi.
- **Privately managed**: LANs are privately owned and managed by the organisation or individual that deploys them. This allows for greater control over security, network policies and resource allocation within the confined environment.
- **Facilitates resource sharing**: LANs enable efficient resource sharing among connected devices. This includes shared access to printers, files, databases and other network resources, fostering collaboration and productivity.

Metropolitan area network

A metropolitan area network, or MAN, covers a larger geographical area, typically encompassing a city or metropolitan region. MANs provide connectivity between multiple LANs within the same locality, allowing for efficient data transmission and communication between them. Key characteristics of MANs are:

- **Intermediate scope**: MANs extend the reach of connectivity to cover a larger area than a LAN, often spanning across a city or metropolitan region. This broader coverage facilitates interconnectivity among different organisations, campuses or institutions on different sites.
- **Interconnectivity**: MANs interconnect multiple LANs within the same locality, enabling seamless communication and resource sharing between various entities. This facilitates collaboration, data exchange and efficient information flow between different groups of users.
- **Service providers**: MANs are often facilitated by telecommunication companies or service providers that offer connectivity solutions to organisations and institutions. These providers ensure reliable and high-performance network infrastructure to support the interconnected LANs.
- **High bandwidth**: MANs provide substantial bandwidth to support the data transmission requirements of interconnected LANs. They offer enhanced speed and capacity compared to individual LANs, ensuring efficient communication across a larger area.

CHAPTER 1 – NETWORKS

Case Study

Belfast Traffic Information and Control Centre

The Belfast Traffic Information and Control Centre (TICC) is at the core of a metropolitan area network (MAN) that effectively manages and optimises traffic flow within the city. It was first deployed in 1981, one of the first in the UK, and has since been updated and expanded as technology has advanced.

The MAN behind the Belfast TICC ensures seamless communication between hundreds of sensors, cameras and traffic signals strategically deployed throughout the city. These are connected to the centralised control centre located next to the Sydenham Bypass, where human operators can monitor the traffic network, while the computer system continually adjusts signal timings in response to road traffic collisions, congestion and weather. In recent years, many of the camera feeds that are part of the TICC have been made available on the internet to allow drivers to see road conditions for themselves in real time.

The impact of the Belfast TICC has been transformative. While it cannot eliminate congestion it can, by dynamically monitoring and adjusting traffic signal timings, reduce congestion where possible, minimise travel times and enhance overall traffic efficiency. It enables better traffic management, particularly during peak hours and special events, resulting in smoother traffic flow and improved safety for road users.

The impact of the TICC is most obvious on the rare occasions when the MAN suffers a network outage, and the traffic signals lose access to the central computer. When this happens, the traffic signals are designed to revert to built-in default timings that cannot take account of current conditions, and traffic congestion rapidly spreads across the city.

By leveraging the MAN, the system can respond in real time to events as they occur. For example, the system can progressively reduce the speed limit on major roads, such as the M1 and Westlink as traffic builds in the rush hour, allowing vehicles to drive more closely together and hence increase road capacity. Similarly, if a road such as the M3 Lagan Bridge is becoming congested, the computer can briefly hold traffic on the onslips with a longer red light to allow it to clear. In recent years, the city's buses have been connected to the MAN so that they can, in certain cases, trigger traffic signals as they approach to give priority to public transport.

Overall, the Belfast TICC is an example of an effective network to manage and optimise traffic within a city. The MAN that connects the hundreds of separate devices across the region is critical to its success.

Wide area network

Wide area networks, or WANs, are the most extensive type of network, spanning vast geographical distances. They connect devices and networks separated by long distances, such as different cities, countries or continents. WANs are the backbone of modern global connectivity, enabling worldwide communication and information exchange. Key characteristics of WANs are:

- **Large scope**: WANs have the broadest coverage, traversing extensive geographical distances across continents and the world. They connect multiple MANs, LANs and remote devices, creating a seamless global network infrastructure.
- **Can be public or private**: WANs can be either publicly accessible or privately owned. Public WANs, such as the internet, facilitate global connectivity and information sharing. Private WANs are deployed by organisations to connect their geographically dispersed branches and offices.
- **Complex network infrastructure**: WANs rely on a complex infrastructure of interconnected routers, switches and other networking equipment to ensure reliable data transmission across long distances. They often utilise leased

lines, satellite links or internet-based virtual private networks (VPNs) to establish connectivity.
- **Higher latency and lower bandwidth**: Due to the vast distances involved, WANs may exhibit higher latency (time taken for data transmission) and lower bandwidth compared to LANs or MANs. However, advancements in technology have enabled WANs to achieve progressively higher speeds and lower latencies, supporting real-time applications, such as live streams and streaming services such as Netflix.

Note: While the internet is an example of a WAN, the two terms do not mean the same thing. There are many WANs in the world, including those used by multinational companies. The internet is simply the most well-known example of a WAN.

Task

Suggest the type of scope each of the following networks has, and why.

1. A network connecting together four campuses of a university within Northern Ireland;
2. A network in a house connecting a doorbell, smart lights and a smart heating system;
3. A network operated by an oil company to allow all its offices and oil production facilities across the world to communicate with each other;
4. The network of the Indian Ocean Tsunami Warning System that connects wave and seismic sensors placed around the Indian Ocean to a centralised computer system;
5. A network that allows every user in an office to connect to a shared server on which to store their data;
6. A network connecting all the libraries in Northern Ireland, allowing a librarian to see what books other libraries currently have in stock.

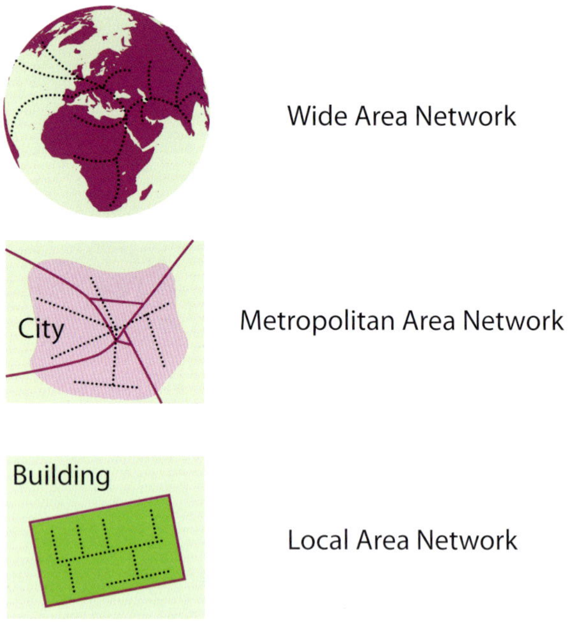

Figure 1.1: Comparison of the scope of LANs, MANs and WANs.

In summary, as shown in Figure 1.1, local area networks (LANs) facilitate communication and resource sharing within a limited geographical area, while metropolitan area networks (MANs) connect multiple LANs within a city or metropolitan region. Wide area networks (WANs) span across vast distances, providing global connectivity and enabling worldwide communication.

1.3 Network Resources

Network resources are the hardware and software components that enable computer networks to function. Network resources are essential for establishing reliable connections, managing network traffic and ensuring secure and efficient data transmission. The CCEA specification requires you to be able to describe the purpose of each of the following network resources.

Network card

A network card, also known as a network interface card (NIC) or network adapter, is a hardware component that enables a device to connect to a computer network. It acts as an interface between the device and the network, facilitating the transmission and receipt of data. Network cards come in various forms, including Ethernet cards and wireless cards, depending on the type of network technology used.

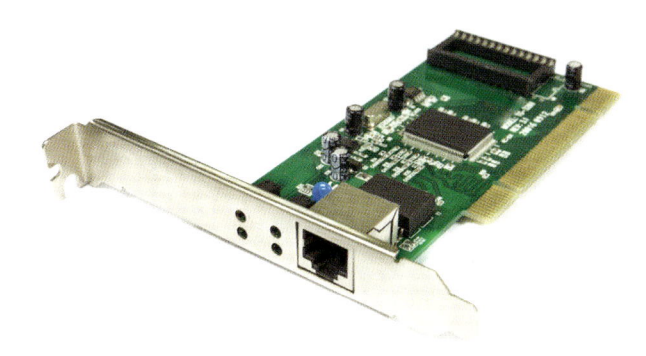

The purpose of a network card is to provide a device with the ability to send and receive data packets over the network. It does this by converting digital signals from the device into a format suitable for transmission across the network medium, such as an Ethernet cable or a wireless signal. Most network cards are identified on the network by a unique hardware address called a MAC address (see section 1.4).

Server

A server is a powerful computer or device that provides services, resources and data to other devices, known as clients, within a network. Servers are designed to handle multiple requests simultaneously and to deliver requested information or services efficiently. They act as centralised repositories of data, applications and other resources that can be accessed by network users.

The purpose of a server is to enable resource sharing, centralised data storage and efficient management of network services. File servers, for example, allow users to store and access files from a central location, promoting collaboration between team members and data consistency. Modern file servers usually incorporate additional functions, such as automated backups, remote file access and protection from cyber attacks. Application servers provide access to specific software applications or services over the network, allowing clients to use them without individual installations. Web servers host websites, making them accessible to users via the internet.

Note: Some servers are large devices, the size of a wardrobe or larger. However, modern servers typically used in offices can be quite small, often smaller than a shoe box.

Task

Imagine a team of six people working on a software project. What would be the possible consequences for the project if the team members did not have a server, and instead the data files had to be stored on each person's personal computer?

Switched hub

A switched hub, often referred to simply as a switch, is a network device that connects multiple devices within a local area network (LAN). It facilitates the exchange of data packets between devices on the same network by directing data to the intended recipient based on their MAC addresses. A typical switch has a dedicated Ethernet cable leading to each device on the network, as shown in Figure 1.2.

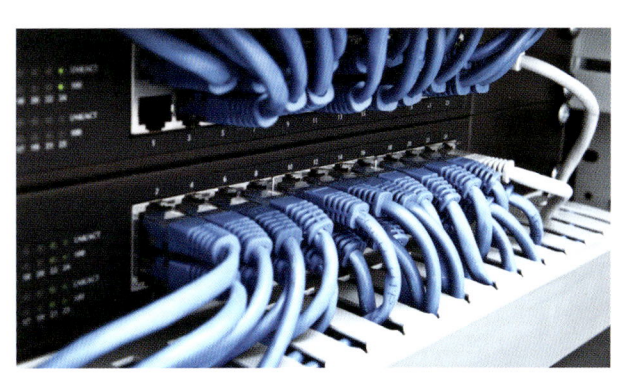

Older hubs simply forwarded all data to all devices on the network, and it was up to each device to determine whether or not the data was intended for them. However, a switched hub is designed to enhance network performance and efficiency by intelligently routing data only to the intended recipient. This reduces the amount of data traffic on the network, improving overall network speed. Switched hubs can cope with simultaneous data transmission taking place between multiple devices without interference.

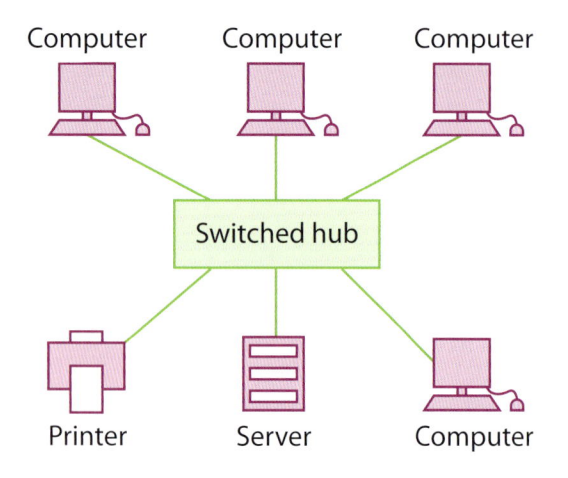

Figure 1.2: How a switched hub is connected to a network.

Wireless access point

A wireless access point (WAP) is a device that enables wireless connectivity within a network. It serves as a central hub for wireless communication, allowing devices equipped with wireless network cards to connect to the network. WAPs transmit and receive data wirelessly, eliminating the need for physical cables. They create a wireless local area network (WLAN) by providing a wireless connection between devices and the wired network infrastructure. WAPs are commonly deployed in public places such as restaurants, airports and universities, as well as in many private homes.

Wireless access points operate on specific radio frequencies and employ various wireless standards, such as Wi-Fi, to facilitate communication between devices. Data packets are converted into radio waves for transmission. They typically have a limited coverage area, known as the wireless coverage range, which can vary based on factors like the transmission power, antenna design and environmental conditions.

To ensure security, wireless access points employ encryption protocols, such as Wi-Fi Protected Access (there are three versions: WPA, WPA2 and WPA3), to encrypt data transmitted over the wireless network (Figure 1.3). Additionally, they may implement security measures like password authentication or network access control to restrict unauthorised access.

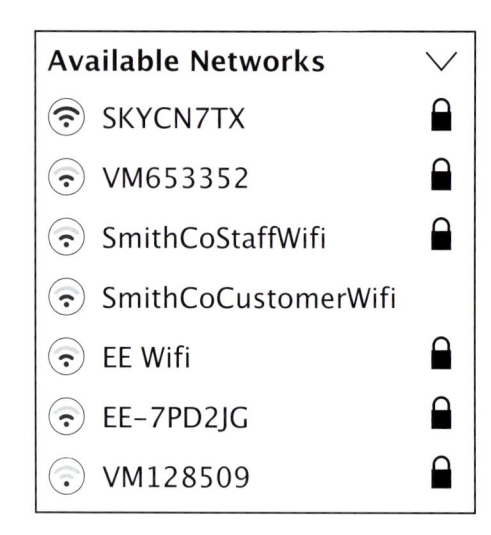

Figure 1.3: A typical list of available Wi-Fi networks. Wireless access points typically employ encryption protocols for security, indicated here by the padlock symbols. If a network is intended for public access, the password protection may be switched off.

In larger networks or areas with high-density user requirements, multiple access points may be deployed to provide seamless coverage and support a larger number of wireless devices. These access points are often connected to a central controller that manages their operation, coordinates wireless network settings and optimises performance.

Repeater

A repeater is a network device that extends the reach of a network (Figure 1.4). It is used in situations where the distance between devices exceeds the maximum transmission limits of the network medium, such as copper wire, fibre-optic cables or wireless signals. Electrical signals in copper wire lose strength over distances of hundreds of metres due to electrical resistance in the wire. Similarly, wireless signals lose strength the further they extend from the wireless access point, so in larger buildings repeaters are used to regenerate the signal and allow devices further away to connect to the network. The purpose of a repeater is to receive and then regenerate the original signal, allowing it to travel further without too much degradation. By amplifying signals, repeaters maintain reliable communication between the devices.

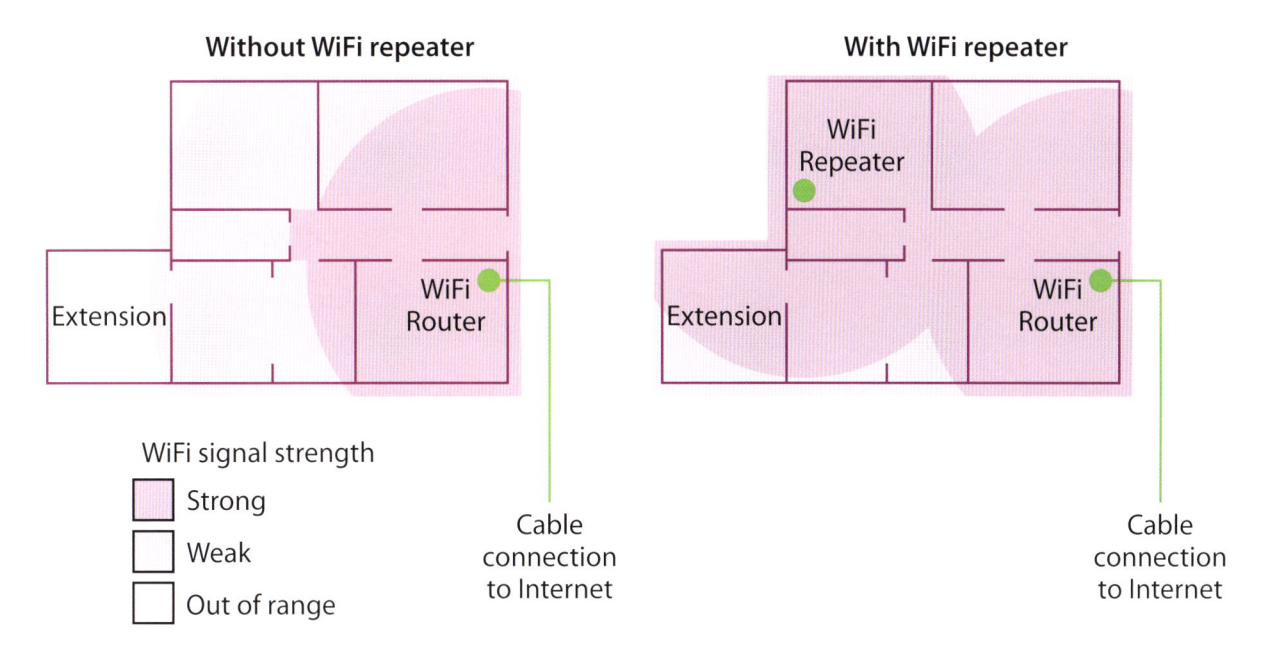

Figure 1.4: A repeater being used to extend the range of a network in a house.

Media converter

A media converter is a device that facilitates the seamless integration of different types of network media, such as copper cables and fibre-optic cables. It serves as a bridge between different types of network cables, enabling smooth data transmission across disparate network segments.

The actual operation of a media converter depends on the media it is designed to work with. For example, one might convert the electrical signals used in a copper cable into optical signals used in a fibre-optic cable, or vice versa. This conversion allows for the compatibility and interoperability of various network technologies.

Media converters are particularly useful in scenarios where the distance between network devices exceeds the limitations of a single media type. Fibre-optic cables, for example, can transmit data over much longer distances compared to copper cables without experiencing significant signal degradation. However, they are often too expensive to use within an individual office. By converting signals between these two media types, media converters allow different transmission technologies to be used where appropriate.

Media converters come in different forms, from basic standalone units to modular devices that can be installed in network equipment racks, providing multiple ports to accommodate different types of media connections.

1.4 Network Addresses

In order for a network to route traffic accurately to its destination, it is necessary for network devices to have unique identifiers. The two main addressing systems are MAC and IP. These are not competing systems – networks use both, as they serve different purposes.

Media access control address

A **media access control**, or **MAC**, address is a unique identifier assigned to the network interface of a device at the hardware level. MAC addresses are assigned by the device manufacturer and remain fixed for the lifetime of the device.

MAC addresses are represented on the network as a 48-bit binary number, but for human readability they are typically written down as six pairs of hexadecimal digits, for example 00:1A:C2:7B:00:47. The first three pairs represent a organisationally unique identifier

(OUI), assigned by the Institute of Electrical and Electronics Engineers (IEEE), which identifies the manufacturer of the device. The remaining three pairs represent the unique device identifier assigned by the manufacturer.

> **Note:** There are 281 trillion possible unique MAC addresses!

MAC addresses play a crucial role in local network communication. When data is transmitted over a network, it is encapsulated with both the source and destination MAC address. These addresses allow devices within the same local network to establish direct connections and communicate efficiently. Network switches and routers use MAC addresses to forward data packets to the correct destination within the network.

Understanding MAC addresses is essential for managing and troubleshooting network connectivity issues, implementing network security measures and ensuring efficient communication within a local network.

IP address

An **IP** address, short for **Internet Protocol** address, is a unique numerical identifier assigned to each device connected to a wide area network. IP addresses play a fundamental role in network communication by providing a means for devices to locate and communicate with each other. They can be either dynamically assigned using protocols, like Dynamic Host Configuration Protocol (DHCP), or statically configured, where a fixed IP address is manually assigned to a device.

Traditional (IPv4) addresses are represented as a 32-bit binary number, which for human readability is written as four numbers separated by periods, for example 192.168.0.1. However, IPv4 only allows for about 4.3 billion unique addresses. With the growth of the internet and the increasing number of connected devices, the adoption of IPv6 has become necessary. IPv6 addresses are 128 bits long, providing a vastly larger address space. For human readability they are written as eight hexadecimal numbers separated by colons, for example 2001:db8:0:1234:0:567:8:1.

IP addresses serve as the foundation of routing across a wide area network, such as the internet. They enable devices to identify each other, establish connections and exchange data packets. While IP addresses used on the internet should be globally unique, IP addresses that are used only within a local area network do not have to be. Certain groups of IP addresses are reserved for use on local area networks, for example addresses in the 192.168.x.x block. This is useful as it means that devices that are only accessed locally, for example a printer, do not need to be assigned an IP address that is unique in the world.

Summary

Figure 1.5 summarises the main differences between MAC and IP addresses.

MAC addresses	IP addresses
Assigned physically at the point of manufacture and cannot be changed.	Assigned via software and can be changed.
Written as six pairs of hexadecimal digits separated by colons.	Written as four numbers separated by periods (IPv4) or eight hexadecimal numbers separated by colons (IPv6).
Globally unique.	Network-specific.
Identifies the device on a local area network.	Identifies the device on a wide area network, such as the internet.

Figure 1.5: The main differences between MAC and IP addresses.

1.5 Peer-to-Peer and Server-Based Networks

We have already considered networks from the perspective of their scope (geographical size). However, networks can also be categorised by the way in which the resources on the network are arranged. Two architectures are common: **peer-to-peer** (P2P) networks and **server-based** networks. Each has a particular structure, functionality and distribution of resources, which gives it both advantages and disadvantages.

Peer-to-peer networks

A peer-to-peer network, or P2P network, is a decentralised network model where individual computers, known as **peers**, communicate and collaborate directly with one another. In P2P networks, each peer has equal capabilities and can act as both a client (requesting resources) and a server (providing services).

P2P networks lack a central server, so the responsibility for resource distribution is shared among the peers. This feature allows for a distributed architecture that can scaled up very effectively, as each peer contributes to the overall network capacity.

P2P networks are commonly used for file-sharing applications, where users can directly access and exchange files with other peers. Examples include popular file-sharing protocols like *BitTorrent*. In these networks, the more peers there are sharing a particular file, the faster the download speeds can be achieved. In addition, P2P networks are resilient: the loss of any one computer from the network is unlikely to lead to a critical failure of the whole system.

However, P2P networks also have certain limitations. Since each peer relies on the resources available from other peers, the overall performance and availability of resources can be inconsistent. If a peer with valuable resources disconnects from the network, those resources become unavailable to other peers. Moreover, the lack of centralised control makes it challenging to enforce security measures and prevent unauthorised access to resources.

Case Study

BitTorrent

BitTorrent is a widely used peer-to-peer computer network system that enables efficient file sharing and distribution over the internet. Developed in 2001 by Bram Cohen, *BitTorrent* has revolutionised the way large files are downloaded and distributed by leveraging the collective resources of its users.

Before *BitTorrent*, downloading large files involved relying on centralised servers, resulting in slow speeds and server overload. *BitTorrent* introduced a decentralised approach where users could simultaneously download and upload files, leading to faster downloads and reduced strain on servers.

BitTorrent operates on a simple principle: a file is divided into smaller pieces, and users who possess those pieces can share them with others. Instead of downloading from a single source, users connect to multiple peers within the network, allowing for faster downloads and increased reliability.

BitTorrent's P2P network system has had a profound impact on digital content distribution. It allows for rapid dissemination of large files, reducing bandwidth costs for content providers and enabling quick access for users. *BitTorrent*'s distributed nature enhances resilience, as the system can continue functioning even if some peers go offline.

Despite challenges and controversies related to copyright infringement and illegal file sharing, *BitTorrent* remains a valuable technology for efficient and decentralised file sharing.

Server-based networks

In contrast to P2P networks, server-based networks employ a client-server architecture. In this model, a central server acts as a dedicated resource provider, and computers are clients that connect to the server to access these resources. The server manages and controls the distribution of resources to clients based on their requests.

The server-based network architecture is highly structured, with a clear division of roles between clients and the central server. Clients primarily request resources and perform tasks, while the server handles resource management, storage and processing. This centralisation allows for efficient resource allocation and control, as well as enhanced security measures.

Server-based networks are utilised in various scenarios. For instance, in an office setting, clients may connect to a central file server to access shared documents and collaborate on projects. Similarly, websites on the internet rely on server-based networks, where web servers respond to client requests and deliver web pages.

One of the key advantages of server-based networks is their robustness and scalability. Since the server holds and manages resources, it can handle a large number of client requests simultaneously. Additionally, server-based networks often employ redundancy (having more than one copy of a resource) and backup mechanisms to ensure data integrity and availability. It is also much easier to implement security on a server-based network, in order to prevent third parties from accessing sensitive data.

However, server-based networks also have their limitations. The reliance on a central server means that, if the server experiences a malfunction, all the clients are unable to access resources. Additionally, the costs associated with maintaining and managing the server infrastructure can be substantial, especially for larger networks.

Case Study

Choosing Between P2P and Server-Based Networks

Zinga Technologies, a growing business with 50 employees, is faced with a decision on the network architecture for its office infrastructure. The company aims to improve collaboration, resource sharing and data security. The two options being considered are a peer-to-peer (P2P) network and a server-based network.

The managers at Zinga Technologies carefully assess the advantages and disadvantages of P2P and server-based networks. They consider factors such as collaboration, resource availability, scalability, data security and cost-effectiveness.

On the one hand, the P2P network model offers decentralised resource sharing and hence cost-effectiveness. It promotes collaboration among employees and allows for easy expansion as the company grows. However, the managers are cautious about potential challenges such as inconsistent resource availability and limited security measures.

On the other hand, the server-based network provides centralised control, enhanced data security and reliable resource access. The managers at Zinga Technologies recognise the benefits of centralised data storage, consistent performance and scalability. They also acknowledge that server-based networks have higher initial investment and maintenance requirements.

After careful consideration, Zinga Technologies determines that a server-based network would best meet their needs. The company prioritises centralised control, data security and consistent resource availability over cost and ease of expansion. They recognise the importance of reliable access to shared resources and centralised backups to mitigate data loss risks.

By choosing a server-based network, Zinga Technologies aims to ensure robust security measures, efficient data management and reliable performance. They are prepared to invest in server hardware, software and maintenance to support their growing business needs. The decision aligns with their long-term goals and the projected growth of the company.

1.6 Network Topologies

Network topologies refers to how devices are physically interconnected within a computer network. The CCEA specification requires you to be able to evaluate three topologies: **bus**, **star** and **ring**. Each topology offers distinct advantages in terms of scalability, performance, fault tolerance and ease of implementation.

Bus topology

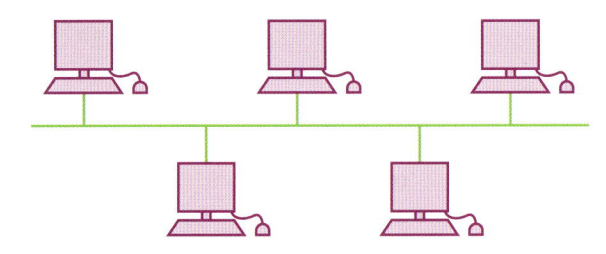

Figure 1.6: The bus topology.

The bus topology, shown in Figure 1.6, features a linear arrangement where devices are connected to a central communication line, known as the bus. This topology is relatively simple to implement and cost-effective, requiring minimal cabling and equipment. It allows for easy additions or removals of devices, making it suitable for small networks. In a bus topology, all devices share the same communication channel, resulting in easy data transmission.

However, the bus topology has limitations. Since all devices share the same communication line, network performance can be adversely affected when multiple devices transmit data simultaneously. Additionally, a single point of failure in the bus, such as a broken cable, can cause the entire network to fail. Troubleshooting and identifying faults in a bus topology can be challenging due to the lack of centralised control.

Star topology

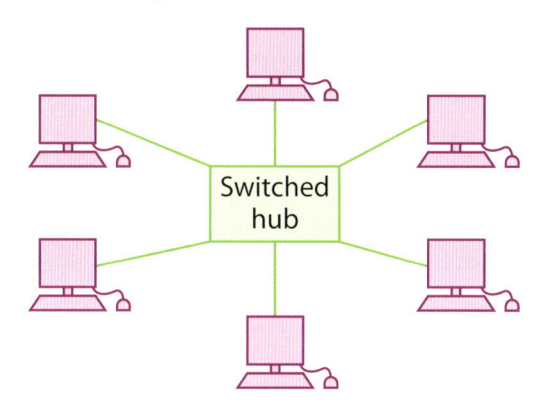

Figure 1.7: The star topology.

In the star topology, shown in Figure 1.7, all devices are connected to a central device, usually a network switch or hub. This central device acts as a connection point, enabling individual devices to communicate with one another. The star topology offers more efficient data transmission than a bus topology, as each device has its own dedicated connection to the central device. It is also easier to scale up, as a new device is simply connected to the central point. Additionally, if one connection fails, it does not affect the entire network, making troubleshooting easier.

However, the star topology has limitations. It requires more cabling compared to the bus topology, which increases costs and complexity. The network's performance relies heavily on the central device; if it fails, the entire network may be affected. The star topology is also less suitable for large networks as it requires significant amounts of cabling and a robust central device to handle the increased traffic.

Ring topology

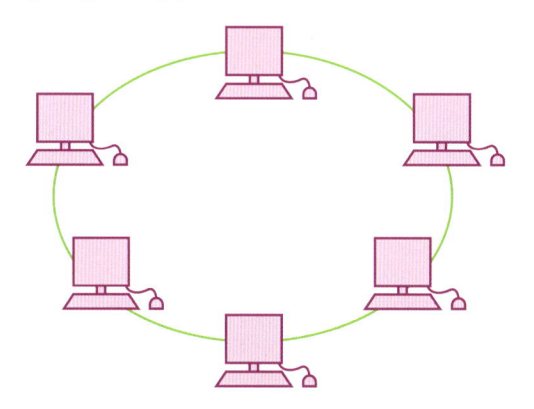

Figure 1.8: The ring topology.

In the ring topology, shown in Figure 1.8, devices are connected in a circle, forming a closed loop. Each device connects to two neighbouring devices, allowing data to flow around the ring in a unidirectional path. The ring topology offers equal access to the network resources for all devices, preventing collisions during data transmission. It provides easy troubleshooting, and fault tolerance, as a break in the ring can be circumvented by rerouting data in the opposite direction.

However, the ring topology has limitations. Adding or removing devices is disruptive to the network, as it requires the circle to be broken for a time. Network performance is reduced by increasing the numbers of devices on the ring, as each device must pass the data packet along to the next device. Although more robust than the bus topology, a single point of failure will slow down the network.

Choosing the right topology

Selecting the appropriate network topology depends on various factors. The bus topology provides simplicity and cost-effectiveness, but it lacks scalability and fault tolerance. The star topology offers better performance and fault tolerance, but it requires more cabling and relies heavily on the central device. The ring topology provides equal access and fault tolerance, but it can be challenging to modify and is sensitive to a single point of failure. Choosing a topology is always a trade-off between competing features.

It is essential to consider the network's size, future growth, required performance, fault tolerance and budgetary constraints when selecting a network topology. Evaluating these factors will guide decision-makers in implementing the most effective topology for their specific network requirements.

Task

Consider your own school. Imagine you have been asked to select an appropriate network topology for a new network for the school. What factors should be considered when choosing the network topology? What topology would you recommend, and why?

Questions

1. What are the key characteristics and advantages of a local area network (LAN)?

2. How do metropolitan area networks (MANs) facilitate communication and resource sharing?

3. What is the role of IP and MAC addresses in computer networks?

4. How does a network card facilitate the connection between a device and a computer network?

5. What is the role of a server in a computer network?

6. How does a switched hub improve network performance compared to older hub models?

7. What is the purpose of a repeater in a network?

8. In a wide area network (WAN), what are the key factors that contribute to higher latency and lower bandwidth compared to local area networks (LANs) or metropolitan area networks (MANs)? How have advancements in technology addressed these challenges to support real-time applications and multimedia content delivery?

9. Compare and contrast the role and functionality of a server in a server-based network with that of a peer in a peer-to-peer (P2P) network. Your answer should discuss how these architectures differ in terms of resource distribution, scalability, security and availability of resources.

10. Write a summary of MAC addresses. Describe how MAC addresses differ from IP addresses in terms of their operation, assignment and role in network protocols. Discuss how MAC addresses are used by devices, switches and routers to facilitate efficient data transmission within a network.

CHAPTER 2
Protocols

> **By the end of this chapter students should be able to:**
>
> - explain the need for communication protocols;
> - describe the Open Systems Interconnection (OSI) network organisation model and each of its component layers; and
> - describe communication protocols:
>   - Transmission Control Protocol/Internet Protocol (TCP/IP);
>   - Ethernet;
>   - Carrier Sense Multiple Access with Collision Detection (CSMA/CD);
>   - token passing;
>   - Wi-Fi;
>   - Bluetooth;
>   - voice over internet protocol (VoIP); and
>   - radio-frequency identification (RFID).

2.1 Introduction

Sports, such as football, have rules that players must follow. These includes physical things like the size of the pitch, the locations of the lines and the number of players. It also includes rules that define how the players interact with each other, how they score, what they can and cannot do, and so forth. A game of football with no rules would quickly descend into chaos as nobody would know what to do or how to play.

In a similar way, **network protocols** are like the rules of a game that all devices in a network must follow. They provide a common language and structure for devices to communicate with each other in a standardised way. Different devices have huge variations in capability and specification, but using common network protocols bring order to this diverse landscape, ensuring that data is transmitted accurately, efficiently and securely.

We will begin by looking at the **Open Systems Interconnection (OSI) model**. The OSI model is a theoretical blueprint for network communication that simplifies a complex process by splitting it into seven layers. Each layer has a specific role and interacts with the layers above and below, creating a structured framework that allows for modular design and compatibility between different devices. We will consider each layer in turn.

We will then turn our attention to an exploration of eight real-world network protocols required by the CCEA specification, each of which implements specific layers of the OSI model. You will likely have heard of the more popular ones like TCP/IP, Ethernet and Wi-Fi. Each protocol serves a specific purpose and caters to different network requirements. Some protocols omit certain layers of the OSI model, and some merge separate OSI layers into one for simplicity.

2.2 The Open Systems Interconnection (OSI) Model

In the early days of computer networking, there was a lack of standardisation, resulting in numerous incompatible networking protocols. This made it challenging for different computer systems to communicate with each other. To overcome these hurdles and establish a common language for network communication, the International Organisation for Standardisation (ISO) developed the OSI model during the early 1980s. The OSI model provided a standardised framework for developers to refer to when building and using computer networks. It breaks networking technology into separate 'layers' each of which deals with a particular aspect of communication.

The OSI model contains seven layers. As we shall see below, the top layer is the most abstract and deals with communication in the way a human would think of it, for example 'send an email' or 'download a file'. The layers get progressively more technical as they descend, until we reach the bottom layer, which deals with physically sending bits (1s and 0s) of data across a physical medium like a wire cable. Each layer can only communicate with the layers directly above or below it.

With the OSI model to refer to, developers can cope with the huge complexity and variations in technology by considering a single layer at a time. In addition, if a manufacturer follows the OSI model, then anything they build that implements a specific layer of the OSI model is guaranteed to be compatible with a product from another company that implements the layer directly above or below.

The widespread adoption of the OSI model allowed devices from different manufacturers to interoperate seamlessly. It enabled the development of networking technologies and protocols that could be implemented universally, fostering global connectivity and collaboration and ultimately facilitated the development of the modern internet.

The main advantages of the OSI model are as follows:

- **Interoperability**: The OSI model promotes interoperability by defining standards and protocols for each layer. This enables devices from different manufacturers to communicate effectively, regardless of the underlying technologies used.
- **Simplified troubleshooting**: With its layered structure, the OSI model simplifies troubleshooting processes. Network issues can be isolated to specific layers, making it easier to identify and resolve problems, resulting in efficient network maintenance.
- **Flexibility**: The modular design of the OSI model offers flexibility, allowing organisations to select and implement protocols specific to their needs. It enables customisation and adaptation to varying network requirements and technologies.
- **Clear hierarchical structure**: The layered approach of the OSI model provides a clear hierarchical structure, allowing network designers and administrators to focus on specific layers during implementation and management. This separation of concerns enhances efficiency and simplifies network design.

Layers of the OSI model

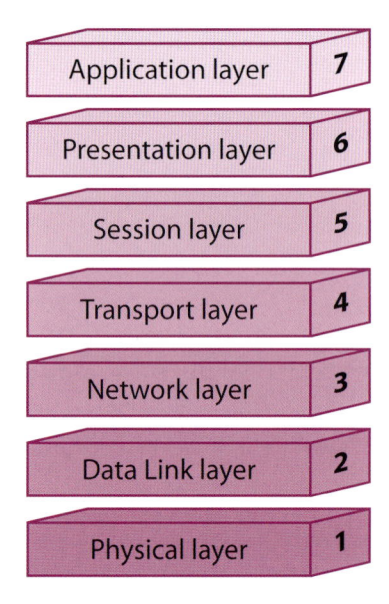

Figure 2.1: The layers of the OSI model.

Figure 2.1 shows the layers of the OSI model, which are as follows, with layer 7 at the top.

7. **Application layer:** At the top of the OSI model, the Application layer directly interacts with users and provides network services to applications. This layer encompasses a wide range of protocols for various purposes, including email (SMTP), web browsing (HTTP) and file transfer (FTP). It enables users to access network resources and services, making it the layer most familiar to us. Examples of the Application layer include email clients, web browsers and file transfer programs.

6. **Presentation layer:** This layer ensures the compatibility of data formats between different systems. It handles data encryption, compression and formatting, making sure that data exchanged between devices is correctly interpreted. This layer plays a vital role in data representation and translation, allowing applications to understand and process data received from the network. Examples of implementations of the Presentation layer

include JPEG and ASCII (which defines how text characters are represented as binary numbers).

5. **Session layer:** This layer establishes, maintains and terminates communication sessions between applications running on different devices. It enables synchronisation and coordination between devices and handles issues such as session checkpoints and recovery from failures. This layer allows for secure and organised communication between applications. An example of the Session layer is Remote Procedure Call (RPC).

4. **Transport layer:** This layer is responsible for providing end-to-end data delivery and ensures reliable and error-free communication between applications. It does this by dividing large data streams into smaller segments, adding sequence numbers and managing flow control. Two well-known protocols in this layer are Transmission Control Protocol (TCP) and User Datagram Protocol (UDP).

3. **Network layer:** This layer focuses on the delivery of data packets from the source to the destination across different networks. It is in this layer that we find the concept of logical addressing, i.e. assigning unique IP addresses to devices. This layer uses routing protocols to determine the best path for data transmission, enabling devices to communicate beyond their immediate network. Examples of implementation of the Network layer include network routers.

2. **Data Link layer:** The Data Link layer is responsible for the reliable transfer of data between adjacent network nodes. It is responsible for detecting transmission errors by ensuring that data packets are transmitted without loss or corruption. This layer also defines protocols for accessing and controlling the physical media, such as Ethernet and Wi-Fi. Real-world examples of the Data Link layer include Ethernet switches and Wi-Fi access points.

1. **Physical layer:** At the bottom of the OSI model, the Physical layer deals with the physical transmission of data over the network. The actual hardware components such as cables, connectors and network interface cards are found at this level. Its primary function is to convert digital bits into electrical, optical or radio signals for transmission across the network. Examples of the Physical layer include Ethernet cables, fibre optic cables and wireless radio signals.

> **Note:** You must be able to name all seven layers in the correct order. It may help to remember the phrase 'A penguin swims to new depths proudly'! The first letter of each word will help you remember the names of the layers.

The Application Set and Transport Set

The top three layers of the OSI model are often grouped together and referred to as the **Application Set** of layers (Figure 2.2). These are the layers that are responsible for how the specific applications running on a computer are using the network. For example, a web browser can be used to look at a website while another application might be copying a file across the local area network.

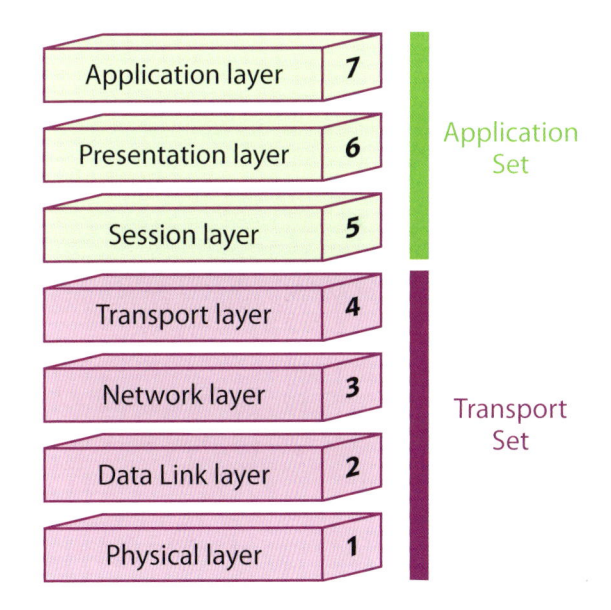

Figure 2.2: The Application Set and Transport Set of the OSI Model.

The four lower layers are referred to as the **Transport Set**. These are the layers that are actually responsible for moving data across the network. These layers are not interested in what the data means; they are only concerned with getting it to its destination.

Understanding the OSI model

To understand the OSI model it may help to consider an analogy. Imagine communicating with someone in France from Northern Ireland by using the postal service:

- The Application layer (layer 7) represents the sender's overall intentions, for example communicating about a house sale.
- The Presentation layer (layer 6) ensures that the communications are sent in a format that both sender and receiver can understand. In this example, the Presentation layer would provide a service to translate the communication from English into French and vice-versa.
- The Session layer (layer 5) considers the process of initiating, maintaining and concluding a conversation. In this example it decides how the overall communication can be split up into a series of separate letters.
- The Transport layer (layer 4) is like selecting a trusted mail service for delivery of an individual letter. It is responsible for ensuring that the letter reaches its destination reliably and intact, for example by using a signed-for postal service.
- The Network layer (layer 3) is like addressing a letter with the correct country and postcode. It determines the route that the letter should take to reach its intended recipient efficiently, making sure it does not get lost in transit. For example, if the address says 'France', the postal service knows it needs to be routed via a ship or an aeroplane to France.
- The Data Link layer (layer 2) acts like the sender and receiver's addresses on the envelope. It ensures that individual letters are correctly addressed to be accurately passed between each of the various postal depots in its journey.
- Finally, the Physical Layer (layer 1) represents the actual physical transmission medium, in this case the physical paper and envelope that contains the message.

Task

Imagine you're building a new social media app. How does each layer of the OSI model play a role in ensuring that users can post, share and interact with content seamlessly and securely?

2.3 Communication Protocols

It is important to grasp that the OSI model is a conceptual framework. While it provides a structured approach to understanding and designing networks, the OSI model is primarily theoretical and does not have a direct implementation in real-world networks.

Real-world network protocols are practical implementations that enable actual communication between devices and networks. Protocols like TCP/IP, Ethernet and Wi-Fi are examples of real-world network protocols. These protocols may not cover all the layers in the OSI model, and may combine two or more of the OSI layers into one for convenience. Unlike the theoretical OSI model, real-world network protocols are designed to maximise efficiency, performance, compatibility and interoperability within the technological constraints of the real world.

The CCEA specification requires you to have knowledge of eight specific real-world communication protocols. These are discussed in the remainder of this chapter.

Transmission Control Protocol/Internet Protocol

Transmission Control Protocol/Internet Protocol, or TCP/IP, forms the basis of communication on the internet. It governs how data is transmitted, routed and received between devices connected to a network.

TCP/IP is often referred to as a **protocol stack** because it actually consists of multiple protocols that work together to facilitate reliable and efficient communication. It takes its name from the two most important protocols in the suite. TCP/IP, shown in Figure 2.3, consists of four layers that are roughly aligned with one or more layers of the OSI model and are as follows:

- **Application layer**: This layer corresponds to the Session, Presentation and Application layers in the OSI model, that is, the upper three layers. It encompasses a wide range of protocols and services that enable user applications to interact with the network. Examples include the HyperText Transfer Protocol (HTTP) for web browsing, the Simple Mail Transfer Protocol (SMTP) for email communication, and the Domain Name System (DNS) for translating domain names into IP addresses.

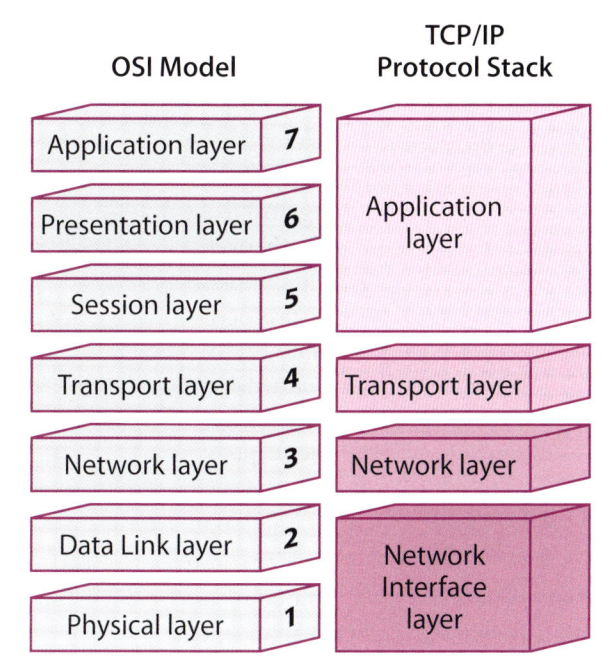

Figure 2.3: The layers of the TCP/IP protocol stack.

- **Transport layer**: This layer corresponds directly to the Transport layer in the OSI model. It is responsible for end-to-end communication between devices and ensures reliable data delivery. The Transmission Control Protocol (TCP) is a prominent protocol in this layer, providing connection-oriented and reliable data transfer. TCP includes mechanisms to check that data has arrived at its destination, and to retransmit it if necessary to guarantee that it does. With this layer taking responsibility for detecting and fixing data errors, the Application layer can assume that data is being transferred reliably.
- **Internet layer**: This layer corresponds to the Network layer in the OSI model. It is responsible for addressing, routing and forwarding data packets across networks. The Internet Protocol (IP) operates in this layer, assigning unique IP addresses to devices and ensuring the packets reach their intended destinations.
- **Network Interface layer**: This layer corresponds to the lowest two layers of the OSI model, the Physical layer and the Data Link layer. It deals with the physical transmission of data over the network medium, including the Ethernet protocol used for local area networks.

TCP/IP has become the de facto standard for networking, enjoying universal support globally across devices and operating systems. This ubiquity enables seamless communication between diverse systems on the internet.

TCP/IP has several key advantages that have contributed to its widespread adoption:

- It has a high degree of scalability, making it suitable for networks of varying sizes and complexities. It can accommodate both small-scale networks, like home networks, and large-scale networks, such as the global internet. This scalability ensures efficient communication regardless of the network's size or growth.
- It is a versatile protocol suite capable of supporting different network technologies, including both wired and wireless networks. It can adapt to various network topologies and is not limited to specific physical or data link layer technologies. This versatility allows TCP/IP to accommodate different network configurations and technologies.
- It provides reliable data delivery through protocols like TCP. As explained above, TCP ensures that data is delivered accurately, in the correct order, and without errors. This reliability is crucial for applications that require the precise transmission of data, such as file transfers and web browsing.

Ethernet

Ethernet (formally known as the IEEE 802.3 standard) is a widely used networking protocol that provides a reliable and efficient means of communication between devices on a local area network (LAN). It only implements the Data Link and Physical layers of the OSI model and is an integral part of the modern networking infrastructure. It defines the rules and procedures for transmitting data packets over a physical network medium, such as twisted pair copper cables or fibre optic cables. It also defines the type of physical connectors to be used.

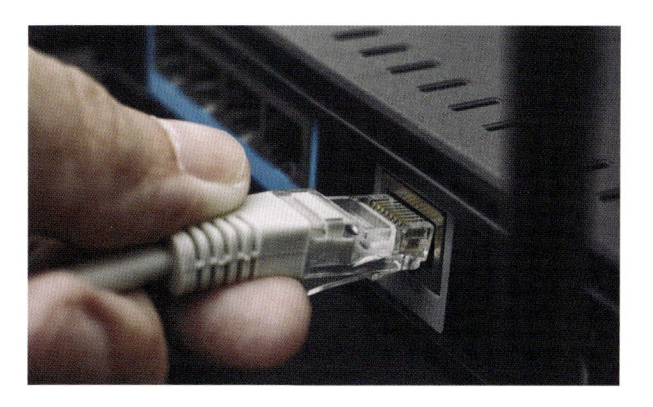

The Ethernet protocol ensures that data is organised into 'frames' and delivers them reliably and efficiently to the intended destination within a LAN. This allows multiple devices, such as computers, printers and servers, to connect and exchange data seamlessly. Ethernet's reliable data transmission ensures that information is delivered accurately and quickly, contributing to improved productivity and collaboration in organisations.

Ethernet has a number of key advantages:

- High degree of versatility and scalability. It supports a range of network topologies, including bus, star and ring (see Chapter 1) making it suitable for various network configurations.
- Ethernet also offers multiple data rates, such as 10 Mbps (mega bits per second), 100 Mbps, 1 Gbps, and even higher speeds, allowing networks to adapt to increasing bandwidth demands.
- Widespread adoption and compatibility. Most networking devices, such as routers, switches and network interface cards (NICs), are Ethernet-compatible. This interoperability allows for easy integration of devices from different vendors.

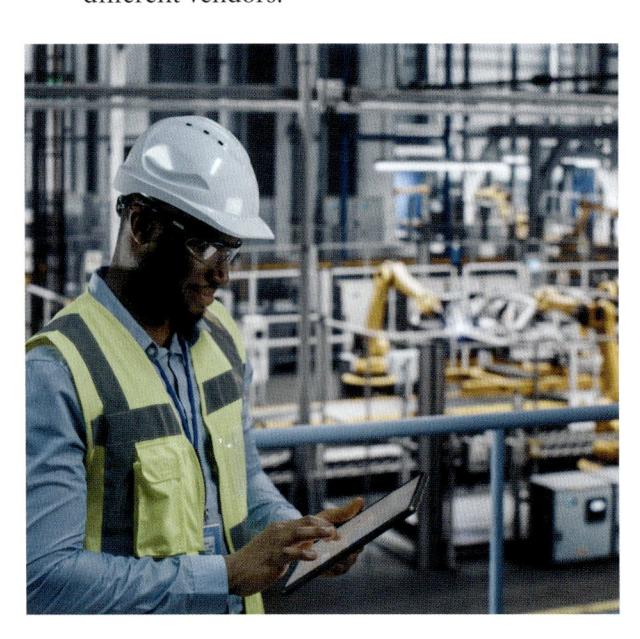

Ethernet has found uses in various environments:

- In office and school environments, Ethernet forms the backbone of local area networks, connecting computers, printers and other devices within a building or campus. It enables file sharing, internet connectivity and supports essential services like email and web browsing.
- In industrial settings, where it forms the foundation of industrial control systems and automation networks. It enables communication between programmable logic controllers (PLCs), sensors, actuators and other devices, facilitating process control and monitoring in manufacturing plants and infrastructure systems.
- In homes, Ethernet is often used create a home LANs, connecting smart devices, gaming consoles, media servers and streaming devices. Ethernet provides the necessary bandwidth and reliability for high-definition video streaming, online gaming and home automation systems. While Wi-Fi has largely taken over this role, Ethernet can still achieve higher data transfer rates than Wi-Fi.

Carrier Sense Multiple Access with Collision Detection

Carrier Sense Multiple Access with Collision Detection, or CSMA/CD, is a protocol that was used historically in Ethernet networks to control access to the network medium and manage data transmission. It operates at the Data Link and Physical layers in the OSI model. It is designed to handle the shared nature of Ethernet networks, where multiple devices contend for access to the network medium and resolve the difficulty of multiple devices trying to use the network simultaneously. The protocol's operation can be summarised in three main steps:

- **Carrier sense**: Before transmitting data, a device using CSMA/CD listens for any ongoing transmissions on the network. If the medium is idle, the device proceeds to the next step. However, if it detects a transmission, it defers its own transmission until the medium becomes available.
- **Multiple access**: Once the device determines that the network is idle, it begins transmitting its data. Since multiple devices may contend for access, collisions can occur if two or more devices transmit simultaneously. CSMA/CD listens for and detects these collisions.
- **Collision detection**: When a collision occurs, CSMA/CD stops transmitting and sends a jam signal to ensure all devices on the network are aware of the collision. Each device then waits for a random period of time before attempting

to retransmit their data. This randomised 'backoff' algorithm helps prevent repeated collisions.

CSMA/CD has a number of advantages:

- It enables efficient utilisation of network resources by allowing multiple devices to share the network medium, leading to increased network throughput.
- It ensures fairness by providing all devices with a fair chance of accessing the network, preventing one device from dominating the network consistently.

However, CSMA/CD is largely obsolete today as it has been replaced by switched Ethernet, where each device is connected by its own dedicated Ethernet cable to a central switch, eliminating collisions. However, it is still found on older Ethernet networks.

Case Study

Collision resolution

Device A and Device B both attempt to send data over a CSMA/CD network at the same time. Device A and Device B both quickly detect the collision. They stop transmitting and each independently waits for a random backoff period before attempting to retransmit.

In this example, Device A completes its backoff period first and retransmits while Device B remains silent. Device A successfully transmits its data without any further collisions. Device B is then able to transmit its data. Each device continues to monitor the network during its transmission to detect any further collisions.

If both Device A and Device B had randomly selected the same time period for retransmission, another collision may have occurred, initiating the collision detection process once again and triggering another backoff period.

Token passing

Token passing is a network access control protocol that allows devices in a network to take turns transmitting data. It is an alternative solution to CSMA/CD and is primarily associated with the ring network topology (see Chapter 1). It also operates at the Data Link and Physical layers of the OSI model.

It operates based on the concept of a **token**, which is a special control message that circulates within the network and grants the right to transmit data to a specific device.

The main advantages of token passing are:

- Its deterministic nature ensures fair and orderly access to the network. Each device in the network holds the token for a specific period of time, allowing it to transmit data without the risk of collisions. This prevents data loss and improves network efficiency.
- It provides a predictable and consistent performance, making it suitable for real-time applications such as industrial control systems, where precise timing and reliable communication are crucial.

While token passing was widely used in the past, its usage has declined with the advent of Ethernet networks. However, token passing still finds applications in specialised environments where determinism, precise control and guaranteed access to the network are critical, such as in industrial automation, process control and certain high-security networks.

Wi-Fi

Wi-Fi (short for wireless fidelity) is a widely used wireless network protocol that ensures convenient and flexible connectivity for various devices. It operates primarily at the Physical and Data Link layers of the OSI model, enabling wireless communication between devices over a local area network (LAN).

Wi-Fi utilises radio frequency signals to transmit data without the need for wires. The effective range of a Wi-Fi network can vary depending on factors such as the transmit power of the devices and the physical environment. But in general, Wi-Fi networks can cover distances ranging from tens to hundreds of metres, allowing for connectivity within a building, across multiple floors, or across open spaces.

Wi-Fi offers several advantages that have contributed to its widespread adoption:

- They eliminate the need for physical cables, which allows mobility, enabling users to access the internet and network resources from different locations within the range of a Wi-Fi network – for example customers in a restaurant.
- They have high data transfer rates. While still not as fast or reliable as Ethernet, Wi-Fi networks are supporting increasingly higher speeds, facilitating activities such as streaming high-definition media, online gaming and large file transfers.
- They are highly scalable, allowing for easy expansion and coverage extension. Additional access points or Wi-Fi range extenders (Chapter 1) can be installed to accommodate larger areas or increase network capacity.

Task

Name as many devices as you can that are able to connect to Wi-Fi.

Bluetooth

Bluetooth is a wireless network protocol that enables short-range communication between devices. It operates primarily at the Physical and Data Link layers of the OSI model, providing a convenient and reliable method for connecting devices wirelessly.

Bluetooth utilises radio frequency signals to establish connections between devices. It operates in the 2.4 GHz band and has special features designed to reduce interference and improve signal reliability. Bluetooth's effective range is affected by environmental factors, such as the presence of walls. The most powerful type, Class 1, can extend up to 100 metres. Class 3 Bluetooth, by contrast, has a much smaller range of about 10 metres. However Class 3 is still widely used because it is cheaper and is sufficient for many devices that only need a short range, such as Bluetooth headphones, an in-car hands-free calling system or a wireless computer keyboard.

Bluetooth offers a number of advantages:

- It is simple and easy to use. Bluetooth devices can be easily paired and connected without the need for complex configuration or setup procedures.
- It is particularly useful for devices which need to communicate with each other within a short range. For example, Bluetooth enables wireless audio streaming from a smartphone to a pair of headphones, or file transfer between two adjacent smartphones.
- It consumes relatively low power, making it suitable for battery-powered devices. This efficiency allows devices like wireless earbuds, fitness trackers and smartwatches to operate for extended periods without charging.

Bluetooth has also found many applications in the Internet of Things (IoT) ecosystem. It enables connectivity between IoT devices, allowing them to exchange data and interact with each other. For example, a smart home system can use Bluetooth to connect and control various IoT devices, such as smart bulbs, smart speakers and smart appliances.

Task

For each of the following decide whether Bluetooth would be an appropriate method of communication between the devices.

1. Between a person's fitness tracker and their mobile phone.
2. Between the International Space Station and Earth.
3. To exchange large files between two laptop computers in the same house.
4. Controlling a drone from a mobile phone.
5. Two friends wishing to exchange photos on their phones.
6. To print a document in an office, from a computer to a printer.

Voice Over Internet Protocol

Voice over internet protocol, or VoIP, is a technology that enables the transmission of voice content over IP networks, allowing users to make phone calls using the internet rather than traditional telephone networks. Traditional phone lines use analogue signals to carry sound, but in VoIP the sound is digitised and sent in binary form. In terms of the OSI model, VoIP primarily operates at the Application layer. *Skype*, *WhatsApp* and *Zoom* are well-known examples of software that utilise VoIP.

The advantages of VoIP are numerous:

- It offers cost savings by utilising the existing IP infrastructure, eliminating the need for separate telephone lines.
- Because it uses existing computer networks, VoIP enables flexible and scalable communication solutions, allowing organisations to easily add or remove users as needed.
- VoIP offers a wide range of additional features and functionalities, including call forwarding, voicemail, video conferencing and integration with other applications.
- Since it can use the global internet, it allows individuals to make long-distance international calls at much lower rates compared to traditional telephone services. This also makes it popular with call centres, which are often located overseas from their customers.

For the above reasons, VoIP was initially adopted in the commercial world, but is increasingly being rolled out in domestic settings too. Despite its advantages, VoIP does come with some challenges:

- Since it relies on IP networks, the quality of VoIP calls can be affected by network congestion, latency and packet loss. This issue can be reduced with proper network management and provision of sufficient bandwidth.
- Security is a concern, as voice and data transmitted over IP networks are susceptible to interception and eavesdropping, requiring the use of encryption protocols.

Case Study

In 2021 BT in the UK began a major project called Digital Voice, which will eventually see all its traditional landlines discontinued and customers switched to VoIP using their broadband network. All landlines are to be switched to VoIP by 2025. The rollout began in the East Midlands, Yorkshire and Northern Ireland in the summer of 2023.

The project is very challenging due to the large number of households that still have an analogue phone, and because some households do not have a broadband connection at all. BT has had to come up with solutions to these problems. Additionally, they have met with opposition from people concerned that a phone system that requires electricity will cease working in a power cut (analogue phone lines are powered separately).

Finally, BT has struggled to explain the benefit of switching to digital to older customers, to whom their analogue landlines appear to be working fine.

There are many advantages of the switchover, however. Analogue phone lines are increasingly obsolete and there are extra costs associated with maintaining two parallel phone networks.

Digital Voice will allow much easier integration of computer technology with the telephone network, as both will use the same internet. This will include the ability to easily block unwanted callers. It will also give much better audio quality – an end to the old problem of getting a 'bad line'.

Radio-frequency identification

Radio-frequency identification, or RFID, is a technology that uses radio waves to automatically identify and track objects or people. It uses tags or labels that contain electronically stored information, and readers or scanners that communicate with the tags to retrieve the information. In terms of the OSI model, RFID operates at the Physical and Data Link layers.

RFID's main advantage is that it provides a non-contact method of identification and tracking, eliminating the need for physical contact or line-of-sight scanning. This eliminates the need for a human being to be involved, for example to scan a barcode. This makes it ideal for applications where convenience, speed and automation are essential, such as tracking goods leaving a factory or stock moving around a building.

Figure 2.4: An RFID scanner at the exit of a clothes shop to prevent shoplifting.

In the real world, RFID is widely used in various domains. In retail, RFID tags are attached to products, allowing for streamlined inventory management, theft prevention and faster checkout processes. For example, some products may have a tag attached to them. The tag is removed or deactivated when purchased. An RFID scanner at the shop exit (Figure 2.4) will trigger an alarm if it detects an active tag passing through.

In logistics, RFID technology enables accurate tracking and tracing of goods, improving supply chain visibility and reducing errors. In healthcare, RFID is utilised for patient identification, medication management and asset tracking in hospitals. It is also used in access control systems, transportation systems and livestock tracking, among other applications.

However, RFID also raises concerns related to privacy and security. The ability to remotely read and track RFID tags can lead to potential privacy breaches. Organisations need to implement appropriate security measures to protect the integrity and confidentiality of RFID data.

Questions

1. How many layers are there in the OSI model, and what are their names? Give them in the correct order.
2. Which layer of the OSI model handles data encryption, compression and formatting?
3. How does the OSI model simplify troubleshooting processes?
4. What are the top three layers of the OSI model collectively referred to as, and what is their role?
5. What does the Transport layer ensure when delivering data to its destination?
6. Explain the purpose of TCP/IP in networking.
7. In what layer of the OSI model does Ethernet primarily operate?
8. In terms of how they handle network access, what is the difference between CSMA/CD and token passing?
9. State three advantages of Wi-Fi for network connectivity.
10. What is the maximum effective range of Bluetooth?

11. Explain the difference between VoIP and traditional phone lines.

12. What is RFID, and how does it work?

13. Explain the concept of interoperability in the context of the OSI model. How does the OSI model facilitate interoperability among devices from different manufacturers, and why is this important for building and maintaining networks?

14. Ethernet has seen widespread adoption in various environments, including offices, industries and homes. What are the advantages of Ethernet for these applications, and how does it compare to other networking technologies like Wi-Fi in terms of reliability, performance and scalability?

15. Evaluate the impact of VoIP on traditional phone services and communication infrastructure. What advantages does VoIP offer, and what challenges must be addressed for its successful implementation?

CHAPTER 3
Transmission Media

By the end of this chapter students should be able to:

- define the terms bandwidth and broadband;
- describe transmission media: metal cable, fibre optic and wireless;
- evaluate these transmission media in terms of volume of data transfer, bandwidth and security.

3.1 Introduction

Transmission media can be thought of as digital highways that enable the exchange of digital information. We will first discuss how the terms **bandwidth** and **broadband** apply to digital communication.

We will then consider three types of transmission media – traditional metal cable, fibre optic cable and wireless communication. In each case we will consider how the technology works, and then compare and contrast the three media in terms of how much data they can reliably accommodate, and how secure they are.

3.2 Bandwidth and Broadband

Bandwidth refers to the amount of data that can be transferred across a transmission medium in a given time. It is usually measured as the number of bits (1s or 0s) that can be accurately communicated per second. For example, a medium that can communicate 56,000 bits of data every second would be said to have a bandwidth of 56 kilobits per second, or 56 kbit/s. Modern Ethernet connections have a maximum bandwidth of 100,000,000 bits per second, written as 100 megabits per second 100 Mbit/s.

Even higher bandwidths are available, such as 100 Gbit/s Ethernet, which is 1000 times faster than the Ethernet described above, although more expensive. In general, the bandwidths that are commercially available increase every year. This is one reason why TV streaming services have only become widespread since around the year 2010.

Broadband

In the early days of home internet use, in the late 1990s, most people connected via a dial-up connection using an analogue phone line. This had a bandwidth of 56 kbit/s. Users had to first connect to the internet, use the service, and then disconnect.

The term 'broadband' was initially coined to distinguish it from dial-up. A broadband connection:

- is always connected, and
- has a high bandwidth capable of transferring multiple signals at once.

The term broadband does not imply the use of any particular type of medium. Broadband connections can be made available by a metal cable, fibre optic or wireless medium.

Worked Example

How long would it take to transfer a 1 GB image file over (1) an Ethernet connection with a bandwidth of 100 Mbit/s (2) a dial-up connection with a bandwidth of 56 kb/s?

1. GB means 1 billion bytes. One byte contains 8 bits. Therefore, the file contains 8 billion bits of data.
   A 100 Mbit/s Ethernet can transfer 100 million bits of data per second.
   So the time to transfer the file over the Ethernet connection is 8 billion divided by 100 million = 80 seconds.

2. A 56 kbit/s dial up connection can transfer 56,000 bits of data per second.
   So the time to transfer the 1 GB file is 8 billion divided by 56,000 = 142,857 seconds or almost 40 hours.

3.3 Metal Cable Transmission Media

Metal cables, often referred to as wired transmission media, are the physical conduits that enable the exchange of data and information between devices in a wide array of applications, from local area networks (LANs) in homes and offices to vast global telecommunications networks.

Metal cables, as the name suggests, are physical cables primarily composed of various metals, most commonly copper and aluminium. These cables serve as the physical medium through which electrical signals, carrying data, travel from one point to another. There are various ways this can be done, but a common method is to repeatedly vary the voltage, with a high voltage representing a '1' and a low voltage representing a '0'. The electrical signals travel along the cable to the destination where the voltages are registered and converted back into '1's and '0's. The electrical signal passes through the metal cable at about 95% of the speed of light.

There are three main types: unshielded twisted pair, shielded twisted pair and coaxial, each of which is suitable for specific environments.

Unshielded twisted pair (UTP)

It is a fact of physics that electromagnetic signals, such as those emitted by radio transmitters, microwave ovens and mobile phones, induce electrical currents in metal conductors that they meet. Electrical currents themselves generate electromagnetic signals, meaning that any cable carrying electricity is also a source of electromagnetic signals, which can, in turn, induce electrical currents in nearby cables.

So, in an environment where there are a lot of electrical devices and cables in close proximity, each is interfering to some degree with those around them.

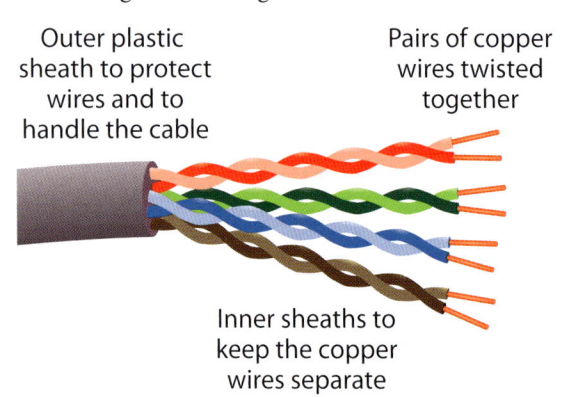

Figure 3.1: An unshielded twisted pair cable.

This is one of the main problems with sending signals along metal cables – if the metal cable is subject to electrical interference, it dilutes the electrical signal being carried. If the interference is sufficiently bad the signal can be swamped and lost.

The main solution is to send the same signal twice, down two wires twisted together, as shown in Figure 3.1. The first wire carries the intended signal while the second carries the same signal in reverse phase (where high voltage becomes low and vice versa). Any interference along the length of the cable affects both wires in the same way because they are close together. However, at the destination, the second signal is inverted for a second time, which also inverts the interference it received. When this is added to the first signal, the interference is cancelled out, leaving a clean signal.

Case Study

The digital signal shown below is to be sent down a cable consisting of a twisted pair of wires.

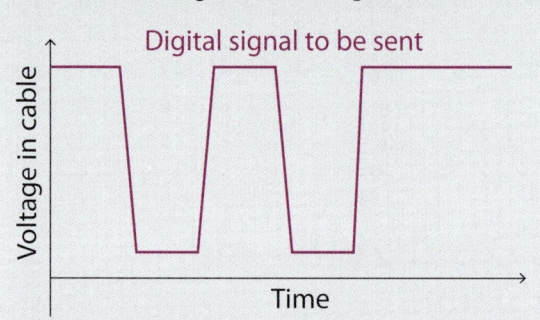

The first signal is sent down one wire, while an inverted form of the same signal is sent down the second wire, as shown:

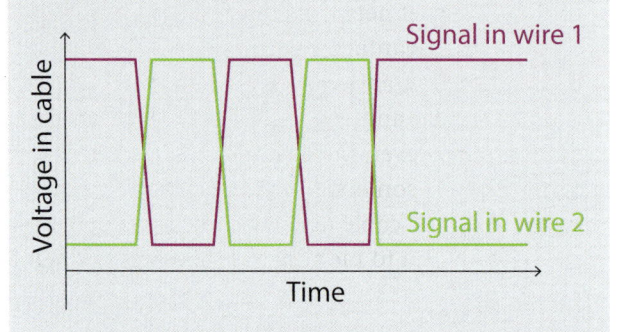

As it passes along the cable, electromagnetic interference from other electrical devices, mobile phone signals and a nearby microwave oven degrades the signal.

The signal received looks like this:

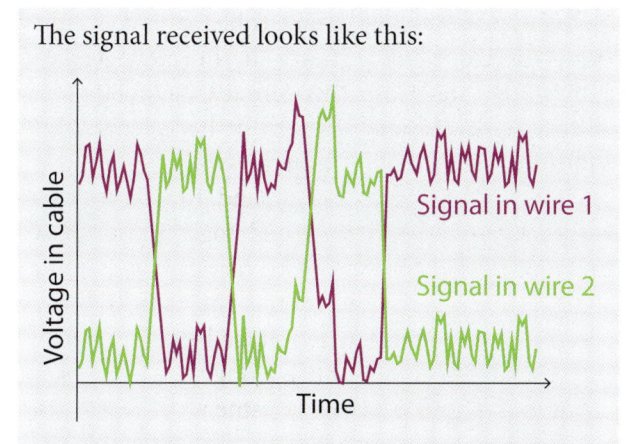

[Graph showing Signal in wire 1 and Signal in wire 2 as noisy inverted signals, with Voltage in cable on y-axis and Time on x-axis]

After the signal arrives at the destination, the one on the second wire is inverted for a second time and added to the first. This eliminates the interference, and the original digital signal is restored.

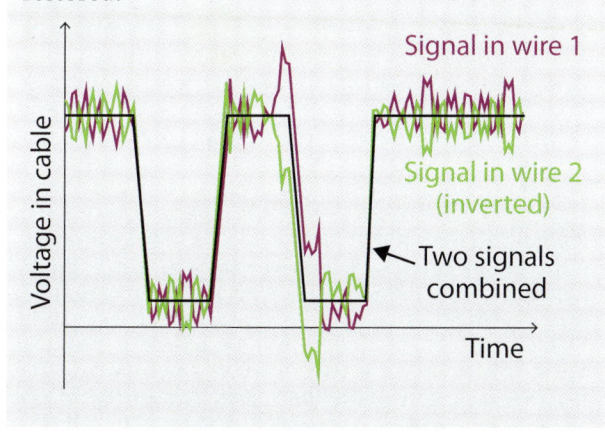

[Graph showing Signal in wire 1, Signal in wire 2 (inverted), and Two signals combined as a clean digital waveform]

UTP cables support data rates ranging from 100 Mbit/s for older versions to 1 Gbit/s for the latest standards, over a length of up to 100 metres in normal environments. They are most commonly found in Ethernet networks in office environments.

The main advantage of UTP cables is that they are cheap to buy and easy to install, because they are both flexible and straightforward to connect at either end. However, their security is low because it is fairly easy for someone to strip the plastic coating off a twisted pair cable and tap into the signal. This would allow them to monitor the data without being noticed.

Shielded twisted pair (STP)

Unshielded twisted pair cables still have two problems:

1. In environments with lots of interference, even the two wires described above are not enough to prevent the signal being swamped by interference, as the two wires can be affected slightly differently.

2. Since electrical currents themselves generate electromagnetic interference, the twisted pair itself can interfere with other wires nearby. There are laws that limit the amount of interference electrical devices are allowed to create to reduce this problem.

For both reasons, shielded twisted pairs, shown in Figure 3.2, contain shielding that both protects the signal being carried and contains the signal to stop it interfering with other nearby cables and devices. Usually either metal foil or braiding is used. In one type of STP cable, each twisted pair of cables is surrounded by a thin layer of aluminium metal foil, which acts as an insulator in both directions. In another type, the twisted pairs are wrapped in a layer of braided copper. Braided copper is particularly effective at shielding high-frequency electromagnetic signals and is flexible, making the cable somewhat easier to bend. Occasionally, where very good insulation is needed, both types are used in the same cable.

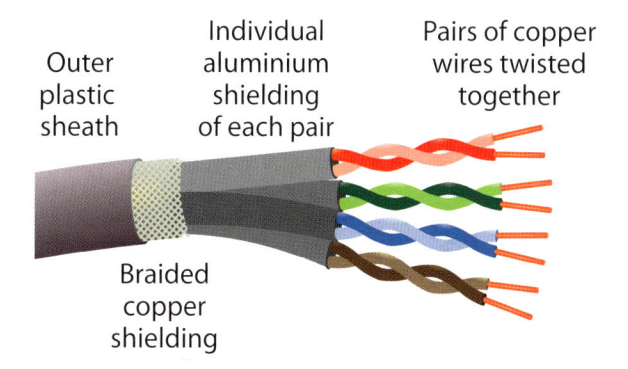

[Diagram of STP cable showing Outer plastic sheath, Braided copper shielding, Individual aluminium shielding of each pair, and Pairs of copper wires twisted together]

Figure 3.2: A shielded twisted pair cable showing both aluminium foil and copper braid shielding. In practice, most STP cables have one or the other.

The bandwidth and distance limit of STP is similar to that of UTP. However, STP cables are typically used in places where electrical interference is a particular issue, for example in factories or near high voltage cables, where a UTP cable would be unable to cope. Because it is more expensive, bulkier and less flexible than UTP cables, it is generally only used in places where it is really needed. Thus, it is unlikely to be used in a typical office Ethernet environment.

Coaxial cables

Coaxial cables, shown in Figure 3.3, offer an alternative solution to the problem of electromagnetic interference. In a coaxial cable there is a single conductor, typically a copper wire, in the centre of the cable, that carries the electrical signal. This is surrounded by a plastic insulator which is itself covered with copper braiding. The copper braiding provides the protection from external electrical interference, while the plastic insulator serves to keep it at a constant distance from the copper conductor in the centre. The whole cable is surrounded by a layer of plastic to protect the copper mesh.

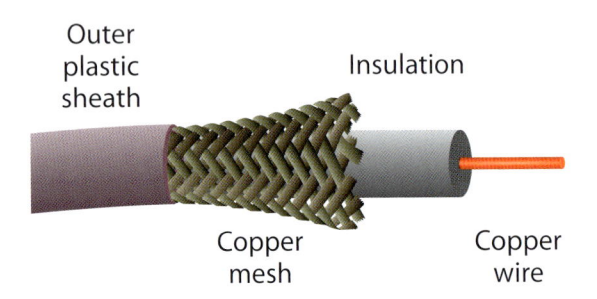

Figure 3.3: A coaxial cable.

The most common use of coaxial cables in a home is to connect a television aerial to a TV set, but it can also be used to carry other digital signals, such as Ethernet.

Their main advantage is that they offer excellent signal protection, and are therefore capable of high bandwidths, typically 1 Gbit/s. They can also send signals over longer distances than STP, typically a few hundred metres. They are also slightly more secure than twisted pair, as they are thicker and require more specialised tools to tap into them. Their main disadvantage is that they are typically inflexible due to the solid copper wire in the centre.

Coaxial cables have a similar cost to STP, so the choice often comes down to specific environmental factors, such as the cable flexibility required, the level of interference expected, transmission distance and what technology is used in existing installations.

3.4 Fibre Optic Cables

Fibre optic cables, shown in Figure 3.4, also carry digital signals, but instead of using electrical currents in a metal conductor, fibre optic cables use beams of light passing along a transparent medium. These cables are primarily composed of incredibly fine strands of glass or plastic known as optical fibres, giving rise to the name. Each optical fibre contains a core strand surrounded by a slightly different type of glass called the cladding. The strand is then encased in an insulating jacket and a tensile material, which protect the delicate glass fibres, give the cable strength and allow it to be handled more easily.

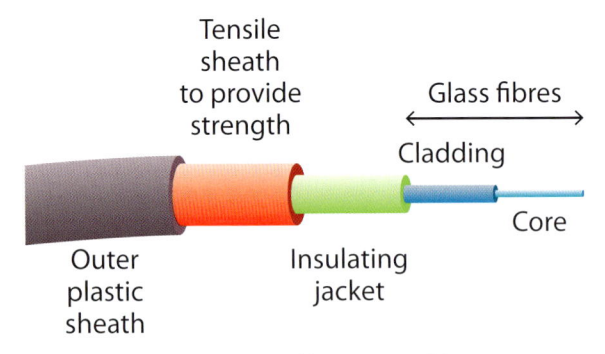

Figure 3.4: A fibre optic cable.

Light normally passes in only one direction along an optical fibre, so a minimum of two fibres are required to facilitate two-way communication. In practice, a typical fibre optic cable carries many strands as this increases the total bandwidth.

Note: Although light typically travels in a straight line, there is a concept in physics called 'total internal reflection', which allows light to be moved round corners, provided it is passing through a layer of glass (the core) that is surrounded by a second layer of glass (the cladding) with a lower refractive index. This is the principle used in fibre optic cables. The CCEA specification does not require you to understand this principle, but it is fundamental to how fibre optic cables work.

In order to be transmitted along a fibre optic cable, electrical signals are converted into optical signals by specialised devices known as optical transmitters, which use lasers or light-emitting diodes to produce the beams of light. A binary '1' is represented by the light being 'on', and a '0' by the light being 'off'.

The light passes along the core of the cable until it emerges at the far end of the cable. As the light is travelling very fast (200,000 km/s in glass) such a beam can cross the Atlantic from Europe to North America in about 1/50th of a second! At the receiving end, optical detectors convert the incoming light signals back into electrical signals that can be processed by computers.

Fibre optic cables come in two types:

- **Single-mode** cables have an extremely narrow core, typically 9 μm. This makes them very expensive to produce, but they are capable of extremely high bandwidths, with some designs reaching 100 Gbit/s or more. They are also capable of carrying signals for very long distances. Depending on their exact design, they have a range from about 50 kilometres to over 1000 kilometres for the highest quality cables. This makes them useful for carrying data between different countries and across seas and oceans.

- **Multi-mode** cables have a wider core, typically about 50 μm in diameter. This makes them much cheaper to manufacture, but the trade-off is that the wider core significantly reduces their range. A typical multi-core cable has a bandwidth of up to 100 Gbit/s, similar to a single-mode cable, but its range is much lower, typically between 300 and 500 metres. They are most commonly used for high-bandwidth connections within a single site such as a university or a data centre.

While traditional broadband connections to homes have used metal cable, these are increasingly being replaced by fibre optic cables. This allows much faster data speeds, facilitating better digital experiences such as streaming movies and faster downloads.

Fibre optic cables have several advantages beyond their high bandwidth and range. Firstly, unlike metal cables, fibre optic cables are immune to electromagnetic interference, making them very useful in locations with a lot of electromagnetic 'noise'. Secondly, they are much more secure than metal cables. Intercepting data from a fibre optic cable is very difficult, as doing so requires physically accessing the very delicate glass fibre. Additionally, any attempt to read light from the cable will disrupt the signal, which is readily detectable at the receiving end of the cable. Finally, because they do not contain any metal, fibre optic cables do not corrode or degrade in the way that metal cables can.

Task

Consider each of the following applications of fibre optic cables and suggest whether a single-mode or multi-mode cable would be the better choice. Give reasons.

1. A cable to connect mainland Scotland to the Orkney Islands.
2. A cable to connect different buildings in a secondary school.
3. A cable to connect a house to a broadband cabinet at the end of the street.
4. A cable to connect a broadband cabinet on a street to a data centre in a nearby city.

3.5 Wireless Transmission Media

Wireless transmission media are so-called because they remove the need for physical cables entirely. They use radio waves to transmit data through the air.

Radio waves are a form of electromagnetic radiation, which also includes visible light. Radio waves are characterised by their frequency, measured in hertz (Hz), which corresponds to the number of oscillations per second. Of all electromagnetic radiations, radio waves have the lowest frequencies, typically below 300 GHz.

Two of the most common forms of wireless transmission media are Bluetooth and Wi-Fi. Both technologies were discussed in Chapter 2, where their main uses and effective ranges were discussed.

Wireless transmission operates in a similar way to fibre-optic cable except that, instead of producing and detecting visible light, radio waves are produced and detected. Unlike visible light, radio waves can pass through solid objects like walls, so they can be transmitted directly through the air towards their destination. Bluetooth uses radio waves at a frequency of 2.4 GHz, while Wi-Fi uses a range of frequencies between 2.4 GHz and 5 GHz, although newer versions can also use the 5.9 GHz to 7.1 GHz range.

In terms of bandwidth, most Bluetooth technology offers between 1 and 2 Mbit/s though some versions can operate at 25 Mbit/s. While this is significantly lower than physical cables, the benefits of not needing cables often outweighs this consideration.

Wi-Fi offers much higher bandwidths than Bluetooth, typically up to 250 Mbit/s. While not as fast as some cable connections, this is sufficient to allow someone to comfortably stream a movie onto a tablet device over a Wi-Fi network in their home.

The main advantage of wireless transmission media is the lack of cables. This allows for much more flexible workplaces, where devices such as laptops and tablets can be moved around freely and remain connected to the network. It also allows people to connect to various networks as they move around the world, such as connecting to a Wi-Fi network in a shopping centre or train station.

However, they also have disadvantages. Wireless technology still does not have the speed or range of physical cables, so cannot yet be used for very high bandwidth or long-distance connections. In addition, because data is moving through the air, it is easy for someone to intercept the radio signal and collect the data. Bluetooth connections are particularly susceptible to this risk, although newer versions offer better protection. Wi-Fi uses strong encryption protocols such as WPA3 to scramble data so that, even if it is intercepted, it cannot be understood. Finally, other common devices, such as microwave ovens, use waves of a similar frequency to Wi-Fi and Bluetooth, which increases interference and reduces the speed of data transfer.

Task

Discuss the relative level of security offered by metal cables, fibre optic cables and wireless transmission media. Is it always worth investing in the most secure technology, even if it is more expensive? Does your decision depend on the type of data being transferred and, if so, how?

3.6 Summary

Figure 3.5 summaries the bandwidth and security levels of the technologies discussed in this chapter.

Technology	Maximum bandwidth*	Security
Twisted pair (unshielded and shielded)	1 Gbit/s	Low
Coaxial cable	1 Gbit/s	Low/medium
Fibre optic cable	100 Gbit/s	High
Bluetooth	25 Mbit/s	Low
Wi-Fi	250 Mbit/s	High

*Approximate figures. The technologies have a very wide range.

Figure 3.5: Summary of the transmission technologies discussed in this chapter.

Questions

1. What does bandwidth refer to in the context of transmission media?
2. How is bandwidth typically measured?
3. What is the maximum bandwidth of modern Ethernet connections?
4. What is meant by the term 'broadband'?
5. What is the main problem encountered when sending signals along metal cables?
6. How do shielded twisted pair cables address interference issues?
7. What are the advantages of coaxial cables over twisted pair?
8. Why are single-mode fibre optic cables more suitable for long-distance connections?
9. What frequency range of radio waves do Bluetooth and Wi-Fi use?
10. What is the typical maximum bandwidth of Wi-Fi connections?
11. Compare wireless and fibre optic communication in terms of bandwidth.
12. Discuss how a twisted pair can be used to reduce the problem of electromagnetic interference in a metal cable.

CHAPTER 4
Error Correction and Detection

By the end of this chapter students should be able to:

- describe and evaluate methods of detecting and correcting data transmission errors: parity bits, checksums, echo checking and cyclic redundancy check (CRC).

4.1 Introduction

Ensuring the integrity and accuracy of transmitted data is of vital importance. For example, in banking, even a single digit error in a bank account number, an amount of money to be transferred or a transaction date could cause significant problems. In industry, an error in a single byte of data could mean the difference between a rocket that successfully reaches orbit and one that fails to do so.

Case Study

On 4 June 1996, the European Space Agency launched its new Ariane 5 rocket for the first time. Just 40 seconds after liftoff, the rocket's guidance system failed. The failure was triggered by an error in a 16-bit number in the spacecraft's guidance software. The error was caused by data being converted incorrectly between two number formats, but the corrupted data was not detected and was sent to the subsystem responsible for directing the rocket's nozzles to keep it on course. The faulty data confused the guidance system, which instructed the rocket to veer significantly off course.

The rocket could not recover from this course deviation and, less than a minute after liftoff, the rocket's self-destruct mechanism was activated for safety reasons. This resulted in the destruction of the rocket and its cargo, which included four scientific research satellites known as *Cluster*. The loss was estimated to be around £300 million in 1996 prices. This incident not only led to a huge financial loss for the ESA, but also caused a significant delay to the Ariane 5 programme and a four-year delay to the *Cluster* mission, as new satellites had to be built and launched.

In the example of Ariane 5 the error was caused by a software fault. However, data errors can occur due to other reasons, such as electromagnetic interference (as discussed in Chapter 3), hardware malfunctions, the weakening of a signal over a long distance and even deliberate security breaches.

The detection of errors is therefore of paramount importance for the integrity of data systems, the reliability of communications, privacy and customer trust. In this chapter we will consider three common ways that communication systems attempt to detect and recover from data errors.

4.2 Parity Bits

Parity bits are extra data bits appended to a data stream to enable the detection of errors that may occur during transmission. A parity bit is added to each block of data to ensure that the total number of '1' bits in the transmitted data (including the parity bit itself) is either odd or even, depending on the chosen parity scheme.

In **even parity**, the total number of '1' bits in the data, including the parity bit, is made even. If the data contains an odd number of '1' bits, an additional '1' parity bit is added to the end of the data to make it even. In **odd parity**, the total number of '1' bits in the data, including the parity bit, is made odd. If the data contains an even number of '1' bits, an additional '1' parity bit is added to the end of the data to make it odd.

If, during the transmission process, a single bit

error occurs anywhere in the transmitted data, the parity check at the receiver's end will reveal the discrepancy. If the number of '1' bits in the received data (including the parity bit) does not match the specified parity, an error is detected. At this point, the data will be discarded, and the sender instructed to retransmit the data.

Note: When a bit is switched from a '1' to a '0', or vice-versa, it is said to have been 'flipped'.

Worked Example

A computer wants to transmit the ASCII character 'S' using an even parity bit for error detection.

First the parity bit is calculated. It counts the number of '1' bits in the 7-bit ASCII character: 1010011. There are four '1' bits. Since 4 is even, and we want to achieve even parity, an additional '0' parity bit is added to the end of the 7-bit ASCII character to make the total number of '1' bits, including the parity bit, even.

The transmitted data becomes: 10100110. This is the original 7-bit ASCII character: 1010011 plus a single parity bit: 0.

The receiving computer receives the data as 10000110. Note that the third bit has been flipped (from 1 to 0) due to electromagnetic interference during transfer. The receiver counts the number of '1' bits in the data, including the parity bit. There are three '1' bits. Since this is not possible under even parity, the receiving computer concludes that the data has been corrupted and asks the sender to retransmit.

The data is then retransmitted and is received as: 10100110. The receiver again counts the number of '1' bits. There are four, which is even, so the receiving computer accepts the data as valid.

Parity bits are a simple and effective method for detecting errors in data transmission. However, they do have limitations that make them unsuitable for certain applications:

- Parity bits can only detect odd numbers of errors. If an even number of bits (including the parity bit) are flipped during transmission, the parity check will not detect the error. This limitation means that parity bits are not robust enough to catch all types of errors, especially when multiple bits are corrupted simultaneously.
- Parity bits can only detect errors but cannot correct them. When an error is detected, the receiver knows that the data is corrupted, but it cannot pinpoint which specific bits are incorrect or try to correct them. More complex error correction techniques, such as Hamming codes (see below), are needed to both detect and correct errors in transmitted data.
- For large datasets, the overhead of adding one extra bit for every eight bits of data (in the case of 8-bit parity) can become inefficient as the additional bits increase the bandwidth and storage requirements.

Hamming codes work by augmenting the original data with additional bits designed not only for error detection but also error correction. During the encoding process, parity bits are calculated based on the positions of certain bits within the data. These parity bits serve as checks, verifying specific combinations of data bits. If an error occurs during transmission or storage, the parity checks fail for the corresponding positions, indicating the presence of an error. By analysing the parity bits, the receiver can identify and rectify the erroneous bit, ensuring the accuracy of the transmitted or stored data.

Note: The CCEA specification does not require you to understand how Hamming codes work.

4.3 Checksums

A checksum is a numerical value derived from a set of data. The primary purpose of a checksum is to verify the integrity of transmitted data. By recalculating the checksum at the receiver's end and comparing it with the checksum actually received, any discrepancies indicate that there are errors in the transmission of the data.

The most basic checksum is to calculate the number of '1' bits in the data and transmit the total as the checksum. However, more complex algorithms can be used to generate checksums. Two common checksum algorithms are discussed below.

Internet checksum (RFC 1071)

Widely used for error detection in network communication, the internet checksum algorithm employs arithmetic to generate a 16-bit checksum.

Suppose we want to transmit the following 16-bit data: 1100110001011010. The data is divided into two 8-bit segments: 11001100 and 01011010. These two 8-bit segments are then added together, giving a total of 100100110 in binary. The '1's and '0's are then reversed to give 011011001 (known as 'one's complement'). This is the checksum that is then transmitted with the data.

Like parity bits, the internet checksum method can only detect an odd number of errors. If two errors occur, this checksum method will not detect it.

Cyclic Redundancy Check (CRC)

CRC checksums are widely used in various applications, including network protocols and data storage. CRC algorithms offer high error-detection capabilities and are often able to detect more than one error.

CRC uses mathematics to generate the checksum. The mathematics are complex, and it is not necessary to know the details. But essentially the data is sent in the form of two numbers, one of which divides evenly into the other. When received, if the two numbers do not evenly divide, then it means that one or more errors has occurred during transmission.

The main advantage of CRC is that it can often detect multiple errors in data transmission. However, it cannot say where the error occurred, only that there is an error. The data needs to be retransmitted if the error is detected.

CRC is used extensively in network protocols such as Ethernet, Wi-Fi and TCP/IP. It is also used to verify data that has been stored on, for example, a hard drive or computer memory. If an error occurs as data is written to or read from memory, a CRC check will detect the error.

Compared to internet checksum, CRC offers higher error detection capabilities and, because it is based on mathematical calculations, is less vulnerable to intentional tampering. These advantages make CRC a preferred choice over internet checksum in critical applications where data integrity and security are paramount.

4.4 Echo Checking

Consider a conversation between two people in a noisy environment. The first person says a sentence to the second person. The second person then repeats the sentence back to the first person. If the sentence that the first person hears at that point is different from what they actually said, then they assume that the sentence has not been received correctly and they repeat the process.

This method is used by airline pilots when they receive instructions from air traffic control (ATC). The pilot repeats the instruction back to the ATC to verify that they have understood it correctly. For example, the ATC may say 'Flight 123, descend and maintain 10,000 feet' to which the pilot will reply 'Descend and maintain 10,000 feet, Flight 123.' If, however, the ATC heard the pilot say '12,000 feet' then they would immediately message that that was incorrect and repeat the instruction. The risk presented by such a message being misunderstood by a pilot is obvious.

In data communications, echo checking (sometimes called 'loopback') operates in a similar way. Data is transmitted to the receiver without any checksum or parity bits. The receiver then retransmits the received data back to the sender. The receiver then compares this to what they originally sent. If the two sets of data are not the same, then an error is assumed to have occurred, and the data is retransmitted.

Note that it is not possible to detect whether the error occurred in the original transmission, or if it occurred in the echo sent back. In both cases the message would be resent. This is one disadvantage of echo checking, i.e. that data may be resent unnecessarily if the error occurred in the echo. A second disadvantage is that it doubles the traffic on the network, since every message is sent at least twice. Finally, it reduces the speed of communication, as it takes time for each message to be transmitted twice to confirm correct receipt.

Nevertheless, despite its inefficiency, echo checking is still used in some situations because it is very simple to implement, as it does not require advanced algorithms. It also has a high level of reliability because it has a low tolerance for errors and is able to detect when multiple simultaneous errors have occurred in the data.

Worked Example

- Computer A transmits the message 'HELLO' to Computer B.
- Computer B receives the message as 'HELLO' and echoes it back to Computer A.
- Computer A receives 'HELLO'. As this is the same as the original message, it concludes that the message has been received correctly.

- Computer A then transmits the message 'OVER' to Computer B.
- Computer B receives the message as 'OVEN' and echoes it back to Computer A.
- Computer A receives 'OVEN'. This is different from the original message, so it detects an error and retransmits the data 'OVER'.
- Computer B receives the retransmitted message as 'OVER' and echoes it back to Computer A.
- Computer A receives 'OVER'. As this is the same as the original message, it concludes that the message has been received correctly.

- Computer A then transmits the message 'THERE' to Computer B.
- Computer B receives the message as 'THERE' and echoes it back to Computer A.
- Computer A receives 'THESE'. This is different from the original message, so it detects an error and retransmits the data 'THERE'. Note that even though the error occurred in the echo this time, the data is still retransmitted.
- Computer B receives the retransmitted message as 'THERE' and echoes it back to Computer A.
- Computer A receives 'THERE'. As this is the same as the original message, it concludes that the message has been received correctly.

After this process, the whole message 'HELLO OVER THERE' has been correctly received.

Questions

1. Why is the detection of errors essential for data systems?
2. What are some common causes of data errors in communication systems?
3. What is the primary function of parity bits in error detection?
4. Describe the difference between even parity and odd parity.
5. How does a receiver detect errors using parity bits, and what action is taken if errors are detected?
6. What are the limitations of parity bits in error detection?
7. Explain briefly how a checksum can detect errors in transmitted data.
8. State two advantages of using CRC over internet checksum.
9. Which is more efficient in terms of network usage – CRC or echo checking? Explain your answer.
10. Compare the use of parity bits and checksums in detecting and correcting errors during data transmission. What are the advantages and disadvantages of each?
11. Discuss how echo checking operates in data communications. Describe some disadvantages of this method, and suggest why it might still be used.

CHAPTER 5
Relational Databases

By the end of this chapter students should be able to:

- describe the main features of a relational database;
- describe the difference between a logical data model and a physical data model;
- define the terms attribute, entity, primary key, composite key, foreign key, relationships, referential integrity, data duplication and data inconsistency;
- produce an entity-relationship (ER) model from the given data requirements for a scenario.

5.1 Introduction

Relational databases are one of the key components of the A2 CCEA specification. This is the first of three chapters that explore relational databases in detail. The initial discussion outlines the basic characteristics of databases, with rows representing records and columns representing fields within the context of a flat-file structure. This allows us to highlight the shortcomings of flat-file databases.

We then introduce relational databases, characterised by multiple tables and defined relationships. The subsequent sections delve into the mechanics of relationships, covering one-to-one, one-to-many and many-to-many scenarios and how these can be implemented in a database.

The chapter then explores additional features such as input validation, querying capabilities with SQL, data modification, access rights and referential integrity. The discussion underscores the significance of referential integrity in preventing contradictory data and ensuring the cohesiveness of the database structure. Finally, the chapter discusses both logical and physical data models and entity-relationship diagrams.

5.2 What is a Database?

A database is a collection of data that is stored in such a way that information can be found easily when required, for example a list of AS/A2 students along with their form class and address. The simplest type of database is a **flat-file** database, which consists of a single table with rows and columns.

Each row represents one entry in the database. In our example, this would be a student. Each column represents one attribute. In our example, these would be attributes such as name, form and address. Each row is called a **record**. Each column is called a **field**.

Figure 5.1 shows a section of a flat-file database with details of school students.

Such a database is very common, and it is easy to carry out simple searches on it. For example, to find out a student's address you simply have to look up the student's record in the database and read the address field. To find out the names of every student in Form 13A, you would simply filter the records to only show those where the Form field contains '13A'.

Imagine that the school now wants to add information about the subjects the students are studying. They could add a column for 'Subject' and add a row for each subject they are studying, as shown in Figure 5.2 overleaf.

Name	Form	Address
Saoirse Doyle	13A	16 Maxwell Street
Peter Marshall	13A	Flat 6, 85 Ballyeaston Street
Declan Kelly	13B	52 Letterbratt Road
Susan Marshall	14A	Flat 6, 85 Ballyeaston Street
John Blair	14A	3 Ballyhannon Park

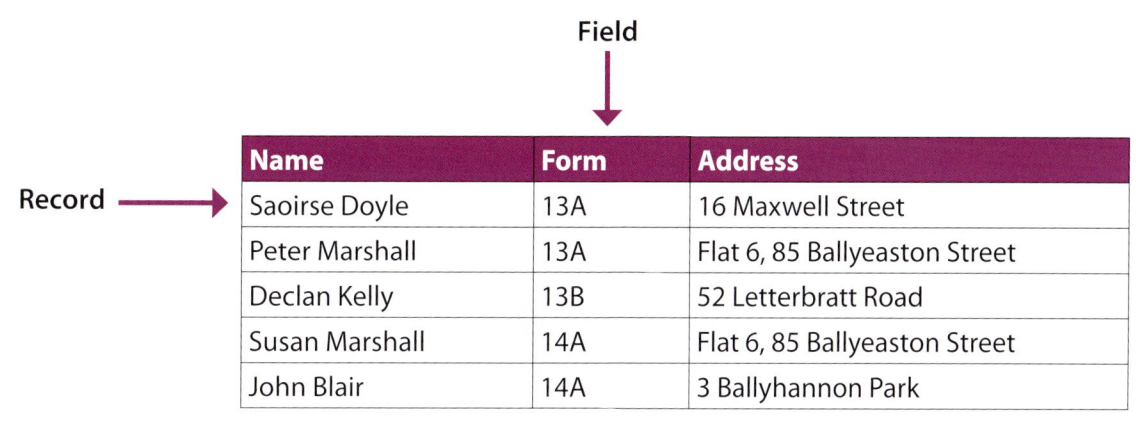

Figure 5.1: An example of a flat-file database.

Name	Form	Address	Subject
Saoirse Doyle	13A	16 Maxwell Street	Mathematics
Saoirse Doyle	13A	16 Maxwell Street	Chemistry
Saoirse Doyle	13A	16 Maxwell Street	Digital Technology
Saoirse Doyle	13A	16 Maxwell Street	History
Peter Marshall	13A	Flat 6, 85 Ballyeaston Street	Religious Studies
Peter Marshall	13A	Flat 6, 85 Ballyeaston Street	Digital Technology
Peter Marshal	13A	Flat 6, 85 Ballyeaston Street	Mathematics
Peter Marshall	13A	Flat 6, 85 Ballyeaston Street	Irish
Declan Kelly	13B	52 Letterbratt Road	Mathematics
Declan Kelly	13B	52 Letterbratt Road	Religious Studies
Declan Kelly	13B	52 Letterbratt Road	Irish
Declan Kelly	13B	52 Letterbratt Road	Chemistry
Declan Kelly	13B	13 King Street	Chemistry
Susan Marshall	14A	Flat 6, 85 Ballyeaston Street	History
Susan Marshall	14A	Flat 6, 85 Ballyeaston Street	Irish
Susan Marshall	14A	Flat 6, 85 Ballyeaston Street	Digital Technology
John Blair	14A	3 Ballyhannon Park	History
John Blair	14A	3 Ballyhannon Park	Mathematics
John Blair	14A	3 Ballyhannon Park	Religious Studies

Figure 5.2: The flat-file database with information about subjects added.

The table is now much longer, because there is now a record for every subject that each student is studying. You may also see the problems that this has introduced:

- There is a lot of **data duplication**. For Saoirse Doyle, for example, her name, form and address are recorded four times, once for each AS subject that she is studying. This not only wastes storage space but makes it more difficult to alter the repeated data. If Saoirse Doyle moves house, then the address has to be updated correctly every time her address appears in the table. This takes time and could introduce an error if the address was not changed correctly in every row. These problems are avoided if Saoirse Doyle's address is only stored once.
- There is **data inconsistency**. For example, Peter Marshall's surname is spelt in two different ways in the database. This error has been introduced because of the problem of data duplication. In the same way, Declan Kelly is listed as studying Chemistry twice, with two different home addresses. As it is, the database offers no clues as to which is the correct spelling of Marshall, and what the current address of Declan Kelly actually is.

These problems show that the flat-file database has poor **data integrity**. Database users are faced with data that they cannot fully rely on. **Relational databases** were initially developed to resolve problems like these, improving data integrity.

5.3 What Is a Relational Database?

A relational database:

- has more than one table, and
- defines the relationships between the tables (hence the term 'relational').

Although this may seem simple at first glance, this

structure gives relational databases immense power. We will explore the advantages of relational databases in this chapter and the two following chapters. But first we will consider the structure of a relational database in more detail.

More than one table

At the heart of a relational database are two important conceptual building blocks: entities and attributes. An **entity** encapsulates a distinct object or concept for which data is stored. In our example, this would be pupils, forms and subjects. **Attributes** define the unique characteristics inherent to each entity. For pupils, attributes might include their names, address and age, while subjects could include attributes like the name of the subject and the teacher in charge.

So, in our school relational database, we would have a table for each entity, and their attributes would look as shown in Figure 3.3.

TABLE Student

StudentName	Address
Saoirse Doyle	16 Maxwell Street
Peter Marshall	Flat 6, 85 Ballyeaston Street
Declan Kelly	52 Letterbratt Road
Susan Marshall	Flat 6, 85 Ballyeaston Street
John Blair	3 Ballyhannon Park

TABLE Form

Form	FormTeacher
13A	Mr Johnston
13B	Mrs Smith
14A	Dr O'Reilly

TABLE Subject

SubjectName	TeacherInCharge
Chemistry	Dr Hamdam
Digital Technology	Mr McKittrick
History	Mr Johnston
Irish	Ms Hagan
Mathematics	Mrs Kincaid
Religious Studies	Miss Porter

Figure 5.3: Three tables in a simple relational database.

As you can see, there is now only one row for each record in each table. Each student appears only once in the Student table, each form appears once in the Form table and each subject appears once in the Subject table. This eliminates many of the problems of data duplication, as it is now often only necessary to change the attributes of a single record to update the database.

Relationships

However, this is not yet a functional relational database. Although we have set up the tables, there is no information about how they relate to each other. We cannot use the database to find out what form a student is in, or what subjects they are studying. For this, we need to somehow link them together, to define the relationships that exist between the various entities.

A **relationship** in a relational database defines how two entities relate to each other. There are three types of relationship:

- A **one-to-one (1:1)** relationship exists where each record in one table is related to no more than one record in a second table. Imagine a situation where each student in a year group has been given a tablet device to help them with their school work. A 1:1 relationship exists between the students and the tablet device. Each student has exactly one tablet device, and each tablet device is assigned to exactly one student.
- A **one-to-many (1:N)** relationship exists where each record in one table can be related to many records in a second table. For example, a single form contains many pupils. However, a student can only be a member of a single form. Therefore, each record in the Form table can be related to many records in the Student table, but each record in the Student table can only be related to one record in the Form table.

- A **many-to-many (M:N)** relationship exists where the records in each table can each be related to many records in the other table. For example, each student is studying many subjects, and each subject is being studied by many students. Therefore, each record in the Subject table can be related to many records in the Student table, and each record in the Student table can be related to many records in the Subject table.

The type of a relationship is known as its **cardinality**.

Now that we have defined the types of relationship that exist, how do we set these up in the database? Obviously, if we are going to link individual entities together, we need to have an unambiguous way to refer to each record. While our table of Students does not contain any students with the same name, this does happen from time to time. In a large school it is quite likely that at some point there will be two students with the same name. So student name is a poor choice for this task.

It is better to create another attribute containing a value that we know is going to be unique. So, in our example, we create an attribute called StudentID that is different for every student. We then use this attribute to refer unambiguously to a single student, as shown in Figure 5.4.

TABLE Student

StudentID	StudentName	Address
1	Saoirse Doyle	16 Maxwell Street
2	Peter Marshall	Flat 6, 85 Ballyeaston Street
3	Declan Kelly	52 Letterbratt Road
4	Susan Marshall	Flat 6, 85 Ballyeaston Street
5	John Blair	3 Ballyhannon Park
6	Saoirse Doyle	27 Knockgreenan Avenue

Figure 5.4: Student table with a unique attribute, StudentID, added.

In the example above, we have imagined that a second student also called Saoirse Doyle has just joined the school. This does not cause problems for the database, however, because the two Saoirses have been given different StudentIDs, so can still be referred to individually.

The attribute that is used to uniquely identify a record in a relational database is known as the **primary key**. In the Student table, StudentID now serves as the primary key. We often underline the primary key, as shown in Figure 5.4.

In the Subject table, we have added a SubjectID to serve as the primary key of the Subject table, as shown in Figure 5.5. You might think that Subject name could serve as the primary key. However, it is possible that the database might contain two subjects with the same name. For example, the school might regard Mathematics at GCSE level as a different subject from Mathematics at AS level. Therefore 'Mathematics' might appear twice, for two different subjects.

TABLE Subject

SubjectID	SubjectName	TeacherInCharge
901	Chemistry	Dr Hamdam
902	Digital Technology	Mr McKittrick
903	History	Mr Johnston
904	Irish	Ms Hagan
905	Mathematics	Mrs Kincaid
906	Religious Studies	Miss Porter

Figure 5.5: Subject table with a unique attribute, SubjectID, added.

For the sake of the example, we will assume that we have also added an attribute, FormID, to the Form table to serve as its primary key.

To show a 1:1 or 1:N relationship, then, it is simply a matter of adding an attribute to the table on the 1: side that will contain a value from the primary key of the related table. For example, to link a student to a form we first add a FormID attribute to the Student table. Then we insert the FormID of each student's form into the FormID field for that student. An attribute that is intended to contain a value from the primary key of another table is called a **foreign key**. The foreign key is often indicated by an asterisk *. So the two tables now look as shown in Figure 5.6.

TABLE Student

StudentID	StudentName	Address	FormID*
1	Saoirse Doyle	16 Maxwell Street	50
2	Peter Marshall	Flat 6, 85 Ballyeaston Street	50
3	Declan Kelly	52 Letterbratt Road	51
4	Susan Marshall	Flat 6, 85 Ballyeaston Street	52
5	John Blair	3 Ballyhannon Park	52
6	Saoirse Doyle	27 Knockgreenan Avenue	51

TABLE Form

FormID	Form	FormTeacher
50	13A	Mr Johnston
51	13B	Mrs Smith
52	14A	Dr O'Reilly

Figure 5.6: The tables Student and Form with primary and foreign keys indicated.

But how do we define a many-to-many (M:N) relationship in a relational database? The approach above, of adding a foreign key to one table, obviously will not work. A foreign key field can only hold one value, but we need to be able to link multiple foreign keys to each entity.

The solution is to create a third table to contain the links. This is known as an associative table. In our example, as we have seen, a M:N relationship exists between Students and Subjects. Each student is studying many subjects, and each subject is being studied by many students. So we can create a third table called Studying to store this information, as shown in Figure 5.7.

Each row indicates that one Student is studying one Subject. Row 1, for example, shows that the student with StudentID = 1 (Saoirse Doyle) is studying the subject with SubjectID = 901 (Chemistry). Note that there are other rows in this table containing StudentID = 1, because Saoirse studies more than one subject. And there are other rows in this table containing SubjectID = 901, because more than one student is studying Chemistry.

Note that both attributes in the Studying table are underlined, because they both form the primary key. Neither attribute on its own can uniquely identify a record in this table. When the primary key consists of more than one attribute it is known as a **composite key**.

Note too that, although we started with a M:N relationship, creating the Studying table has replaced this with two 1:N relationships. There is a 1:N relationship between Student and Studying (each Student is linked to many records in the Studying table) and there is a 1:N relationship between Subject and Studying (each Subject is linked to many records in the Studying table).

TABLE Studying

StudentID	SubjectID
1	901
1	902
1	905
2	902
2	904
2	905
2	906
3	901
3	904
3	905
3	906
4	902
4	903
4	904
5	903
5	905
5	906

Figure 5.7: An associative table used to link many Students with many Subjects.

5.4 Other Features of Relational Databases

We have seen that the two fundamental features of a relational database are that it has many tables, and that there are relationships between them. However, relational databases usually have other features that make them even more useful.

Constraining input/validation

Relational databases usually allow the developer to define what values are and are not allowed to be entered into a field. For example, a field that is meant to hold a date can be defined to only accept input that is in the form of a date, for example '6 June 2024' or '36/9/24' but not 'Sarah Smith'. When entering the name of a school form we could define a rule saying that it must consist of up to two digits followed by one letter, so it would accept '14A' or '8G' but not 'Year 8'. This reduces the chances of errors occurring at a later date due to faulty data, or data that is in an unexpected format.

Running queries

A relational database allows users to carry out simple or complex 'queries' on the database using a powerful system called Structured Query Language (SQL). SQL is discussed in more detail in Chapter 7. An example of query is to find the names and addresses of all pupils whose FormID is 50.

Data modification

A relational database will allow users to add a new record to a table, delete a record from the table and modify data in an existing table, often using SQL. We shall consider data modification in more detail under 'referential integrity' later in this section.

Access rights

A relational database typically allows the developer to create usernames and passwords, which users of the database must use to 'log in' to the database. These users could have different levels of access. So, for example, the headmaster might be the only person who has the ability to add, delete or modify entries in the Subject table, but all staff could have 'read only' rights to that table. This prevents unauthorised or inexperienced staff creating problems by accessing or modifying data that they should not.

> **Task**
>
> Consider the scenario where a school administrator wants to implement access rights in a relational database. Discuss the potential challenges and benefits of assigning different levels of access to various users. How might this impact data security and overall database management within an educational institution?

Referential integrity

Because a relational database holds information in related tables, deleting data from one table has implications for other tables. For example, if a student is deleted from the Student table, then all entries connected to that student should also be deleted from any related tables, in this case the Form table and the Studying table. If this did not happen, it would mean (for example) that the StudentID foreign key in the Form table would contain a reference to a student who did not exist, which would make no sense. Records which contain a foreign key that does not exist in the primary table are called **orphan** records. This leads to contradictions in the database that could potentially cause serious errors in the future. To prevent contradictory data, a relational database enforces **referential integrity**.

Under referential integrity, if a user deletes, say, John Blair from the Student table, then the database will automatically also delete all his associated entries in the Form table and the Studying table. Therefore, deleting a single record from the Student table actually results in multiple records across three different tables being deleted.

Similarly, if a user attempts to add a record to the Studying table, the database will only let the user do so if the StudentID they entered exists in the Student table, and the SubjectID they entered exists in the Subject table. If either does not, the database will enforce referential integrity by refusing to add the record.

Case Study

A roads authority carries out bridge inspections on a regular basis to ensure that bridges are safe for road users. This information is stored in a relational database where each bridge is stored as a record in a table called Bridge. Each Inspection is stored in a second table with a 1:N relationship with the Bridge table, as each bridge can be inspected more than once. Finally, repairs are stored in a table called Repair. This table is related to the Inspection table with a 1:N relationship, since an inspection may result in more than one repair. Repair teams use the Inspection records to decide when to carry out Repairs. The structure of the tables and some sample data are shown in the following tables.

TABLE Bridge

BridgeID	BridgeName	Structure
1	Arthur Bridge	Steel beam
2	Bellevue Bridge	Concrete beam
3	Collin Bridge	Steel beam
4	Hightown Road	Steel beam
5	Templepatrick	Concrete beam
6	Donegore Footbridge	Concrete arch

TABLE Inspection

InspectionID	BridgeID*	Date	Inspector
11	1	30 Apr 2024	McCarthy
12	2	4 May 2024	Kumar
13	6	7 May 2024	McCarthy
14	2	4 Jun 2024	Smith
15	4	5 Jun 2024	Kumar

TABLE Repair

RepairID	InspectionID*	DateOfRepair	Task	Team
61	15	10 Jun 2024	Rust treatment	A
62	14	12 Jun 2024	Spalling repair	B
63	11	26 Jul 2024	Barrier repair	B
64	14	26 Jul 2024	Parapet repair	A

On one occasion an engineer inspects a bridge and finds a serious defect in one of the main beams of the bridge. He creates a new Inspection record and registers the fault. However, he enters the ID of a bridge that doesn't exist with the result that the Inspection record becomes an orphan record. A few days later, the repair team consults the database for a list of Bridge records that have recently had an Inspection. Because of the error, the Inspection does not appear in the list. As a result, no repair is carried out, meaning that the bridge is left in a dangerous condition and may collapse. It is only the vigilance of a passing engineer who notices the condition of the structure that a failure is avoided.

On a second occasion, a team carries out a repair to a bridge after an inspection. Afterwards, the team manager creates a new Repair record, intending to link it to the Inspection record to show that the work has been done. However, she enters the wrong InspectionID, creating an orphan record. Later in the month another team notices that the Inspection has no associated Repair and, assuming no repair has been carried out, sends a team to carry out the work. Only when they have closed the road, erected their scaffolding and started work do they realise the job has actually already been done. Thousands of pounds and a day of time are wasted.

Neither of these issues could have happened if the database had enforced referential integrity. Because of the waste of resources and the narrowly-avoided bridge failure, the roads authority rebuilds their database to enforce referential integrity.

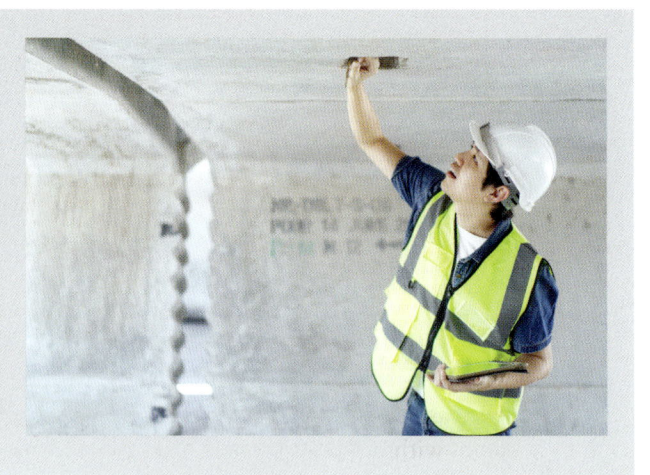

Portability

Because the relational model is a widely used standard, it is fairly straightforward to transfer a database structure, and the data it contains, between different database applications. This is because database software developers usually follow the same standards for defining tables and the relationships between them.

5.5 Data Modelling

Logical model

When a developer considers creating a new relational database, they first create a **logical model** of the system. A logical model defines:

- the entities to be included;
- the relationships between them;
- the attributes of the entities;
- the primary key for each entity (i.e. how to uniquely identify each entity).

The purpose of a logical model is to provide a high-level view of the overall structure of the data that is to be modelled. At this point, we are not yet considering how it would be implemented in an actual database.

A summary of a logical data model can be represented using an **entity-relationship (ER) diagram**. Different ways of drawing ER diagrams exist, but one of the most common is to use **crow's feet** notation (Figure 5.8). In this notation, entities are represented by rectangles, and relationships by lines with 'crow's feet' to show the 'many' ends of relationships.

A summary of the logical model of the school system described above is shown as an ER diagram in Figure 5.9.

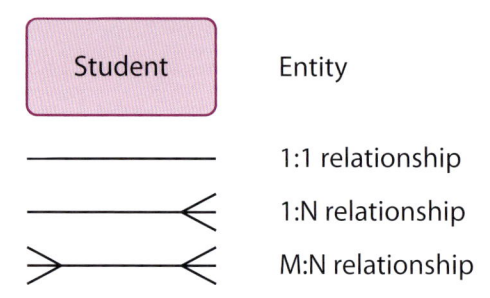

Figure 5.8: Guide to crow's feet notation.

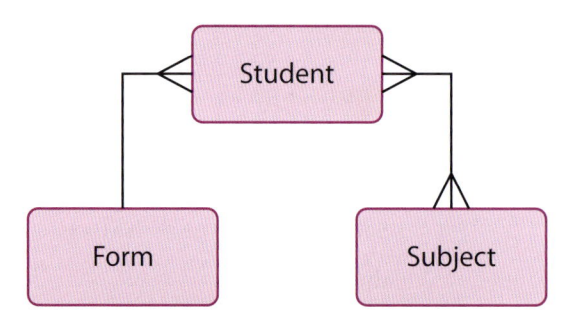

Figure 5.9: ER diagram representing the logical model of the school system.

Note: The ER diagram in Figure 5.9 is only an *overview* of the logical model. The logical model must also include details of each entity's attributes and primary keys.

Data model

Once the logical model has been agreed, the developer then considers how to implement it in an actual database. This means creating a **data model**. A data model defines:

- the tables to be created;
- the names of the fields in each table;
- the data type of each field;
- the primary key of each table;
- any input constraint/validation rules.

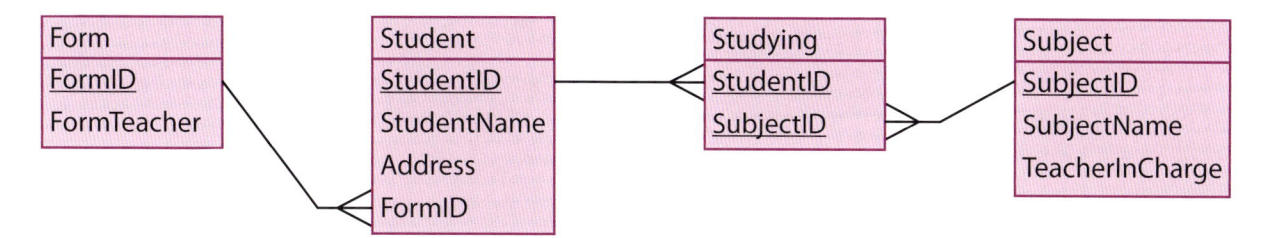

Figure 5.10: ER diagram representing the data model of the school system.

In particular, it is important to remember that we cannot create a M:N relationship directly in a relational database. Any M:N relationships needs to be replaced with an extra table and two 1:N relationships, as discussed in section 5.4.

Figure 5.10 shows a summary of the data model for the previous logical model. You can see that, as discussed, it lists the tables, attributes, primary keys and relationships as well as the additional Studying table. The links connect attributes from the primary key to their equivalent foreign key, using crow's feet notation.

Note: The ER diagram in Figure 5.10 is only an overview of the data model. The data model must also include information on data types and input constraint/validation rules.

Questions

1. What is a flat-file database?
2. Why were relational databases developed?
3. State two main differences between a flat-file database and a relational database.
4. Explain what an entity is in the context of a relational database.
5. What is a primary key in a relational database?
6. What is a foreign key and how is it used in a relational database?
7. How is a many-to-many relationship handled in a relational database?
8. What is meant by referential integrity in the context of a relational database?
9. Why is a primary key important in maintaining referential integrity?
10. List five features that you would expect a relational database to offer users.
11. What is the purpose of Structured Query Language (SQL) in a relational database?
12. Why is constraining input/validation important in a relational database?
13. What is an ER diagram, and how does it represent relationships?
14. Distinguish between a logical model and a data model in a relational database.
15. A library contains many Books and many Borrowers (the people who borrow books). There are also Authors, who write the books. Each author can write many books, and each book can have many authors. Each borrower can borrow many books but each book can only be borrowed by one borrower at a time. Each Author has a unique AuthorID, each Book has a unique ISBN and each Borrower has a unique BorrowerID.

    (a) Construct an ER diagram to model the library system and the relationships between the three entities: Book, Borrower and Author.

    (b) The library system is to be implemented as a relational database. Identify the tables that should be created, including the relationships between them and suggesting suitable primary and foreign keys where appropriate.

16. Consider the concept of referential integrity in relational databases. Why is it essential for maintaining data consistency, and what challenges could arise if referential integrity is not enforced? Provide real-world examples to illustrate your points.

17. Discuss the potential issues that might arise if primary keys are not carefully chosen.

CHAPTER 6
Optimising Databases

By the end of this chapter students should be able to:

- describe the characteristics of data in un-normalised form, first normal form (1NF), second normal form (2NF) and third normal form (3NF);
- describe the advantages and disadvantages of normalisation;
- normalise data requirements for a scenario to 3NF;
- describe the components of a data dictionary.

6.1 Introduction

In the previous chapter we explored how a relational database is constructed from a series of tables and relationships between them. We briefly discussed how splitting data into different tables reduces data redundancy and helps to prevent error. In this chapter we will consider this process in a more formal way.

The term **database optimisation** refers to the general process of refining the structure and arrangement of data in a database to enhance its integrity, its accessibility and its performance.

There are number of ways this can be done. In this chapter we will focus on the process of **data normalisation**, beginning with data in un-normalised form, and then following its progression through first, second and third normal forms (1NF, 2NF and 3NF). We will illustrate this process using a detailed worked example. The chapter will then discuss the advantages and disadvantages of normalisation.

Finally, we will explore the integral components constituting a **data dictionary**, an additional method of database optimisation. A data dictionary is an important tool in the creation of well-structured and easily-understood databases.

6.2 Understanding Data Normalisation

Normalisation is a formal process of organising data in a relational database by creating and modifying tables and the relationships between these tables. In this section we will explore data normalisation through a worked example with the following scenario:

Worked Example

Zinga Technologies is a company that sells computer products through its website. The company wishes to create a relational database to store the details of its products and to record sales to customers.

As a first step, a software engineer has created a flat-file database of the system with a row for each order. A section of the database is shown in Figure 6.1.

OrderID	OrderDate	CustID	CustName	CustAddress	ProdID	Product	Cost	Qty
14	5 Mar 24	256	Donnelly	5 Doagh Rd	2	PC Econ	£399	3
14	5 Mar 24	256	Donnelly	5 Doagh Rd	4	Printer iRC2	£129	2
14	5 Mar 24	256	Donnelly	5 Doagh Rd	7	PC Max	£689	1
15	8 Mar 24	214	Johnston	76 Main St	4	Printer iRC2	£129	1
15	8 Mar 24	214	Johnston	76 Main St	2	PC Econ	£399	2
15	8 Mar 24	214	Johnston	76 Main St	9	Printer 56HK	£159	1
16	13 Mar 24	256	Donnelly	5 Doagh Rd	2	PC Econ	£399	20
16	13 Mar 24	256	Donnelly	5 Doagh Rd	8	Hub 16r34	£39	2

Figure 6.1: A section of Zinga's flat-file database.

CHAPTER 6 – OPTIMISING DATABASES

We can see from the table that a customer can place a number of orders and that each order can refer to more than one product. Therefore, there is one complete row for every product involved in each order. This results in a lot of duplication, as information about the order itself, and about the customer who made the order, are repeated for every product in an order. As we saw in Chapter 5, this data redundancy wastes space and may lead to data inconsistencies.

> **Note:** You may sometimes see a row or a record in a table referred to as a **tuple**. The terms are interchangeable.

Notation

Firstly, it is necessary to set out some of the notation we will use in this chapter. The worked example shows data presented in the form of a table. We can write down the structure of this table more succinctly like this:

ORDER(OrderID, OrderDate, CustID, CustName, CustAddress, ProdID, Product, Cost, Qty)

You can see that this consists of:
- a table name, often written in uppercase, for example ORDER;
- a list of attribute names written within a pair of brackets, with commas between them.

Keys

The example table of data given above is a flat-file database that does not have any keys defined. Therefore, no attribute names are labelled as keys at this point.

However, we will use the following notation to identify keys:
- Primary keys are underlined.
- Foreign keys are indicated with an asterisk* after the name.

Zinga Technologies wish to go through a data normalisation process to produce a more efficient and reliable database structure.

This notation will be used in the next section.

6.3 The Process of Normalisation

Un-normalised form

The data in the example table from Zinga Technologies is a single table, containing all the data in a flat-file format. Data in such a form can be considered to be **un-normalised**.

Un-normalised data often contains **repeating groups**. A repeating group is a set of data that contains multiple values for the same entry. In the example from Zinga Technologies, each single order in the table contains multiple products, costs and quantities. For example, the single order with OrderID 14 placed by customer Donnelly contains three different products: a PC Econ, a Printer iRC2 and a PC Max. These attributes therefore form a repeating group.

Redrawing the table allows us to see the repeating group more clearly, as shown in Figure 6.2.

The last four columns of the table are the repeating group.

OrderID	OrderDate	CustID	CustName	CustAddress	ProdID	Product	Cost	Qty
14	5 Mar 24	256	Donnelly	5 Doagh Rd	2	PC Econ	£399	3
					4	Printer iRC2	£129	2
					7	PC Max	£689	1
15	8 Mar 24	214	Johnston	76 Main St	4	Printer iRC2	£129	1
					2	PC Econ	£399	2
					9	Printer 56HK	£159	1
16	13 Mar 24	256	Donnelly	5 Doagh Rd	2	PC Econ	£399	20
					8	Hub 16r34	£39	2

Figure 6.2: Zinga's database redrawn to highlight the repeating group.

We use curly brackets { } to indicate a repeating group when writing down the structure of this table. Thus, the structure of the un-normalised data can be written as follows (note how the curly brackets are used to indicate which attributes are in a repeating group).

ORDER(OrderID, OrderDate, CustID, CustName, CustAddress, {ProdID, Product, Cost, Qty})

First Normal Form (1NF)

Data is said to be in 1NF if:

- all attributes are atomic; and
- entities do not have repeating groups.

An **atomic** attribute is one that cannot, or need not, be broken down further. Data in an attribute is not atomic if it contains two or more pieces of information that the database needs to be able to treat separately. An example of a non-atomic attribute might be a person's full name 'Steven Donnelly'. This contains both a first name and a surname. Having two separate pieces of data in a single attribute is considered bad practice in a relational database as it can create inefficiencies. For example, it makes it difficult to sort customers using their surnames, as their first names and surnames are stored together and not separately.

In the example from Zinga Technologies, we can see that the Product attribute contains two pieces of information: the product category (e.g. Printer, PC etc) and the model for each product. Thus, printer model iRC2 and printer model 56HK are two separate products. This is not a useful way to store the data, because it makes it difficult to consult the database to find (for example) all PCs, regardless of their specific model.

To ensure the data is in 1NF all attributes must be atomic. Therefore, the attribute Product needs to be split into two attributes, one for the Product category and one for the Model. Once done, the table looks as shown in Figure 6.3.

The new data structure can be written as follows:

ORDER(OrderID, OrderDate, CustID, CustName, CustAddress, {ProdID, ProdCat, Model, Cost, Qty})

The data now meets the first criteria for 1NF. However, it does not meet the second criteria because it still contains a repeating group. This can be resolved by separating out the attributes in the repeating group into a new table. This results in two tables. The ORDER table is now as shown in Figure 6.4.

OrderID	OrderDate	CustID	CustName	CustAddress
14	5 Mar 24	256	Donnelly	5 Doagh Rd
15	8 Mar 24	214	Johnston	76 Main St
16	13 Mar 24	256	Donnelly	5 Doagh Rd

Figure 6.4: The ORDER table after the repeating group has been removed.

The new ORDER_PRODUCT table is as shown in Figure 6.5.

OrderID*	ProdID	ProdCat	Model	Cost	Qty
14	2	PC	Econ	£399	3
14	4	Printer	iRC2	£129	2
14	7	PC	Max	£689	1
15	4	Printer	iRC2	£129	1
15	2	PC	Econ	£399	2
15	9	Printer	56HK	£159	1
16	2	PC	Econ	£399	20
16	8	Hub	16r34	£39	2

Figure 6.5: The new ORDER_PRODUCT table.

The relationship between the two tables is preserved by using keys. In the table ORDER, the attribute OrderID has been defined as the primary key, and the same attribute is included in the table ORDER_PRODUCT as a foreign key.

OrderID	OrderDate	CustID	CustName	CustAddress	ProdID	ProdCat	Model	Cost	Qty
14	5 Mar 24	256	Donnelly	5 Doagh Rd	2	PC	Econ	£399	3
					4	Printer	iRC2	£129	2
					7	PC	Max	£689	1
15	8 Mar 24	214	Johnston	76 Main St	4	Printer	iRC2	£129	1
					2	PC	Econ	£399	2
					9	Printer	56HK	£159	1
16	13 Mar 24	256	Donnelly	5 Doagh Rd	2	PC	Econ	£399	20
					8	Hub	16r34	£39	2

Figure 6.3: Zinga's database with the Product attribute split into two attributes.

Note also that the table ORDER_PRODUCT has a primary key consisting of two attributes, since both the OrderID and the ProdID are needed to uniquely identify a row. The same OrderID can appear in a number of rows. The same ProdID can appear in a number of rows. Only by using both OrderID and ProdID can a single record in the table be identified unambiguously.

The structure of the data in 1NF can now be written as:

ORDER(OrderID, OrderDate, CustID, CustName, CustAddress)

ORDER_PRODUCT(OrderID*, ProdID, ProdCat, Model, Cost, Qty)

Second Normal Form (2NF)

Data is said to be in 2NF if:

- it meets the criteria for 1NF; and
- all non-key attributes are fully dependent on the primary key.

Attribute A is said to be **dependent** on attribute B if the value of attribute A can be determined by knowing the value of attribute B.

For example, consider a table that stores details of cars, their manufacturer and dates when they have had an MOT test. Cars above a certain age are required to pass an MOT every year, so the same car can have more than one entry in the table. Such a table might look as shown in Figure 6.6.

NumberPlate	MOTDate	Manufacturer
MIL 1234	31 Jan 2024	Peugeot
DEF 567	14 Dec 2023	Hyundai
CY51 XYZ	5 Jul 2024	Ford
CGZ 5064	31 Jan 2024	Vauxhall
YDZ 788	20 Sep 2024	Tesla
DEF 567	12 Dec 2024	Hyundai

Figure 6.6: A table storing details of cars and when they have had MOT tests.

First, consider the Manufacturer attribute. A number plate uniquely identifies a car and, since a car can only have one manufacturer, it is possible to determine the manufacturer of a car solely by knowing its number plate. To put it another way, if you are given a number plate you can use that to identify an individual car and, by doing so, you can then determine its manufacturer.

So, when talking about the structure of this data we would say that the Manufacturer attribute is **dependent** on the NumberPlate attribute.

On the other hand, knowing the date of an MOT is **not** sufficient to determine the manufacturer of the car. This is because multiple cars can have an MOT test on the same date. In the example table, you can see that two different cars had tests on 31 January 2024.

So, when talking about the structure of this data we would say that the Manufacturer attribute is **not dependent** on the MOTDate attribute.

Next, consider the primary key of the table. You can see that the primary key consists of two attributes – NumberPlate and MOTDate. As we have seen, a car can have more than one MOT test, so NumberPlate alone is not enough to uniquely identify a row in the table. And, of course, more than one car can have an MOT test on the same date, so MOTDate is not enough to uniquely identify a row. Both NumberPlate and MOTDate are needed to identify an individual row, thus both have to form the primary key.

A **partial dependency** occurs when there is an attribute that is dependent only on **part** of this primary key. In our example, we have seen that the Manufacturer attribute is dependent on NumberPlate but not on MOTDate. This is a partial dependency.

Partial dependencies are inefficient because they lead to data duplication and can result in errors if the data is modified in one record but not in another. In the example, you can see that for the car with the number plate DEF 567, the manufacturer is stored twice, once for each time that it appears in the table. This is unnecessary duplication.

For a database to be in 2NF all the non-key attributes (attributes that are not part of the primary key) must be fully dependent on the primary key. This is another way of saying that for a database to be in 2NF, partial dependencies must be eliminated.

Now let us apply this to the example from Zinga Technologies. First, consider the table ORDER_PRODUCT:

ORDER_PRODUCT(OrderID*, ProdID, ProdCat, Model, Cost, Qty)

The primary key consists of two attributes, OrderID and ProdID. The final attribute (Qty) is fully dependent on the primary key, because the quantity of a particular product being ordered depends on both the product and the specific order. However, the remaining three attributes (ProdCat, Model, Cost) are only dependent on ProdID. This information is unrelated to the OrderID, as it is the same every time that specific product is ordered. So, all three of these attributes are partial dependencies.

With the way the database is currently structured, the category and model of each product along with its price is still duplicated every time it is ordered. As we have seen, this creates data redundancy and could lead to errors.

The solution is to separate the partial dependencies out into a separate table, in this case called PRODUCT. This new table has ProdID as its primary key:

PRODUCT(ProdID, ProdCat, Model, Cost)

The existing table ORDER_PRODUCT now contains fewer attributes, while the existing attribute ProdID in this table is now a foreign key to preserve the link with the PRODUCT table. The PRODUCT table looks as shown in Figure 6.7.

ProdID	ProdCat	Model	Cost
2	PC	Econ	£399
4	Printer	iRC2	£129
7	PC	Max	£689
8	Hub	16r34	£39
9	Printer	56HK	£159

Figure 6.7: The new PRODUCT table.

Note that this table has fewer rows because the data duplication has been eliminated.

The ORDER_PRODUCT table now looks as shown in Figure 6.8.

OrderID*	ProdID*	Qty
14	2	3
14	4	2
14	7	1
15	4	1
15	2	2
15	9	1
16	2	20
16	8	2

Figure 6.8: The table ORDER_PRODUCT that links a product to an order.

The table now contains a link to a specific order via OrderID and a link to a specific product via ProdID. The only additional piece of information that it holds is the quantity of that product that is part of that order.

The structure of the data in 2NF can now be written as:

ORDER(OrderID, OrderDate, CustID, CustName, CustAddress)
ORDER_PRODUCT(OrderID*, ProdID*, Qty)
PRODUCT(ProdID, ProdCat, Model, Cost)

With this structure, all non-key attributes are fully dependent on the primary key. Therefore, the data is now in 2NF.

Note: The table ORDER was not considered here because its primary key consists of a single attribute. This means it is not possible for it to have partial dependencies. Only tables with composite primary keys need be considered at the 2NF stage.

Third Normal Form (3NF)

Data is said to be in 3NF if:

- it meets the criteria for 2NF; and
- there are no non-key dependencies.

Consider a table that stores details of employees in a company. Every employee in this table has a supervisor. The table records details of the employee and their supervisor, as shown in Figure 6.9.

Each Employee is uniquely identified by an EmployeeID. Every other attribute in this table is dependent on EmployeeID. Knowing an EmployeeID is enough to uniquely identify an individual row in this

EmployeeID	EmployeeName	Department	SupervisorID	SupervisorName
3	Declan	Marketing	30	Alice
4	James	Sales	34	Samuel
5	Nora	Sales	34	Samuel
6	Suzanne	Marketing	30	Alice
7	Michael	Sales	31	Aoife

Figure 6.9: Table storing details of employees in a company.

table, so EmployeeName, Department, SupervisorID and SupervisorName can all be determined from the EmployeeID. So this table is already in 2NF.

Now consider the last two attributes. These are SupervisorID and SupervisorName. However, a Supervisor can be uniquely identified by a SupervisorID, which means that SupervisorName is dependent on SupervisorID.

The problem with this is that SupervisorID is not part of the primary key of this table. This is called a **non-key dependency**. A non-key dependency (or **transitive dependency**) occurs when an attribute depends on another attribute that itself is not part of the primary key.

You can see in the example table that SupervisorID 30 appears twice, and their name (Alice) is also stored twice. Similarly, SupervisorID 34 also appears twice, along with their name (Samuel). This is an unnecessary duplication of data.

For a database to be in 3NF all non-key dependencies must be eliminated. Non-key dependencies are inefficient for the same reason that partial dependencies are inefficient. They lead to data duplication and can result in errors if the data is modified in one record but not in another.

Now let us apply this to the example from Zinga Technologies. First, consider the table ORDER:

ORDER(OrderID, OrderDate, CustID, CustName, CustAddress)

In this example the CustName and CustAddress are dependent on the CustID, which is itself dependent on the primary key, OrderID. This is a non-key dependency.

Since the CustID is unique to each customer, we do not need to include their name and address in every order. Instead we store their name and address once in a separate table. So the non-key dependencies are placed in a new table called CUSTOMER which looks as shown in Figure 6.10.

CustID	CustName	CustAddress
256	Donnelly	5 Doagh Rd
214	Johnston	76 Main St

Figure 6.10: The new CUSTOMER table.

Note that this table has fewer rows because the data duplication has been eliminated, thus reducing the risk of errors.

The ORDER table now looks as shown in Figure 6.11.

OrderID	OrderDate	CustID*
14	5 Mar 24	256
15	8 Mar 24	214
16	13 Mar 24	256

Figure 6.11: The new ORDER table.

The relationship between the two tables is established by using primary and foreign keys. In the table CUSTOMER, the attribute CustID has been defined as the primary key, and the same attribute is included in the table ORDER as a foreign key.

Only tables with non-key attributes need be considered at the 3NF stage. The table PRODUCT does not contain any non-key attributes, nor does the table ORDER_PRODUCT, so they do not need to be altered.

Therefore, the data is now in 3NF.

Worked Example

Having completed the process of normalisation, Zinga Technologies now have data structured in 3NF, which can be written as:

CUSTOMER(CustID, CustName, CustAddress)
ORDER(OrderID, OrderDate, CustID*)
ORDER_PRODUCT(OrderID*, ProdID*, Qty)
PRODUCT(ProdID, ProdCat, Model, Cost)

The data can be represented as an ER diagram in order to show the types of relationship between them. To work out the cardinality of the relationships, we note that:

- A CUSTOMER can have many ORDERs.
- An ORDER can have many ORDER_PRODUCTs.
- A PRODUCT can also appear in many ORDER_PRODUCTs.

Therefore, the ER diagram is as shown in Figure 6.12.

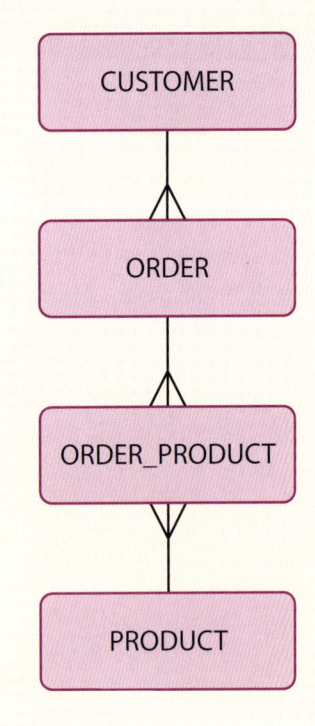

Figure 6.12: ER diagram of the data structure of Zinga's database.

The data structure is now ready for Zinga Technologies to implement in a relational database.

Note: In an exam you are likely to be asked to go through the normalisation process for a specific set of data, so you should pay particular attention to the practical illustration featuring Zinga Technologies, and specifically the use of the appropriate database notation, to ground your understanding of theoretical concepts in a real-world scenario.

Practical limitations of normalisation

There are cases where the strict process of normalisation may require the creation of a new table, but the developer may nevertheless decide not to create the extra table in order to avoid unnecessary extra complications for users or system processing. For example, consider a table that stores a UK postal address:

ADDRESS(AddressID, HouseNumber, StreetName, Town, County, Postcode)

A UK postcode always refers to a single street: so, in fact, only the HouseNumber and Postcode are required to uniquely identify the address. Therefore this table is not in 3NF because it contains a non-key dependency, since the StreetName, Town and County are all dependent on the Postcode which is itself dependent on the AddressID. To structure this data in 3NF it would be necessary to create an additional table as follows:

ADDRESS(AddressID, HouseNumber, Postcode*)
POSTCODE(Postcode, StreetName, Town, County)

This data is in 3NF as the non-key dependency has been removed. In practice, however, a database developer would be unlikely to structure the data like this.

Firstly, it would make data entry cumbersome as the user would have to enter the Postcode into the database first, defining its StreetName etc, and then add the address as a second step by combining a HouseNumber with the pre-defined Postcode. From a user's perspective this would be an unnecessarily complex process that most would think of as a single step – entering an address.

Secondly, unless the database was storing millions of addresses, it is unlikely that much storage would be saved by using two tables. Since it is likely that most postcodes will appear just once, or only a small number of times, in the database, the duplication that would be prevented is likely to be minimal.

Finally, it would make it unnecessarily complex to search the database as (for example) finding all addresses in a given town would involve joining two tables together. Additional computer processing would be required but with little practical benefit.

Overall, it is important to see that, while optimising a data structure to 3NF is very useful, in some cases the benefits of strict normalisation may be outweighed by practical considerations related to user experience and system performance.

Task

In groups, discuss the trade-off between the benefits and drawbacks of normalisation in the context of database design, considering factors like data integrity, redundancy and system performance.

6.4 Advantages and Disadvantages of Normalisation

Normalisation has significant benefits for database design. Some of these are as follows.

- **Improved data integrity:** Normalisation significantly improves data integrity by eliminating redundancy and dependencies. In a normalised database, information is stored in a single location, reducing the risks associated with a user updating data inconsistently. In the example from Zinga Technologies, customer information is stored in a single table in the normalised database, eliminating data redundancy as customer information is segregated from other data. This separation simplifies data maintenance and guards against discrepancies stemming from alterations in customer information.
- **Reduced redundancy:** Because normalisation serves as an effective mechanism against redundant data, data is stored more efficiently and takes up less storage space. By splitting data into logical tables, normalisation ensures each set of information is stored just once. Consider the un-normalised database from Zinga Technologies where product details were replicated for each order. In the normalised version, a specialised table houses unique product information, while the order table only stores references to these products. This eliminates redundant product details in each order entry, conserving storage space.
- **Query performance enhancement: simplifying retrieval:** Normalisation contributes to improved query performance by simplifying data retrieval and analysis. With a normalised database structure, queries (discussed in Chapter 7) become more straightforward as data is logically organised, alleviating the processing burden on the system.
- **Flexibility and adaptability:** Normalisation enhances the adaptability of databases by simplifying modifications to existing data or the assimilation of new information. In a normalised structure, changes are localised, averting systemic reverberations. Consider the un-normalised database from Zinga Technologies. Changes to a product's details need to be modified in multiple records. In the normalised structure, the adjustment can be made to just one record, and is then reflected across all locations it is referenced without necessitating modifications in every order entry.
- **Scalability:** The structured data resulting from normalisation is more conducive to scalable database systems. As organisations grow, the structured framework allows for the addition of new tables, or modification of existing ones, without triggering cascading changes throughout the system.

However, it is important to note that normalisation does have some drawbacks, including the following.

- **Increased join operations:** One prominent drawback of normalisation lies in the need to 'join' two or more tables in order to extract data. As databases undergo normalisation, data fragments into distinct tables,

necessitating joins to reconstruct comprehensive datasets during queries. While mitigating redundancy, the separate tables do impose computational overhead, potentially impeding query performance.
- **Complexity in implementation:** Normalisation produces a more complicated design than a flat-file database, which is therefore more complex to implement in real-life database software. As databases progress through normalisation stages, intricate relationships emerge, demanding meticulous attention to detail. Establishing and maintaining referential integrity across these tables requires precision, posing challenges for both initial implementation and subsequent modifications.
- **Performance of updates:** Normalisation can adversely affect operations to modify data, due to increased dependencies and distributed data. A normalised database enforces referential integrity, so in scenarios where multiple tables interconnect, modifying records many generate a cascade of additional updates, incurring additional computational overhead. For example, in the Zinga Technologies example, deleting a customer will also trigger the deletion of all their orders in the database, which will in turn trigger the deletion of multiple lines from the table holding order/product data.
- **Performance of strict normalisation:** In some cases, strict normalisation may be counterproductive. The example of a UK postcode, discussed earlier in this chapter, is a scenario where the benefits of strict normalisation are outweighed by practical considerations. Another example might be a developer who decides to create an attribute to store the total value of an order in the Order table, even though this can be calculated by adding up the individual lines in the Order/Product table. The developer would do this to reduce the amount of processing that the database software has to do when querying the data. Striking the right balance requires consideration of specific use cases, query patterns and real-world performance requirements.

In conclusion, while normalisation is a vital process in database design, its significant advantages coexist with distinct disadvantages. The astute developer will understand the tension that exists and will aim to design a database that optimally balances the benefits of normalisation with practical, real-world considerations.

6.5 Data Dictionaries

A **data dictionary** serves as a comprehensive guide for a database, ensuring clarity and consistency in understanding and managing data. Essentially, it acts as a manual, providing essential details about the contents of a database, its organisation and its significance. Since it contains data *about* data, the contents of a data dictionary are often called 'metadata'.

When a database developer is designing a database, they will first go through the process of data normalisation. But their task is not complete without also creating a data dictionary for the database they have designed. Although initially created by the developer, data dictionaries can be used by many people, including database administrators, managers and end users.

The primary objective of a data dictionary is to enable database developers and other users to understand the database, via a common language, in order to streamline the process of managing the database.

A data dictionary typically contains the following four types of information:

1. **Definitions of data elements:** This section defines each data attribute in detail, describing its name, data type, length, default value and any limitations on values it can store. This precision ensures a comprehensive understanding of the individual data elements. For example, it might define an attribute called 'OrderDate' that must be in the form of a valid date, and which cannot be less than, say, 1 January 2024. It may also contain a default value. For example, when a new customer is added, an attribute containing the date the customer was last contacted may default to today's date.
2. **Descriptions of the data structure:** This part describes the overarching structure of the database. It provides information on each table

CHAPTER 6 – OPTIMISING DATABASES

Entity (Table)	Attribute	Is Key?	Data type	Must contain a value?	Restrictions
Customer	CustID	Primary	Integer	Yes	
Customer	CustName		Text	Yes	
Customer	Name		Text	Yes	
Customer	DepartmentID	Foreign	Lookup	Yes	
Customer	LastContactDate		Date	No	Must be after 1 Jan 2024

Figure 6.13: Example of metadata from a data dictionary.

it contains, and listing the attributes that are stored in each one.

3. **Data relationships:** This section focuses on relationships between tables, describing the connections between primary and foreign keys, and rules about how referential integrity is to be enforced. In a data dictionary, a foreign key is usually described as having the data type 'lookup'. This means that it must contain a value 'looked up' from the primary key of another table.

4. **Other metadata for database management:** This final part contains any additional information required. This might include details of how data is indexed to speed up performance, lists of users and access permissions.

An example of some metadata from a data dictionary is shown in Figure 6.13. It lists all the attributes in a given table (entity) along with further information about them, where appropriate.

Data dictionaries have many advantages, including the following.

- They provide lasting and structured documentation beyond the development phase, offering a reference guide for later database users.
- By using a common language, the data dictionary facilitates communication between both technical and non-technical users of the database.
- The precision in defining data elements within the data dictionary ensures standardised storage, retrieval and adherence to rules, safeguarding data integrity.

To summarise, a data dictionary enables a shared understanding between different types of user, ensures data coherence and guides users in navigating the database effectively. As databases grow in complexity, a data dictionary becomes an indispensable asset for managing the system.

Questions

1. State what is meant by an 'atomic attribute', providing an example.
2. In the context of normalisation, what is a repeating group?
3. Why is it important to eliminate partial dependencies in a normalised database?
4. State the requirements for a database to be in (a) 1NF (b) 2NF (c) 3NF.
5. Why might a developer choose not to strictly adhere to normalisation principles in certain cases?
6. What is a non-key dependency, and why is it a concern in normalisation?
7. What is the purpose of defining primary and foreign keys in a normalised database?
8. State three advantages of normalisation.
9. State and explain one disadvantage of normalisation.
10. What is the primary purpose of a data dictionary in a database?
11. State the four main elements present in a data dictionary.

12. *Forest* is an online bookshop that sells school textbooks. Currently all data about orders is stored in a single table as shown below.

OrderID	OrderDate	CustID	CustName	CustAddress	BookID	Book	Cost	Qty
100	1 Jan 2024	2	Smith	5 Doagh Rd	20	Biology, 2nd Ed	£15.99	2
					88	Dig Tech, 1st Ed	£11.99	1
					47	Biology, 3rd Ed	£17.99	1
101	2 Feb 2024	7	Mackey	76 Main St	88	Dig Tech, 1st Ed	£11.99	4
					20	Biology, 2nd Ed	£15.99	2
					11	Dig Tech, 2nd Ed	£14.99	1
102	6 Feb 2024	2	Smith	5 Doagh Rd	20	Biology, 2nd Ed	£15.99	1
					53	Physics, 3rd Ed	£15.99	2

(a) Explain why this table is not in 1NF.
(b) Normalise the data in the table to 1NF. Give your answer by writing out the data structure of each table in the form TABLE_NAME(Attributes, …).
(c) Normalise the data in the table to 2NF.
(d) Normalise the data in the table to 3NF.
(e) Produce an entity-relationship (ER) model for the data in the table. It should not include any many-to-many relationships.

13. Discuss the concept of a data dictionary and its role in effective database management. Provide examples of information that should be included in a data dictionary and explain how it contributes to maintaining a shared understanding between different users of a database.

CHAPTER 7
Using Databases

> **By the end of this chapter students should be able to:**
> - use Structured Query Language (SQL) to create tables and to retrieve, update, insert and delete data in a relational database;
> - evaluate Query By Example (QBE) as an alternative to SQL.

7.1 Introduction

The previous two chapters have explored why and how a relational database can be created. This chapter explores how end users can access and manipulate the information in a relational database. This task is referred to as **querying** the database, and individual commands designed to extract or alter information are referred to as **queries**.

The two most common ways of constructing queries are **Structured Query Language (SQL)** (often pronounced 'sequel') and **Query By Example (QBE)**. SQL requires a bit more technical knowledge to use but is the more powerful. QBE is easier for novices to use, but lacks the power needed for more complex queries.

In this chapter we will explore SQL in detail, and then look at QBE. At the end of the chapter we will compare and contrast the two approaches.

The example screenshots in this chapter are all from Microsoft *Access*, a powerful general-use database program. However, most modern relational database software supports both SQL and QBE.

7.2 What Is SQL?

SQL was invented by computer scientists at IBM in the 1970s who needed a standardised way to manipulate relational databases. It has since become the global standard and is used daily by millions of people worldwide. It is used to create, access and manipulate the databases of major companies, including those that run large websites that store data, such as Instagram, Facebook and Amazon.

SQL is a very complex high-level programming language in which database users must type their requirements in the form of an SQL **command**. However, one of the most useful aspects of SQL is that the user only has to specify what data they want, not how it is to be extracted from the database. This makes it intuitive and user-friendly and makes it possible for non-programmers to use SQL by only learning a small subset of SQL commands.

Each SQL command is entered as a single line of text into the SQL interface provided by the database software. The first word/words of the command identify what type of operation the user is trying to accomplish. The SQL commands covered in this chapter are:

- SELECT: Used to display existing data from a database.
- CREATE TABLE: Used to create a new table in a database.
- INSERT INTO: Used to add new rows/records to a table.
- UPDATE: Used to change values in an existing table.
- DELETE: Used to delete rows/records from a table.

As you can see, these commands cover all the basic functions needed to access and manipulate a relational database. In the exam you are likely to be asked to write commands in SQL, so it is important to memorise the syntax of these commands and how to use them.

Microsoft *Access* allows users to enter SQL commands via a text interface, as shown in Figure 7.1. Once entered, the user clicks the button 'Run' to execute the SQL command, which will then, if appropriate, display the results on screen. *Access* also offers user-friendly tools that can generate SQL code for you, as will be discussed in section 7.8.

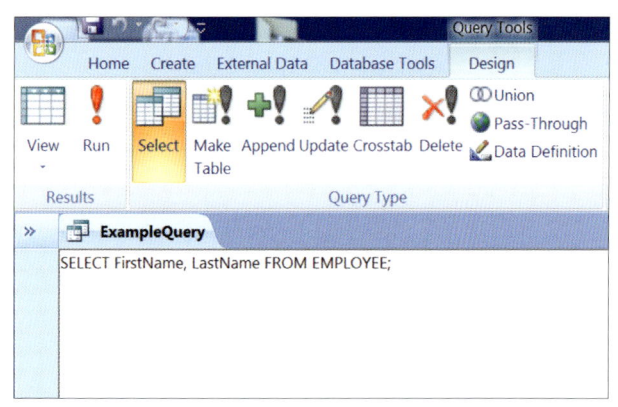

Figure 7.1: The SQL text interface in Microsoft Access.

7.3 The SELECT Command

In this section we will refer repeatedly to an example table from Zinga Technologies.

Worked Example

Zinga Technologies keep details of staff in a relational database. The basic staff information is contained in a table with the following structure:

EMPLOYEE(EmployeeID, FirstName, LastName, Department, Salary)

Figure 7.2 shows the first six rows of the database.

Figure 7.2: Staff information stored in a table in Microsoft Access.

We will use this table to illustrate the various SQL commands.

The SELECT command forms the core of SQL queries, facilitating the retrieval of data from one or more tables. It is the command that database users are likely to use most often. Note that a SELECT command does not modify any data; it simply retrieves a copy of data that already exists.

Its basic structure involves specifying the attributes (often referred to as 'columns' in SQL) that are of interest, after the SELECT keyword. This is then followed by the keyword FROM and then the name of the table the data is to come from. For example, to get a list of the names of all staff, the following SQL command would be used:

SELECT FirstName, LastName FROM EMPLOYEE;

This will cause the following data to be displayed:

Note: The keywords in SQL (in this case SELECT and FROM) are normally written in capital letters. Note also that SQL commands always end with a semicolon.

If you simply want all columns from the table, you can replace the list of attributes with an asterisk * as a shortcut. So, for example, the SQL command:

SELECT * FROM EMPLOYEE;

will display the entire contents of the EMPLOYEE table, with all attributes.

The WHERE clause

The WHERE clause in the SQL SELECT command acts as a filter mechanism, allowing users to extract specific subsets of data from tables. The clause allows you to define criteria that the rows returned must have. Any row that does not meet the criteria is not displayed.

For example, the SQL command:

SELECT FirstName, LastName FROM EMPLOYEE WHERE LastName = 'Brown';

will cause the following data to be displayed:

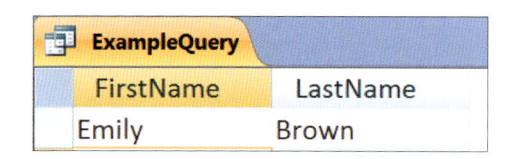

Notice how only rows where the LastName column contains the value 'Brown' are displayed.

WHERE can also be used with other types of value, such as dates and numbers. The following SQL command:

```
SELECT * FROM EMPLOYEE WHERE
Salary > 62000;
```

will return the following data, i.e. all employees whose salary is more than £62,000.

EmployeeID	FirstName	LastName	Department	Salary
4	Emily	Brown	Finance	65000
5	Sean	White	IT	70000

You can also use <> to mean 'not equal to', for example:

```
SELECT * FROM EMPLOYEE WHERE
Department <> 'Marketing';
```

which will return the following data, i.e. all employees not in the Marketing department:

EmployeeID	FirstName	LastName	Department	Salary
1	John	Smith	HR	50000
2	Aoife	Murphy	IT	60000
4	Emily	Brown	Finance	65000
5	Sean	White	IT	70000

Aggregate functions

SQL provides users with functions that allow them to get information on the overall characteristics of data. For example, the following command:

```
SELECT COUNT(*) FROM EMPLOYEE;
```

will return the number 6, being a count of the number of rows in the EMPLOYEE table. Remember that the asterisk * is a shortcut to refer to all the data in a row. This command:

```
SELECT AVG(Salary) FROM EMPLOYEE;
```

will return the average (mean) value of all values in the Salary column, namely 60000.

Aggregate functions can be used with the WHERE clause. For example:

```
SELECT COUNT(*) FROM EMPLOYEE
WHERE Department = 'IT';
```

will return the number 2, being the total number of rows where the Department column contains the value 'IT'.

Three other useful aggregate functions are:
- SUM(): Gives the total of the values that meet the specified criteria.
- MIN(): Gives the minimum of the values that meet the specified criteria.
- MAX(): Gives the maximum of the values that meet the specified criteria.

The ORDER BY clause

Since data from a SQL SELECT query is to be displayed to a user, it can be useful to sort the data into a particular order. This can be achieved with the ORDER BY clause. It allows you to specify one or more columns that data should be ordered by. For example, the following query:

```
SELECT FirstName, LastName FROM
EMPLOYEE ORDER BY LastName;
```

will display the names of all employees in alphabetical order by last name:

FirstName	LastName
Emily	Brown
Mike	Johnson
Sarah	Lee
Aoife	Murphy
John	Smith
Sean	White

Dates and numbers can also be arranged in order. You can arrange them in the opposite order by adding the word DESC. For example, the following query:

```
SELECT FirstName, LastName, Salary
FROM EMPLOYEE ORDER BY Salary DESC;
```

will return a list of employee names, ordered by descending salary.

FirstName	LastName	Salary
Sean	White	70000
Emily	Brown	65000
Sarah	Lee	60000
Aoife	Murphy	60000
Mike	Johnson	55000
John	Smith	50000

Note: Sometimes two rows have the same value. The order in which these rows appear is not defined. However, more advanced users can specify multiple columns in the ORDER BY clause to deal with this eventuality, if they so wish.

Note: The CCEA specification requires only a basic understanding of SQL commands as covered in this chapter. However, SQL can do considerably more than is discussed here. For example, SELECT can be used to join two or more tables together in various combinations, and to group data by category with aggregate totals for each group. This makes SQL very powerful for large enterprise-size database systems.

Task

A table has the following structure:

BOOK(BookID, Title, AuthorSurname, Price)

Practice writing SQL SELECT queries to display:

- All book titles in the table.
- All book titles with their author surname, in alphabetical order by the surname.
- All books that cost more than £9.99
- All books written by an author with the surname Hamza.
- All books with their prices, ordered from cheapest to most expensive.
- All data in the table.
- All books that cost exactly £12.99

7.4 The CREATE TABLE Command

SQL allows users to create new tables using the CREATE TABLE command. This can be useful in certain circumstances, for example if the results of the next query are to be saved permanently in a new table, rather than just displayed on the screen. The syntax of the command is as follows:

```
CREATE TABLE TableName(
    Field1 DataType,
    Field2 DataType
    …
);
```

You can add as few or as many fields (columns) as you like to the new table. The data types must be one of the following:

- INT: Holds any integer, such as 0, 76 or −201.
- VARCHAR(N): Holds text. You must specify how many characters it can hold in brackets. So VARCHAR(12) will create a field that can store up to 12 text characters.
- DATE: Holds any date.
- DECIMAL: Used to store numbers with a decimal point. (It is not necessary at this level to know the precise details of how the DECIMAL data type works.)

For example:

```
CREATE TABLE Pupil(
    FirstName       VARCHAR(20),
    LastName        VARCHAR(20),
    DateOfBirth     DATE,
    NoOfSubjects    INT
);
```

creates a table that can store a pupil's name (with up to 20 characters for each), their date of birth and the number of subjects they study (as an integer).

After each field name and data type, you can also specify some additional information. For example, to specify that a particular field must contain a value, add the text 'NOT NULL'. To specify that a field is the primary key add the text 'PRIMARY KEY'. For example:

```
CREATE TABLE Pupil(
    StudentID       INT PRIMARY KEY,
    FirstName       VARCHAR(20),
    LastName        VARCHAR(20),
    DateOfBirth     DATE NOT NULL,
    NoOfSubjects    INT
);
```

In this case, a new field called StudentID has been defined as an integer and marked as the primary key of the table. In addition, we have also specified that the date of birth cannot be left blank (null) whenever a record is created or modified.

7.5 The INSERT INTO Command

The INSERT INTO command in SQL is used for adding new records to a table. This can be very useful, especially if a series of SQL commands are being run automatically. The syntax of the command is as follows:

```
INSERT INTO Table(Field1, Field2, …)
VALUES  (Value1, Value2, …);
```

This creates a new record in Table with the given values. Note that the values provided must be in the same order as the field names, as this is how the SQL command determines where to put them. For example, the following command:

```
INSERT INTO Employee(EmployeeID,
FirstName, LastName, Department,
Salary)
VALUES (7, 'Sam', 'Stevenson',
'Finance', 62000);
```

will add a new row to the table containing employee data for Sam Stevenson. You can specify more than one new row by adding more sets of values, each row enclosed in brackets and separated by commas. For example the following command adds two rows:

```
INSERT INTO Employee(EmployeeID,
FirstName, LastName, Department,
Salary)
VALUES (7, 'Sam', 'Stevenson',
'Finance', 62000),
(8, 'Donal', 'Kelly', 'IT',
57000);
```

Note: More advanced users can use SQL to combine INSERT INTO with a SELECT query, which allows them to add data that has been extracted from one table into another table.

7.6 The UPDATE Command

The UPDATE command in SQL is used for modifying values in the existing records of a table. The syntax of the command is as follows:

```
UPDATE Table
SET Column1 = Value1, Column2 =
Value2, ...
WHERE Condition;
```

This changes the value of Column1 in every record in the table that meets the given Criteria to Value1, and so forth. For example, the following command:

```
UPDATE Employee
SET Salary = 61000
WHERE Department = 'Marketing';
```

will change the salary of everyone in the Marketing department to £61,000.

Note: You can omit the WHERE clause but, if you do, the query will alter every record in the table. In this case it would change every employee's salary to £61,000. Great care is needed in executing SQL commands that modify data.

The following example will change the surname of a single employee:

```
UPDATE Employee
SET LastName = 'Ferguson'
WHERE EmployeeID = 4;
```

You can also enter an expression in the SET part of the command, which allows you to make changes specific to each record. For example, this command:

```
UPDATE Employee
SET Salary = Salary * 1.1;
```

will increase every employee's salary by 10% (by multiplying their existing salary by 1.1).

Note: As with INSERT INTO, more advanced users can use SQL to combine UPDATE with a SELECT query which will allow them to alter data based on information from another table.

7.7 The DELETE Command

The final SQL command that you need to know is DELETE. It is used to delete records from a database. For this reason, great care needs to be taken before executing a DELETE command. The syntax is as follows:

```
DELETE FROM Table
WHERE Condition;
```

For example, the following command:

```
DELETE FROM Employees
WHERE Department = 'IT';
```

will delete all employees in the IT department from the table. And this command:

```
DELETE FROM Employees
WHERE Salary > 67000;
```

will delete all employees with a salary greater than £67,000.

> **Note:** Omitting the WHERE clause will cause every record to be deleted from the table.

When deleting records, it is important to recall the significance of referential integrity in relational databases (discussed in Chapter 5). Deleting records from a table in a well-designed relational database will lead to cascade deletions of records from related tables. For example, deleting an Employee from the Employees table might also delete all records in a table called Team that lists which members of staff are in which teams. This is normally what is desired, as it maintains the integrity of data.

However, poorly planned deletions can have catastrophic consequences. Using the DELETE command to delete all the records from an important table could lead to cascade deletions in other tables that results in large data losses. In a worst-case scenario it could result in the loss of all data in the database. In a relational database, tables are rarely completely independent of each other. Therefore, the impact of deletions must be carefully considered.

Task

Consider again the table that has the following structure:

BOOK(BookID, Title, AuthorSurname, Price)

Practice writing SQL queries to:

- Create the table.
- Insert a new book with BookID 30, title 'Rathlin Island', author surname 'Free' and price £12.99.
- Change every author with the surname 'McShane' to 'MacShane'.
- Increase the price of every book by 10%
- Increase the price of every book by the author with surname 'Free' by £2
- Delete all books that have a price below £6
- Delete all books by the author 'MacShane'.

7.8 Query By Example

While SQL offers a powerful language for creating tables and interacting with relational databases, Query By Example (QBE) provides an alternative approach, one that is especially useful for those who are less confident in writing complex SQL queries.

Developed by Moshé Zloof in the 1970s, QBE simplifies the process of constructing queries by using a more user-friendly, graphical interface. Rather than composing complex SQL statements, users can express their queries by constructing visual examples of what they want.

In a typical QBE interface, users work with a grid that mirrors the structure of one or more of the tables in the relational database. Each column represents an attribute of the table. Rows within this grid allow the user to further refine what they want.

Figure 7.3 shows the initial QBE interface provided by Microsoft *Access*. The structure of the table to be queried is displayed at the top, and the grid below is initially empty.

One of the strengths of QBE lies in its interactive elements, often featuring drag-and-drop functionality. QBE allows users to specify which attributes/columns they want to include in the query result by dragging them from the structure of the table down onto the grid. By interacting directly with the columns in the grid, users can then express their preferences regarding the data they wish to retrieve. Figure 7.4 shows a query designed to obtain a list of employee names, ordered by descending salary.

> **Note:** All three columns are marked to be 'displayed' in the results, while the user has told *Access* to order the results by the Salary field.

Users can also specify criteria for the query. The QBE interface provides a 'criteria' row in the grid, where users can type values directly into cells to define conditions that must be met for the data to be displayed.

For example, if the user wants to limit the list of employees to those with a salary over £60,000 they simply have to type '> 60000' in the 'criteria' section of the QBE grid for the Salary attribute, as shown in Figure 7.5 overleaf.

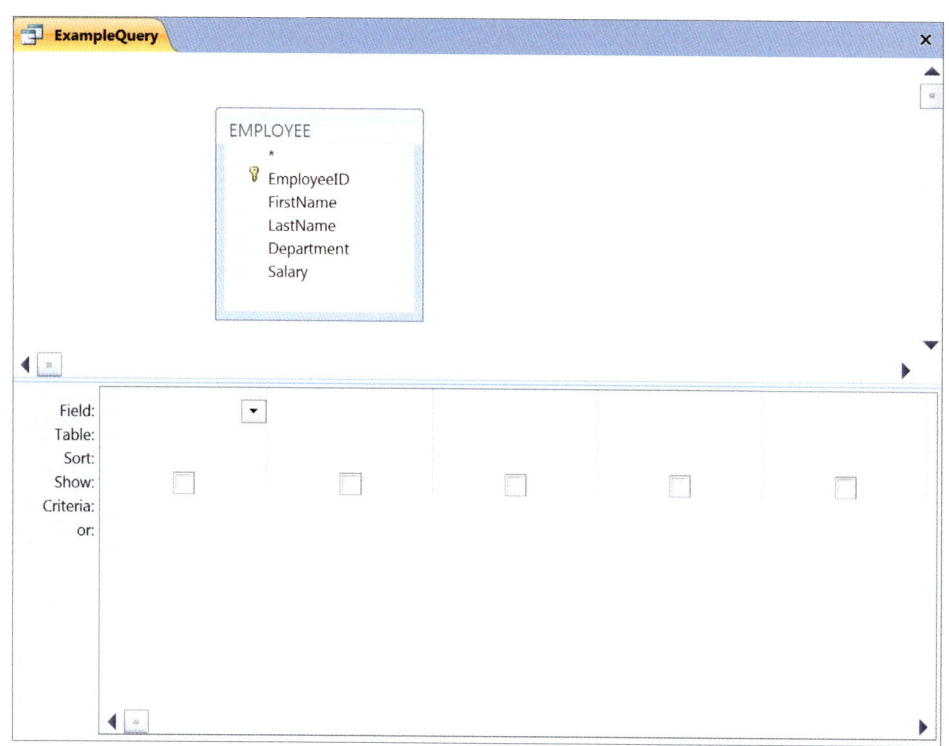

Figure 7.3: The QBE interface as provided by Microsoft Access.

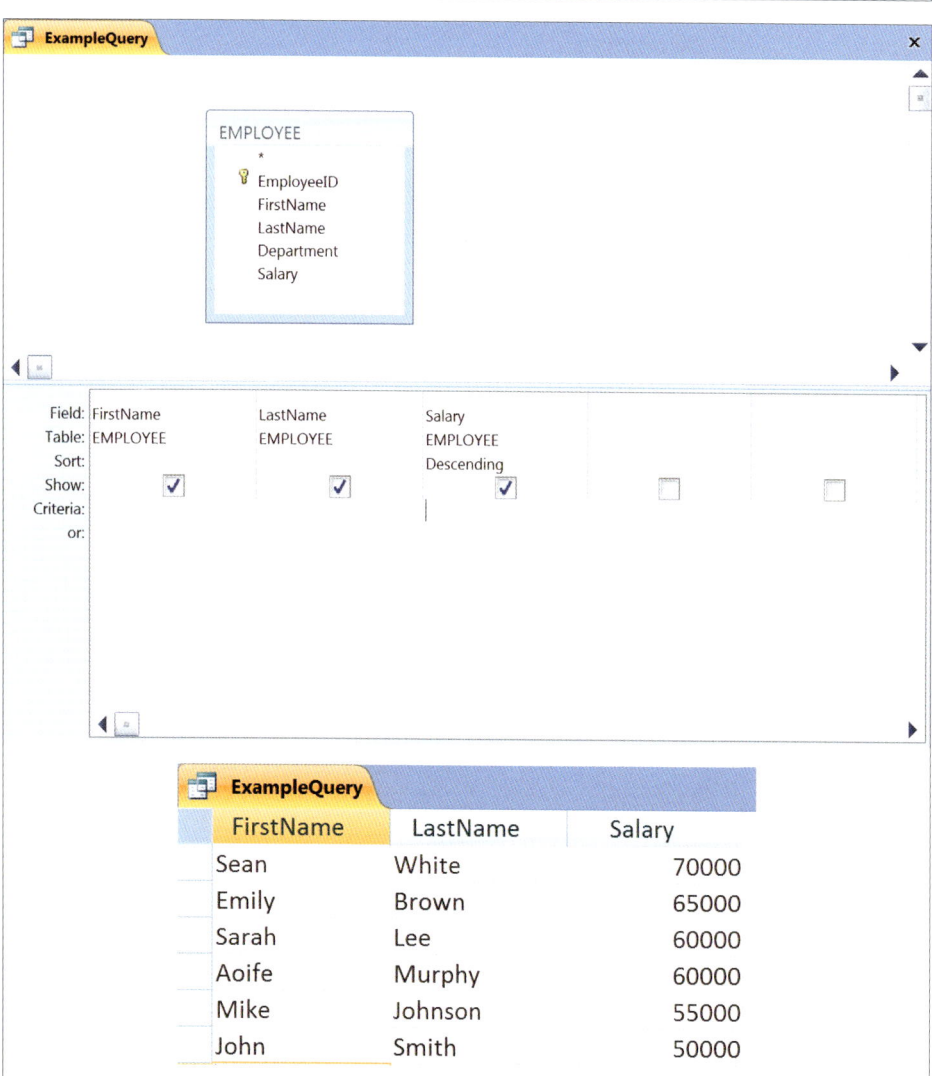

Figure 7.4: Query designed using QBE in Microsoft Access, and the data that is displayed by running the query.

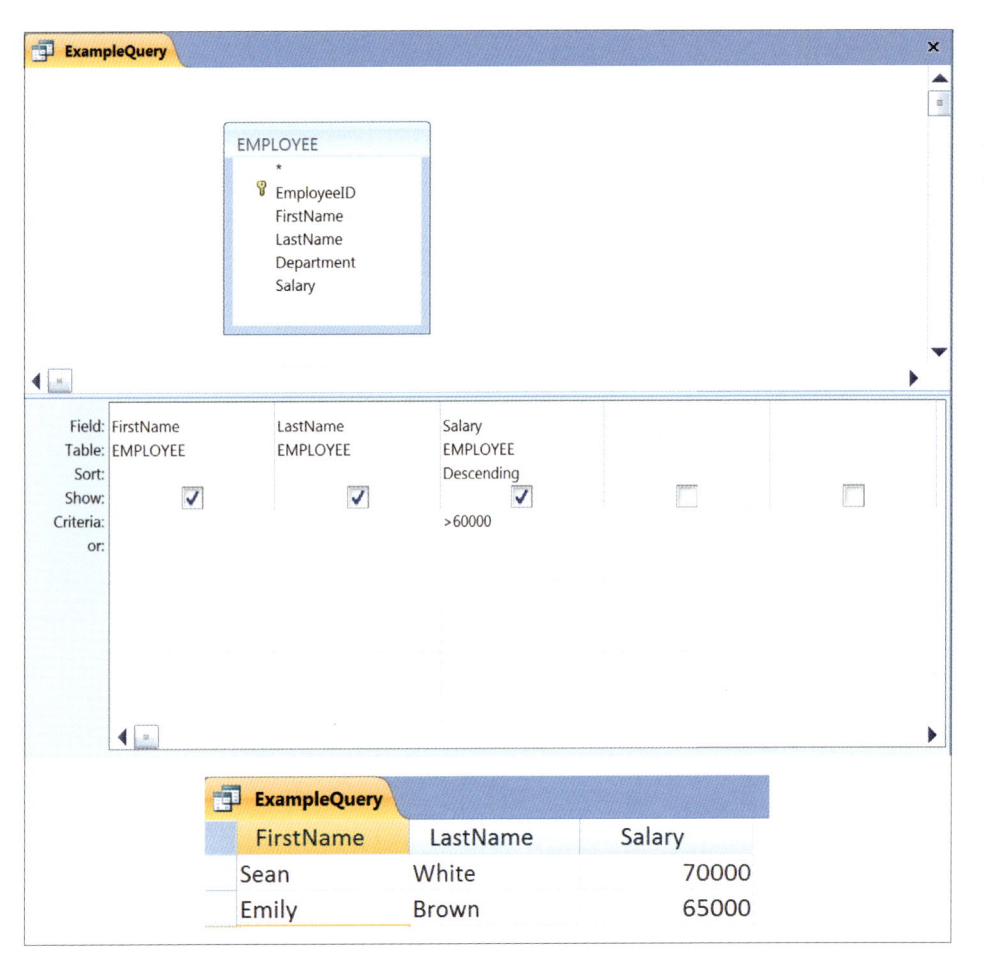

Figure 7.5: QBE query showing criteria specified for one attribute, and the data that is displayed by running the query.

Most database software will allow the user to convert a completed QBE query into SQL automatically. This allows novice users to generate their own SQL code without needing to know the exact syntax of the command.

Users can visually link tables together to express relationships, facilitating the retrieval of data from multiple tables. For example, two tables can be joined together by clicking on a foreign key in one table and dragging it onto the primary key of the linked table, as shown in Figure 7.6.

Most database software allows users to create the equivalent of UPDATE, INSERT and DELETE SQL queries in QBE. This is done by changing the query type through the graphical user interface, and the

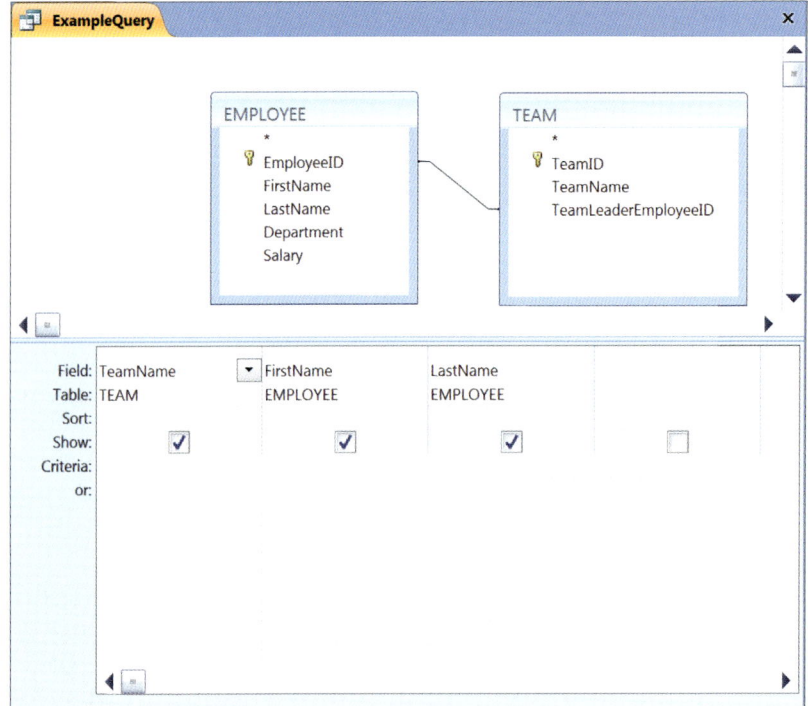

Figure 7.6: Two related tables appearing in a single query in QBE in Microsoft Access. (This example displays the names of all team leaders.)

query grid then changes in a corresponding way. For example, Figure 7.7 shows a QBE query that updates the salaries of all users in the Marketing department to £61,000. The user has done this by clicking 'Update' at the top of the screen, which tells *Access* that this query should change data rather than just display it. You can see that a new row called 'Update To' has been added to the grid below, into which the user has entered the required new salary level. The query is executed by clicking 'Run' at the top of the screen.

QBE can do many more things than is outlined in this introduction. Nevertheless, despite its user-friendly approach, QBE does have limitations. These are discussed in the next section.

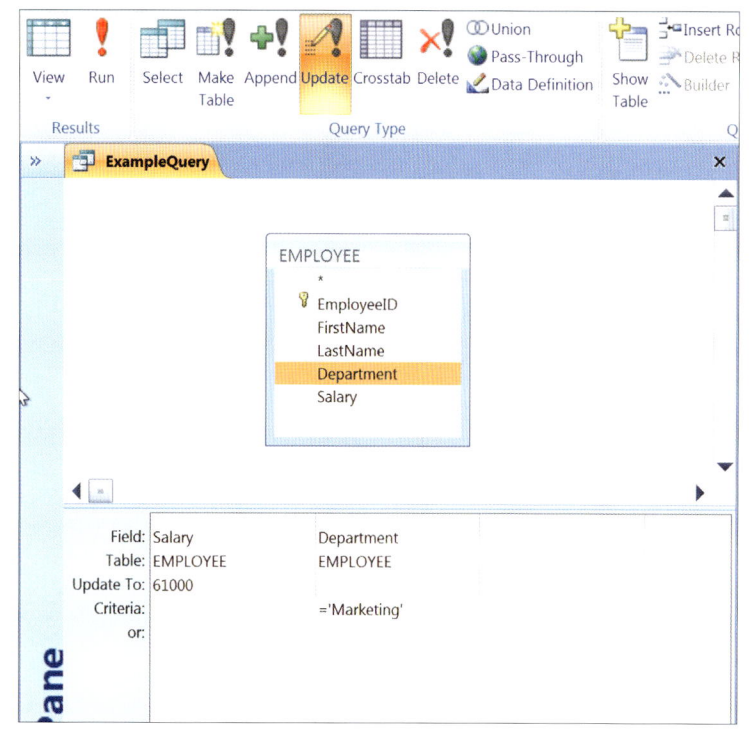

Figure 7.7: An UPDATE query designed in QBE in Microsoft Access.

7.9 Evaluation of QBE

SQL, with its powerful capabilities for interacting with relational databases, is a universal standard for database professionals. However, the syntax and structure of SQL can be a hurdle for individuals who are not familiar with programming or database management systems. Recognising this barrier, QBE provide a more intuitive means of constructing queries. However, QBE has both advantages and disadvantages over SQL.

Advantages of QBE

The main advantages of QBE are:

- **Accessibility and user-friendliness**: QBE's key advantage is that it provides a user-friendly and largely graphical interface, particularly beneficial for individuals lacking extensive programming experience. The grid format mirrors a database table, and users interact with it visually, simplifying the process of query construction process.
- **Reduced syntax complexity**: Unlike SQL, where the use of precise syntax is crucial, QBE users express queries through examples and interactive elements. This reduces opportunities for syntax errors and makes query building more accessible to a broader audience.
- **Faster learning curve**: The visual representation of data and direct interaction in QBE contribute to a faster learning curve. This is advantageous for beginners or those transitioning into roles involving database interaction.
- **Error reduction**: QBE's interactive nature minimises errors by allowing users to click, drag, and drop to define criteria and projections. This not only enhances the user experience but also contributes to the overall reliability of queries.

The main disadvantages of QBE, however, are:

- **Limited complexity**: QBE excels in simplifying basic and moderately complex queries. However, because it works by simplifying complex tasks, it may struggle

with highly intricate database operations that SQL handles adeptly. Its capabilities may therefore be insufficient for more advanced tasks.
- **Less useful for SQL experts**: QBE is very useful for novice users. However, an SQL expert may actually find it quicker and more convenient to type an SQL command than use drag-and-drop to construct a query by QBE.
- **Lack of universal standard**: The absence of a universal standard is a limitation. QBE interfaces vary between different systems, meaning that users familiar with one system have to adapt when switching platforms. This lack of consistency can impact user training and cross-system usability.

Ultimately, the decision to use QBE as an alternative to SQL hinges on the balance between accessibility and functionality. For users with limited programming backgrounds, or those seeking a more intuitive means of interacting with databases, QBE can be a game-changer. For example, a business manager seeking specific information about customers who made purchases exceeding a certain amount could use QBE to interactively fill in a row indicating the condition for the purchase amount and select the desired columns for the output. However, a database manager at the same company may prefer to use an SQL SELECT query with a WHERE clause to achieve the same result. In practice, both forms of query may be used within the same database system.

Questions

1. Write down the syntax of the SQL SELECT command.
2. In SQL, what does the asterisk (*) represent when used in the SELECT command?
3. How can the WHERE clause be used in the SQL SELECT command? Provide an example.
4. How does the ORDER BY clause affect the output from SQL SELECT queries? Provide an example.
5. What is the syntax for creating a new table using the CREATE TABLE command in SQL?
6. Explain the purpose of the INSERT INTO command in SQL and provide its syntax.
7. How does the UPDATE command in SQL modify values in existing records? Provide an example.
8. What precaution should be taken when using the DELETE command in SQL?
9. How does QBE differ from SQL in terms of user interaction?
10. Briefly list the main advantages and disadvantages of QBE compared to SQL.
11. A second-hand car showroom uses the following table to keep track of cars that are for sale: CAR(CarID, Make, Model, Price)
    (a) Produce SQL code to display all cars with the make 'Ford', displayed in descending order by price.
    (b) Produce SQL code to add the following record to the table:
    CarID: 56, Make: Renault, Model: Zoe, Price: £13000
    (c) Produce SQL code to delete all cars with a price less than £5000 from the table.
    (d) An input error has been discovered in some of the records. Produce SQL code to update all records with a Make of 'Rneault' to 'Renault'.
12. Evaluate the use of QBE as an alternative to SQL for creating database queries.

CHAPTER 8
Artificial Intelligence

By the end of this chapter students should be able to:

- explain what is meant by artificial intelligence (AI);
- explain the significance of the Turing test in defining what is meant by AI;
- describe the main features of neural network modelling.

8.1 Introduction

Artificial intelligence, often abbreviated to AI, has transformed the way we perceive and interact with technology. Although it can trace its origins to the 1950s, AI has rapidly become an integral part of our daily lives, influencing everything from the way we shop and communicate to the manner in which we access information.

The significance of AI lies in its ability to process vast amounts of information swiftly and make complex decisions with minimal human intervention. This capability has paved the way for ground-breaking applications across various industries, enhancing efficiency and driving innovation. From virtual personal assistants like *Siri* and *Alexa* to chatbots on eCommerce sites and recommendation algorithms on streaming platforms, AI is already seamlessly integrated into our daily routines.

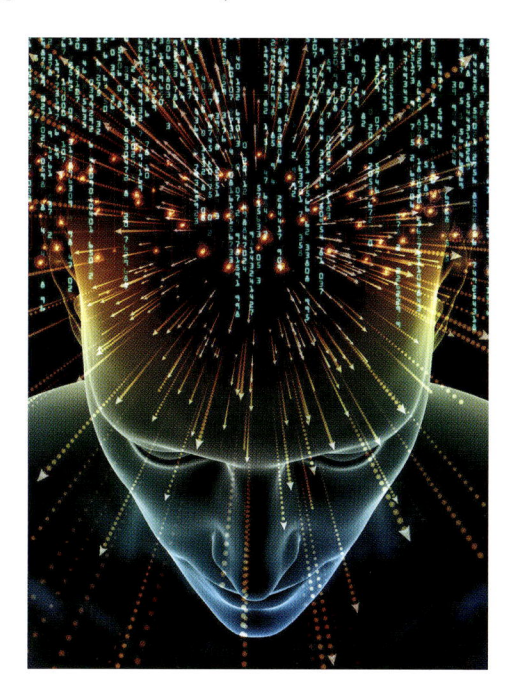

The field of AI is developing very rapidly. On the one hand it presents exciting possibilities for the future, including developments such as self-driving cars, advanced robotics, smart cities and advances in medicine. AI has even demonstrated its ability to compose music, generate art and write text. On the other hand, it raises new questions that society will have to address, including those related to privacy, copyright, the possible impact of AI on warfare and even whether AI may be considered a form of life. There are already intriguing debates about the limits and ethical impacts of AI.

When studying AI it is important to remember that it is a fast-moving technology that is impacting the world now and will continue to rapidly advance in the near future. It will become an increasingly important aspect of the work of anyone involved in Digital Technology.

8.2 What Is AI?

AI refers to the ability of machines to perform tasks that typically require human intelligence. It encompasses a broad spectrum of capabilities, ranging from basic rule-based systems to sophisticated learning algorithms that can adapt from experience. This capacity for learning allows AI systems to improve their performance over time, making them valuable tools in various fields.

In traditional programming, humans meticulously code instructions that outline how a computer should execute a task. The program follows these predetermined steps without the ability to deviate or adapt to changing circumstances. AI systems, however, instead of relying solely on explicit programming, use special algorithms that enable them to learn from data. This ability, known as **machine learning**, enables AI to recognise patterns, make predictions and enhance its performance through exposure to new information.

Machine learning

Machine learning is categorised into two main types.

- **Supervised learning** involves training the algorithm on labelled data, meaning the input data is labelled in some way to help the machine work out what it is meant to be doing. For example, a machine-learning algorithm designed to weed out junk mail is first given a set of existing emails, each labelled either 'junk' or 'not junk'. The system then analyses the two types of email, trying to detect and learn patterns that typically accompany each. It then analyses new emails and attempts to determine whether or not they are 'junk'. A human operator then 'marks' the system's attempt and feeds the results back in. The machine analyses the new information and learns from both its successes and its failures.

- **Unsupervised learning** involves feeding the algorithm with unlabelled data; it must then find patterns or relationships within the data on its own. This type of learning is more exploratory, allowing the system to discover hidden structures or trends. For example, a business may want to see if there are patterns in what its customers are buying. The system is given data on customer purchase history, including items bought, frequency of purchases and the total amount spent. Importantly, this data does not have predefined categories or labels. The algorithm explores the data, looking at various features like types of products purchased, spending habits and the time of purchases to try to find any patterns or clusters of behaviour. For instance, one cluster might comprise frequent buyers of electronics, while another might be fashion enthusiasts. The resulting knowledge allows the business to tailor marketing strategies, promotions and product recommendations to each cluster.

Everyday examples of AI

AI can be found in many places in our daily lives. For example:

- Virtual personal assistants such as *Siri*, *Google Assistant* or *Alexa* employ AI to understand voice commands, process natural language and provide relevant information or execute tasks.
- Recommendation algorithms on platforms like *Netflix* or *Spotify* use AI to analyse a user's viewing or listening history, predicting their preferences and offering personalised content suggestions.

- The health sector uses AI to assist with medical diagnosis. AI can analyse medical images, such as X-rays or brain scans, and rapidly flag up concerning images for a human doctor to check.
- Drugs researchers can use AI to rapidly go through thousands of possible combinations of drugs and check whether they are likely to be of use without manual testing. Such a process can reduce the time taken to do initial drug tests from years to days.
- Chatbots on eCommerce websites are programmed with details about a company's products or services and can then respond to user's queries using natural language. AI allows them to deal with a much greater range of queries than could be programmed directly using a traditional programming algorithm.
- In computer games, AI-controlled characters can add realism for gamers by providing opponents that are able to respond with more sophistication to the user's actions.
- AI is being used to develop autonomous vehicles, for example Tesla's *Autopilot*. The AI is trained with thousands of hours of real-life road experience to learn how to respond to numerous situations. At the time of writing, AI can already drive a car in limited environments such as on a motorway, but the technology is not yet sufficiently developed to allow self-driving vehicles in all situations, for example a busy city street with roadworks in heavy snow.

- AI image generation software, such as *GenCraft* or Adobe *Photoshop*, can be used to generate very lifelike images from textual input. The commercial availability of reliable AI imagery is a very recent development, only becoming widely available in 2023, but is likely to expand rapidly.

Task

Think of examples of AI that you come across in your everyday life. How many can you list? Discuss how helpful each one is to you – is it essential, useful or just a curiosity?

Case Study

Because AI is able to respond to queries other than those the programmer has specifically anticipated, controls need to be put in place to ensure this does not cause a problem.

In January 2024 media reported a user interacting with delivery company DPD's online chatbot. The chatbot was designed to respond to queries about deliveries, but the user found that a lack of sufficient 'guardrails' in the AI meant that it could be instructed to swear, criticise DPD and even to write a poem in the form of a haiku insulting the company. DPD said that it had been the result of a software update and disabled that element of the AI.

In the same month, an American user persuaded an online chatbot of a dealer of Chevrolet cars to offer to sell them a brand-new car for $1. The company only became aware of the issue when they noticed unusual levels of traffic on their site as the phenomenon went viral on social media. However, the company found that the AI application had resisted most attempts to wrongfoot it.

Both these incidents highlight that AI is, to some degree, 'intelligent' and therefore introduces an inherent degree of unpredictability when it is used. Developers need to be very careful that using AI does not create unwelcome problems.

General chatbots

We have already seen how chatbots can be used in limited situations, such as helping users to choose a product. One of the most successful to date is *ChatGPT*, which launched publicly in 2022. *ChatGPT* is a type of AI called a language model, trained using millions of individual documents gathered from all over the internet. This gives it extensive knowledge of most areas of human knowledge.

ChatGPT is able to respond to a whole range of user queries ranging from recipes to technical explanations and philosophical questions. It can also create its own fictional prose and poetry and can respond in multiple languages. It can even tailor its writing style: for example it could be asked to describe the water cycle in the style of Jane Austen. As such, *ChatGPT* has become immensely popular very rapidly and is now being joined by other chatbots.

Because it is a language model, it has limitations. For example, at the time of writing, it is poor at performing mathematics and often makes errors when asked to do so. To avoid creating significant problems, *ChatGPT*'s owners have limited its responses to certain types of query. For example, it will refuse to describe how to make a bomb, and will generally not take a position on issues with which there is widespread disagreement, such as the existence of God. Finally, it is not always clear whether the output of the system is factually correct so, if its responses are to be relied upon, they should be checked by a human.

All of the uses discussed above are examples of **narrow** (or **weak**) AI, which is designed to perform specific tasks, or narrow sets of tasks. They excel in their carefully-contained domain but lack the broad cognitive abilities associated with human intelligence.

A **general** (or **strong** AI), on the other hand, would possess the ability to understand, learn and apply knowledge across a wide range of tasks, essentially mirroring human intelligence. At the time of writing, true general AI remains a theoretical concept and has not been fully realised. If it is ever invented, it would achieve or even surpass the capabilities of a human being. This makes it a subject that raises profound scientific and ethical questions.

However, regardless of how an AI functions, the question of how to determine whether it is truly intelligent can be addressed by the Turing Test.

8.3 The Turing Test

The Turing Test was proposed by the visionary British mathematician and computer scientist Alan Turing (Figure 8.1) in 1950 as an attempt to determine when AI becomes as 'intelligent' as a human. At its core, the Turing Test is designed to evaluate a machine's ability to exhibit intelligent behaviour indistinguishable from that of a human during a natural language conversation.

Figure 8.1: Alan Turing in 1936.

The test is carried out with a human judge (the 'player') and two respondents – one a human respondent and one the candidate machine, as shown in Figure 8.2. It is the role of the human to be themselves and respond naturally to questions posed. The candidate machine must attempt to respond to questions in as human a manner as possible. The player is located in a different room from the respondents and can only communicate with them via a computer screen where they can type questions and send replies to each other. This prevents them from making judgements based on the voice or visual appearance of the respondents.

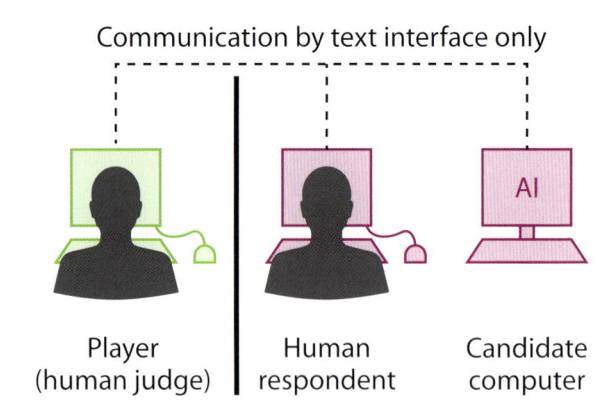

Figure 8.2: Setup for the Turing Test.

Once the test begins, the player asks questions of both respondents. The judge can ask any question on any topic they wish, and the respondents respond. If, after a set period of time has passed, the judge cannot reliably determine which respondent was the machine and which was the human, the machine is considered to have passed the Turing Test.

The Turing Test provides a practical and accessible benchmark for assessing the capabilities of AI systems. Rather than relying on complex technical criteria, the test focuses on the observable outcome – the machine's capacity to engage in human-like conversation. This emphasis on behaviour aligns with the broader goal of AI development, concentrating on functionality and performance in real-world scenarios. There has been more than one claim by AI researchers in recent years that a system has passed the Turing Test but, at the time of writing, none that has been widely accepted by scientists.

The Turing Test was one of the earliest attempts to grapple with the question of machine intelligence. Alan Turing's proposition not only provided a pragmatic method for evaluating AI but also initiated a philosophical discourse on the nature of consciousness, intelligence and the potential of machines to simulate human thought processes. While the test has its critics and limitations, its enduring relevance underscores its foundational role in shaping the trajectory of AI research and development.

CHAPTER 8 – ARTIFICIAL INTELLIGENCE

Task

Read the following between a human player and a respondent sitting the Turing Test, which could be either the machine or the human.

Human: Hi, how are you?

Respondent: I'm very well thank you. And you?

Human: Not bad, thanks! Let's get started. What do you like to do for fun?

Respondent: I enjoy many different things. I like playing tennis with my friends, but you can't beat sitting with a good book either.

Human: Tell me something you remember from your childhood.

Respondent: I remember one time there was a storm. I must have been very young, and I was scared. My parents let me sleep with them in their bed. I still remember the warm smell and the feeling of security I had.

Human: Sounds nice! What's your take on ethics in the field of AI?

Respondent: That's a good question! I advocate for ethical AI development, emphasising transparency, fairness and minimising biases. It's crucial for the responsible evolution of technology.

Human: A principled stance. Can you tell me a joke?

Respondent: Sure. Why did the quantum computer start a band? It wanted to perform in multiple states simultaneously!

Human: Very funny! But did you find it funny?

Respondent: Yes, I did. I appreciate the elegance in clever wordplay and conceptual humour. It's a testament to the intricacies of language.

…

Human: Thank you for talking to me today.

Respondent: It was my pleasure. Enjoy the rest of your day.

Based on this interaction, do you think the candidate is a human or a machine mimicking a human? Why or why not? Different people in your class may disagree.

This illustrates the challenge of assessing whether or not an AI has actually passed the Turing Test.

8.4 Neural Network Modelling

Many AI systems use neural networks to process their inputs. A **neural network** is a computational model that emulates the way the human brain processes information, enabling machines to learn and make predictions from data.

A neural network, shown in Figure 8.3, consists of interconnected nodes or units (artificial neurons, which are intended to mimic the neurons in human brains). These units are organised into layers. These layers include an input layer, one or more hidden layers, and an output layer. The input layer receives data from the outside world, and the output layer represents the conclusions that the neural net has made.

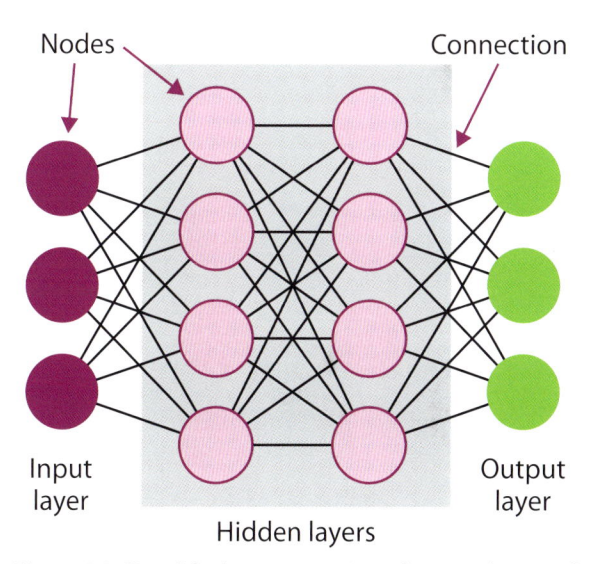

Figure 8.3: Simplified representation of a neural network.

Each unit is typically connected to each other unit, but the connections are weighted to adjust their strength and nature. The units each apply a function to the weighted sum of their inputs and generate a series of outputs from that layer. If a given output is sufficiently strong it is passed on to the next layer for further processing, while weak outputs are discarded. This is known as 'feedforward' propagation of data. The weights are initially set during a training process where the network learns from example data and improves its performance. However, the neural network is able to continue learning and adjusting these weights as it encounters real data. As such, it can learn and adapt by itself.

Provided there are enough units, the neural network starts to function like a brain and is able to process information, learn patterns and make predictions based on the input data. Neural networks have demonstrated particular success in tasks such as image recognition, natural language processing and various other machine-learning applications. A neural network designed for image recognition can have hundreds of thousands of nodes, while those used for natural language processing typically have over a million. For comparison, a human brain contains about 100 billion neurons (nodes).

Case Study

Consider a scenario where we aim to develop a simple neural network for image classification. The task at hand is to differentiate between images of cats and dogs. The system has a training dataset that consists of black and white images, each 28 by 28 pixels, and is labelled with the corresponding class (cat or dog), as shown.

Dog   Cat   Dog
Cat   Dog   Cat

Our neural network will have a straightforward architecture with one hidden layer between the input and output layers. Each pixel in the input images corresponds to a unit in the input layer, resulting in 784 input units (28×28 pixels). The hidden layer contains, for simplicity, 128 units, and the output layer has two units (one for cat, one for dog). Every unit in each layer is connected to every unit in the next layer, meaning there are over 200,000 connections, each with its own weight.

The neural network is trained using a supervised learning approach. During training, the weights connecting the units are adjusted in a logical way using one of several algorithms designed for this purpose, with the aim of finding the arrangement of weights that leads to a set of outputs that most closely matches the actual class of animal pictured in the images from the training set.

Next, to assess the model's generalisation capabilities, it is evaluated on a separate set of images not used during training. If the neural network makes mistakes, the user informs it of this, as shown in the following diagram.

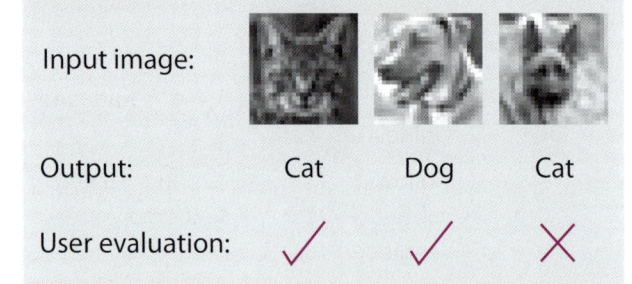

Input image:
Output: Cat   Dog   Cat
User evaluation: ✓   ✓   ✗

The neural network uses this new information to further adjust the weights between its units. This training process continues until the neural network is producing reliable output. The eventual result is a neural network that can distinguish images of cats and dogs with a high degree of reliability.

It is important to understand that, if you could look 'inside' the trained neural net, you will not find an explicit algorithm for recognising cats and dogs. Nor are any actual images of cats and dogs contained in it. Rather, a trained network of interconnected nodes is doing the work.

Questions

1. Define artificial intelligence (AI) and explain its principal uses in daily life.
2. What distinguishes supervised learning from unsupervised learning in machine learning?
3. State the purpose of the Turing Test.
4. Explain how the Turing Test is carried out.
5. Differentiate between narrow (weak) AI and general (strong) AI.
6. Explain the concept of neural networks and their role in AI systems.
7. Describe the main features of a neural network.
8. Assess the benefits of AI to the human race.
9. Explain how the Turing Test determines whether a computer can exhibit intelligence equivalent to a human.

CHAPTER 9
Expert Systems

By the end of this chapter students should be able to:

- describe the structure of an expert system;
- describe the purpose of the knowledge base and inference engine in an expert system;
- explain the following terms in relation to expert systems: shell; heuristics; fuzzy logic; and knowledge engineer;
- evaluate the use of expert systems in medicine, car engine fault diagnosis and life insurance.

9.1 Introduction

What are expert systems?

Expert systems use artificial intelligence (AI) to emulate the decision-making capabilities of human experts in specific domains. At their core, expert systems are computer programs that combine knowledge, reasoning and problem-solving to produce intelligent solutions to a range of problems. However, unlike traditional software, which uses predefined algorithms, expert systems use AI to provide a wider range of solutions and can cope with a very wide range of problems within their domain.

Their significance lies in their ability to replicate human expertise within the field that they are designed to operate, known as their 'knowledge domain'. This knowledge is acquired from human experts and encoded into a format that the system can comprehend and manipulate. The adaptability of expert systems makes them valuable tools in situations where human expertise is scarce, inconsistent or impractical. As a result, they have become instrumental in enhancing decision-making processes across diverse industries.

The origin of expert systems can be traced back to the 1960s and 1970s, coinciding with the rise of AI as a field. Early computer scientists developed rule-based systems, laying the groundwork for intelligent decision-making. In subsequent decades, advances in technology, improved computing power and better algorithms led to the widespread adoption of expert systems in the 1980s and 1990s. As the field matured, the integration of expert systems with machine learning and AI further enhanced their capabilities, allowing them to adapt and learn from experience, leading to the powerful expert systems in use today.

The role of expert systems

The overarching role of expert systems is to provide intelligent decision support across a very wide range of industries, exploiting and then building on the capabilities of human experts, and enabling more informed choices and decisions to be made. Examples of industries that make use of expert systems are as follows.

- **Healthcare**: Expert systems aid in medical diagnosis by analysing symptoms, medical history and research findings to suggest diagnoses and recommend treatment plans to medical professionals. This not only enhances the speed of diagnosis but also contributes to the accuracy of medical decisions.

- **Finance**: Expert systems are employed for risk assessment, management of investments and fraud detection. These systems can analyse vast datasets, identify patterns and make real-time recommendations, enabling financial institutions to speed up decision-making while mitigating risks.

- **Manufacturing**: Expert systems trained with the knowledge of seasoned engineers are used for quality control, optimisation of production processes and to predict when maintenance will be required, helping manufacturers to achieve consistent product quality, reduce downtime and enhance operational efficiency.

- **Marketing**: Expert systems aid in targeted advertising and market analysis, optimising campaign strategies based on historical data and current trends.

- **Environmental monitoring**: Expert systems analyse data from sensors and satellites to predict environmental changes, such as hurricanes or longer-term climate shifts. This proactive approach allows for timely interventions and decision-making to mitigate potential risks.

Expert systems do not replace humans, but rather serve as valuable decision support tools to humans, relying on the capabilities of professionals, and enhancing them, in a wide variety of domains.

9.2 Structure of an Expert System

Expert systems, as we have seen, are designed to replicate human decision-making capabilities. At its core, an expert system (Figure 9.1) is made up of two fundamental components: the **knowledge base** and the **inference engine**. These are made accessible through a **user interface**.

Knowledge base

The knowledge base serves as the reservoir of information, encapsulating the extensive domain-specific knowledge that has been acquired from actual human experts. This information comes in two types:

- **Factual** knowledge, which will include data and information about the real world of the particular domain, such as the length of a road, the different income tax brackets in the UK, or what the law says about the use of particular chemicals.
- **Heuristics**, which consists of the rules that the experts have provided. These rules do not have to be true in every single case; rather, they are rules that experts have found to be generally true and therefore of value in deciding a course of action. For example, it may say that people with children are more likely to respond to adverts that emphasise healthy food, or that a persistent cough means a person is more likely to be suffering from a lung condition, or that a particular set of symptoms occurring in the same group of people suggests a particular health condition. These rules are often based on domain-specific knowledge, past experience

and the intuition of a human expert, allowing the expert system to make informed decisions even in situations where complete information is not available or practical to obtain.

Both types of knowledge are combined within the knowledge base. The factual knowledge can generally be input as statements directly into the system, while the heuristics are typically written as statements of the form:

IF <condition> THEN <possible conclusion>
ELSE <different conclusion>

Heuristics in expert systems typically make use of fuzzy logic, which is discussed later in this section.

Inference engine

Complementing the knowledge base is the inference engine, which is the part of the system that analyses new input data. This component is responsible for drawing inferences, reasoning through the available knowledge, and generating solutions or recommendations. The inference engine uses the factual knowledge and the heuristic knowledge (rules) from the knowledge base. It applies this knowledge to the input data by using various reasoning techniques to provide useful output. Note that, although AI is often used with expert systems, inference engines themselves do not typically use AI for generating outputs.

In many expert systems, the knowledge base can continue to evolve and refine itself through learning, facilitated by the inference engine or, more commonly, by having their knowledge base updated by human experts. For example, an expert system in finance will need to change and adapt its recommendations based on politics, which can make certain countries or sectors more or less desirable places to invest. Similarly, the knowledge base of a marketing expert system will need to evolve as new social media platforms rise in popularity and old ones decline.

User interface

An expert system is, of course, useless without a means for the user to interact with it. The user interface provides this mechanism, facilitating communication between the expert system and its users. The interface must be tailored to the specific domain within which it works.

For example, a medical expert system designed to analyse mammograms may have a user interface that allows the user to input a scan image, as well as data about the patient, such as age and any other medical conditions and current medication. An environmental expert system may be automatically fed data from sensors located in the ocean, land or in space. However, it still needs a user interface through which scientists can request data, such as the predicted wind speed in a particular city over the next 72 hours, or the forecast annual average temperature in an area of woodland over the next 30 years.

The user interface can be either a command line interface or a WIMP (windows, icons, menus, pointer) interface. A command line interface is often preferred by users who are comfortable with typing commands and navigating through text-based interfaces quickly and offers more options for automating commands. WIMP interfaces are generally more intuitive and user-friendly, especially for users accustomed to graphical interfaces commonly found in modern software applications but are also more resource-intensive and may be frustrating for users who prefer to operate at speed with a keyboard.

How the components work together

In an expert system (Figure 9.1), the user interface and the inference engine are typically grouped together, as it is the inference engine that the user interface is directly interacting with. The interference engine then interrogates its knowledge base when processing its response.

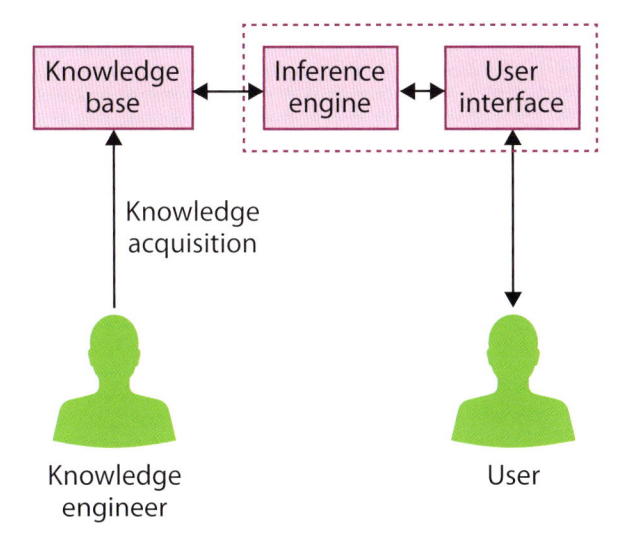

Figure 9.1: Structure of an expert system.

Case Study

An expert system is being asked to suggest a good marketing strategy for a new range of baby food that a supermarket is seeking to launch. The supermarket wants to know which customers to target, how, and what the emphasis should be.

The expert system has a knowledge base that been programmed with human knowledge about the success of various types of advertising, which demographic of customers typically buys certain types of products, and what factors typically influence people of that demographic. It also has knowledge about the type of media that each demographic uses. It also contains data about competing products that are already on the market.

The system then receives information about the new product through its user interface. The user interface asks for information about the new product, who it is designed for (babies in this case), data on its nutritional content, its price and its regional availability.

After applying its inference engine to all this data, the expert system recommends that the product would be best advertised to mothers in their 20s and 30s in the UK and Ireland, and that the focus of the adverts should be on the good nutritional value of the food rather than the price, which is actually higher than average. It further recommends that the marketing should last two months and consist of video shorts on social media, print adverts in parenting magazines and adverts on daytime television, as these are the places this demographic is most likely to see them. It also recommends that a free sampler pot should be included in a home shopping delivery of people in this demographic.

The supermarket's human marketing managers are, of course, free to ignore or alter this advice, but the output of the expert system provides an important series of first steps that save the marketing team valuable time since they do not have to analyse everything manually.

Fuzzy logic

Expert systems often have to deal with imprecise information. **Fuzzy logic** allows for the representation and manipulation of imprecise or uncertain information. Unlike traditional binary logic, which operates with values of either true or false, fuzzy logic acknowledges and accommodates the inherent uncertainty and ambiguity present in many real-world situations.

Fuzzy logic is particularly useful in expert systems because it enables the system to handle vague descriptions and make decisions based on degrees of truth rather than absolute values. It deals with the imprecision inherent in natural language expressions. These are variables that can take on values such as 'very low', 'low', 'medium', 'high' and 'very high', rather than precise numerical values. Fuzzy logic also employs fuzzy inference mechanisms to derive conclusions from these rules. This flexibility allows expert systems to mimic human decision-making processes more accurately, as humans often deal with uncertain or subjective information and make decisions based on degrees of certainty or confidence.

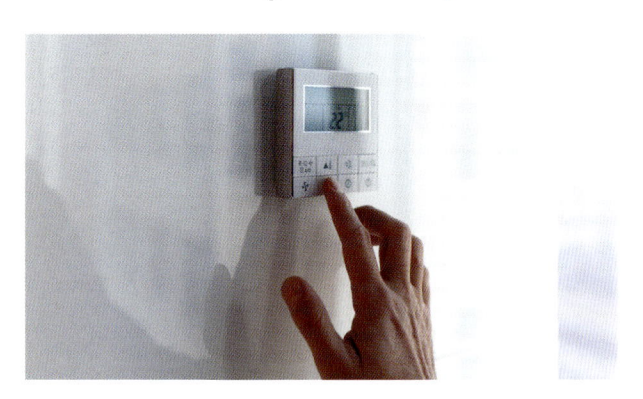

For example, consider an expert system designed to control the temperature of a room based on user comfort. Traditional logic might dictate that if the temperature is above 25 degrees Celsius, the air conditioning should be turned on; otherwise, it should be turned off. However, in reality, users may have different perceptions of comfort, and the decision to turn on the air conditioning may depend on factors such as humidity, air circulation, and even whether the user has been sitting all morning or has just come in from a run. Fuzzy logic allows the expert system to consider these subjective factors and make decisions based on fuzzy rules such as 'if the temperature is somewhat high and the humidity is somewhat high, and the user has been indoors for a while, then increase air conditioning slightly'.

Overall, fuzzy logic enhances expert systems by enabling them to handle uncertainty and imprecision in decision-making, thereby making them more adaptable and effective in real-world applications.

9.3 Deploying an Expert System

The shell

In order to create an expert system, the developer starts with a template called a **shell**. As the name suggests, a shell consists of all the components of an expert system, but without the content required to make it usable. Its purpose is to provide the essential infrastructure and components necessary for the functioning of the expert system. These components include:

- **Knowledge base management system**: Integral to the shell is the knowledge base management system, which facilitates the organisation, storage and manipulation of the system's factual and heuristic knowledge. This component allows developers to add, modify or delete rules, facts and other domain-specific information essential for the functioning of the expert system.

- **Inference engine:** Central to the shell is the inference engine, which will produce the output from the system. The inference engine is ready to operate once the rules have been set up in the knowledge base and the user interface has been configured.

- **User interface**: The shell includes a template user interface which, as we have seen, is the gateway through which users interact with the expert system. It is ready to be configured to ask for whatever information the expert system is designed to help with. This means that the developer does not need to create a user interface from scratch. Instead, they can quickly define the text boxes or other information to be filled in by the user.

- **Explanation facility**: Some shells also include an explanation facility, which would provide explanations for the system's outputs, i.e. descriptions of how the system reaches its conclusions and what kind of heuristics are being used. It is up to the developers to tailor the content of the explanations to align with the domain-specific knowledge and inference processes of the expert system.

Using a shell has several benefits. Firstly, by providing a pre-existing framework, it speeds up the development process of expert systems. Secondly, the shell hides much of the technical complexity involved in building an expert system, allowing developers to focus primarily on the domain-specific aspects such as defining the facts and rules. Thirdly, the use of a generic shell allows the same developers to build expert systems over a wide range of domains without having to start from scratch each time. Finally, by providing a pre-existing, customisable user interface the shell takes care of the details of communication between the user and the expert system.

Knowledge engineer

The developer who has the task of turning a shell into a working expert system is called a **knowledge engineer**. The knowledge engineer is an individual responsible for acquiring, organising and encoding the domain-specific knowledge of human experts into a format that can be utilised by the expert system.

The primary responsibilities of a knowledge engineer include:

- understanding the domain thoroughly;
- collaborating with domain experts (doctors, meteorologists, marketing specialists etc.) to extract relevant knowledge. The deep knowledge, expertise and first-hand experience of domain experts is essential for creating an accurate, effective and reliable expert system, and it is up to the knowledge engineer to accurately capture this knowledge;
- structuring and representing the acquired knowledge in a way that can be entered into the shell;
- developing the rules governing the decision-making processes;
- validating and testing the knowledge base and rules;
- maintaining and updating the system's knowledge base after deployment.

The knowledge engineer plays a critical role in bridging the gap between domain experts and the expert system, facilitating the transfer of expertise from human experts to the machine. Their expertise in knowledge acquisition, representation and validation is essential for the successful development and deployment of effective expert systems.

9.4 Applications of Expert Systems

The CCEA specification requires you to be able to evaluate the use of expert systems in three specific domains: medicine, car engine fault diagnosis and life insurance. We will consider the role of expert systems in each of these domains in turn.

Medicine

Expert systems play a pivotal role in medical diagnosis by using inference techniques and domain-specific knowledge to assist doctors to make accurate and timely diagnoses. These systems are designed to emulate the decision-making processes of human medical experts: analysing patient data, symptoms, medical history and diagnostic tests to generate different diagnoses and treatment recommendations. By providing decision support to doctors, expert systems enhance diagnostic accuracy, reduce diagnostic errors and improve patient outcomes.

There are many examples of real-world expert systems in the area of medicine. For instance, in dermatology, systems like *DermExpert* utilise image recognition algorithms to assist dermatologists in diagnosing skin conditions based on photographs of skin lesions. The results can often be returned within seconds of the images being uploaded.

Case Study

IBM *Watson for Oncology*, developed in partnership with Memorial Sloan Kettering Cancer Center in the USA, is an AI-powered expert system that has revolutionised cancer care. By swiftly analysing vast medical literature, patient records and clinical data, it provides evidence-based treatment recommendations to healthcare professionals globally. With cancer treatment evolving rapidly and new research constantly emerging, *Watson for Oncology*'s ability to sift through immense volumes of data ensures that oncologists are equipped with the most up-to-date information to tailor treatments to individual patient needs.

Users of the system input individual patient factors, such as medical history, genetic profile and disease stage, and the system responds with personalised treatment options tailored to that individual. This saves oncologists valuable time, allowing them to spend more time with patients.

Moreover, because it is based on the knowledge of top oncology experts, *Watson for Oncology* ensures consistency in treatment protocols across different healthcare settings, thereby enhancing treatment quality and patient outcomes.

The integration of expert systems into healthcare has yielded significant benefits in terms of patient care and accuracy of diagnosis. By allowing doctors of all experience levels to avail of the skills of the world's top medical professionals, expert systems contribute to better patient outcomes, reduced mortality rates and improved quality of life. This is especially true when a patient presents with symptoms that a particular doctor has not seen before, or where the doctor may not be fully up to date with the latest drugs and their recommended usage.

Moreover, expert systems help standardise diagnostic processes, ensuring consistency and adherence to evidence-based practices, such as NHS guidelines. These systems enable timely interventions and preventive measures, leading to early detection of diseases and improved prognosis for patients.

However, it is essential to recognise that medical expert systems are not intended to replace human expertise but rather to complement and enhance the capabilities of healthcare professionals. Therefore, ongoing evaluation and refinement of these systems are essential to optimise their performance and ensure their continued effectiveness in improving patient care and diagnosis accuracy.

Car engine fault diagnosis

As vehicles have become more complex in recent decades, more and more electronics and software have been built into their systems. While in the 1980s a car mechanic could repair a car engine by checking and replacing faulty parts, a modern engine can develop faults that can only be diagnosed, and even repaired, electronically. As every car manufacturer has their own system, it has become impossible for a car mechanic to be sufficiently knowledgeable about all types of engine to be able to work on the wide range of vehicles they will typically encounter.

As a result, many car manufacturers and third-party companies have developed expert systems that a mechanic can simply 'plug' into a car engine. These systems examine the car's sensor readings, engine performance data and historical maintenance records. With this information they then consult a vast knowledge base of known engine problems and solutions determined by human experts to identify problems and suggest solutions.

Case Study

Image ©Actron.

Auto Scanner Plus is a hand-held expert system produced by Actron. It is compatible with the systems from multiple car manufacturers and contains over four million repairs in its knowledge base, all originally derived from, and verified by, human mechanics.

When a car develops a fault, the mechanic (or even the car's owner) can plug the *Auto Scanner Plus* directly into the car. The system will examine the data from the car's systems and, using its inference engine, make suggestions for what fault has caused the problem, ranked in order of likelihood. Once the mechanic has selected a problem the system will provide them with instructions for how to carry out the repair, what spare parts are needed and will even display where the part is located in the engine and how to access it.

Auto Scanner Plus not only diagnoses the symptoms, but also considers factors like the age of the car (as some problems are more likely to occur in older cars) and even the manner in which it is typically being driven, as this too can make certain failures more likely.

The use of such expert systems allows engineers to both use their time more efficiently and be more successful in diagnosing problems, benefitting not only their own professional work but the vehicle owners as well.

Life insurance

Life insurance is a financial product that provides a cash payout upon the death of an insured individual, offering financial protection and support to loved ones in the event of loss. Policyholders pay a monthly premium to the insurer. The premium charged depends directly on how likely the person is to die during the lifetime of the policy, and it is in determining this risk that expert systems have a role. An insurance company that underestimates risk can go bankrupt if it has to pay out more than anticipated, while one that overestimates risk will be uncompetitive because it will charge higher premiums than competitors.

Risk can be influenced by many factors, for example:

- **Age**: an older person has a higher likelihood of death than a younger person.
- **Gender**: statistically, men have a lower life expectancy than women.
- **Health history**: a person who suffers from underlying health conditions is at a higher risk than a person who has been healthy all their life.
- **Lifestyle**: smokers have a higher risk of death, as do the those with high cholesterol, and even those who partake in high-risk sports such as BASE jumping.

Expert systems employed in life insurance risk assessment leverage advanced domain-specific knowledge to analyse these various factors and assist the insurance company to accurately assess the risk profiles and set appropriate insurance rates.

The adoption of expert systems in life insurance offers numerous benefits to insurers, policyholders and the industry as a whole. Firstly, expert systems streamline the underwriting process by automating routine tasks and data analysis, reducing manual effort and improving operational efficiency. Secondly, these systems help the company to assess risk in the most accurate way. Finally, expert systems enable insurers to identify emerging trends, and adapt underwriting guidelines in response to changing market conditions, regulatory requirements and customer preferences.

It is worth noting that, despite their significant advantages, the application of expert systems in the insurance sector does raise ethical issues. The use of historical data may inadvertently perpetuate existing biases in underwriting and claims assessment. For example, if historical data shows that individuals of a certain race or gender are statistically more likely to file claims, the system may unfairly penalise individuals belonging to those groups by charging higher premiums, even if a person's individual circumstances do not warrant such treatment. Insurers must therefore adhere to strict ethical guidelines to safeguard confidence in the insurance industry.

Task

'Expert systems eliminate the need for human experts'. Discuss this statement. Do you agree? Why or why not?

9.5 Evaluation of Expert Systems

The use of expert systems has many advantages. The main ones are:

- They help users to make informed and consistent decisions based on expert knowledge and reasoning.
- They reduce the manual effort required to make decisions, improving the efficiency of the organisation.
- They make subject-specific expertise accessible to users regardless of their own level of expertise in the subject matter.
- They ensure consistency in decision-making and problem-solving, reducing variability and errors that may arise from human judgment or fatigue.
- They are able to handle large volumes of data and are therefore able to 'scale up' to accommodate growing organisational needs and data complexity.
- They can be used as tools for training and education, providing users with interactive learning experiences and real-time feedback on their decisions.
- They can be updated and refined over time, incorporating new knowledge, feedback and insights to improve performance and adapt to changing circumstances.

However, they are not without their problems, some of which are as follows:

- The initial acquisition of domain-specific knowledge from experts can be time-consuming and costly.
- Because they are domain-specific, expert systems are often unable to deal with problems that are even slightly outside their area of expertise.
- The decision-making processes of expert systems can be difficult for users to understand, meaning that there can be issues with developing trust in the system's recommendations, especially in complex or critical situations, such as medicine.
- The ongoing maintenance required to remain accurate and relevant can be expensive.
- Overreliance on expert systems may lead to dependency among users, diminishing critical thinking skills and actually reducing the number of human experts.
- Expert systems must be programmed correctly, as incomplete, outdated or biased data sources will result in poor recommendations. If the users are not aware of the issue, they, in turn, will make poor decisions.
- They may struggle to adapt to new or unforeseen situations, limiting their effectiveness in rapidly evolving environments.

Questions

1. What is the primary purpose of expert systems?
2. Describe the significance of expert systems in decision-making processes.
3. Outline, with the aid of a diagram, the structure of a typical expert system and describe the role of each component.
4. Explain what is meant by the term 'shell'.
5. Explain what is meant by the term 'fuzzy logic'.
6. Explain what is meant by the term 'heuristics'.
7. Briefly outline the role of a knowledge engineer.
8. Describe the two types of user interface that expert systems can have and state an advantage of each.
9. Briefly outline the advantages and disadvantages of using an expert system in the diagnosis of medical conditions.
10. Briefly describe an ethical issue associated with expert systems and how the problem can be reduced.
11. Evaluate the use of an expert system in diagnosing faults in car engines.
12. Zinga Technologies wishes to implement an expert system to help market its new products more effectively to its existing customers. Outline the process that should be followed to build the expert system. Include references to the roles of the different people required.
13. Evaluate the use of an expert system in calculating insurance premiums.

CHAPTER 10
Natural Language and Voice Recognition

By the end of this chapter students should be able to:
- describe the technology required for natural language and voice recognition systems;
- evaluate the use of natural language and voice recognition systems.

10.1 Introduction

Natural language processing (NLP) is a branch of artificial intelligence (AI) that focuses on enabling users to communicate with computers in a natural way, through the use of human language. The challenge of NLP is not merely to allow computers to receive input in the form of human speech (through voice recognition systems), nor is it to allow computers to speak to humans using natural language. While both of these are technologically complex in their own right, the deeper challenge is to create computer systems that can actually understand the meaning behind the human language.

We are all aware of how imprecise human language can be. For example, consider the sentence 'I saw a piece of wood'. Does this mean that you simply saw one with your eyes, or were you actually sawing it in two at the time? The answer would lie in the context of the sentence. Similarly, consider the sentence 'I gave it to him'. This contains both a reference to a thing and a reference to a person. What was it that the speaker gave? And who did they give it to? The answer, again, would lie in the context.

These examples show how it is not sufficient for a NLP system to recognise the individual words that have been spoken, but it must also be able to determine their meaning too. Once the meaning has been understood, NLP can be used to perform many tasks, such as:

- Extracting information from unstructured text data, such as articles, emails, social media posts or documents, to identify key concepts, entities, sentiments and relationships.
- Translating text from one language to another, utilising technology such as neural nets to produce accurate and fluent translations.
- Indexing and searching through vast amounts of textual data, enabling users to find relevant information quickly and efficiently;
- Identifying and removing spam email before it enters a user's inbox.
- Analysing the sentiment or emotional tone expressed in text, allowing organisations to gauge public opinion or customer satisfaction;
- Allowing users to ask questions in natural language and providing them with accurate and relevant answers. Examples include search engines or virtual assistants such as *Siri*.
- Generating human-like text, such as articles, stories or dialogue, based on input prompts or contexts, often leveraging techniques such as language modelling or natural language generation.

As there is significant overlap between natural language processing and AI generally, this chapter will focus specifically on the technologies involved with natural language and voice recognition. For a more general look at AI, refer to Chapter 8.

10.2 Working Principles of Natural Language Processing

To understand and interpret human language, an NLP system must not only understand the individual words being received, but their meaning when taken together. There are different levels of meaning, and an NLP system must take account of them all:

- **Syntax** considers how words are arranged. In English, for example, sentences usually follow the structure subject–verb–object. So the sentence 'Seamus bites the sandwich' makes sense but 'Bites Seamus the sandwich' does not. In the same way, because English uses this order, the sentence 'The sandwich bites Seamus' has a very different meaning to the original sentence, even though the individual words are the same.

- **Semantics** considers how the meaning of words depends on what is around them. For example, the following three sentence all contain the word 'apple' but the meaning is very different each time: 'She picked an apple from the tree', 'His baby is the apple of his eye', 'I just bought a new Apple computer'. The meaning can only be determined from the context.

- Spoken language is a continuous sound wave. **Phonology** is an awareness of what these sounds mean. This is made more complicated when certain sounds can mean different things. For example, the words 'their', 'there' and 'they're' all sound identical when spoken.

- **Morphology** considers how words relate to other words. For example, in the sentence 'I like the red car' the sentence consists of a noun ('I'), a verb ('like'), a definite article ('the'), an adjective ('red') and a noun ('car'). This knowledge is important, for example, when the NLP system is translating into another language where the morphology is different. French, for example, puts most adjectives after the noun, so the colour 'red' would need to come after the noun 'car' in French, giving 'J'aime la voiture rouge'.

- **Pragmatics** considers the deeper meaning beyond what has literally been spoken. For example, if a waitress asks 'Do you have any special dietary requirements?', a literal answer would be 'yes' or 'no'. However, the answer 'yes' would be an inadequate response to this question. An NLP system would be expected to realise that the waitress is also seeking details on what the requirements are. This is difficult to teach computers, as it is the type of knowledge that humans pick up through everyday experiences, whereas computers do not live in human society.

Task

An 'idiom' is group of words that have a meaning not deducible from the meaning of the individual words, for example 'I am over the moon'. Write down a few more examples of idioms. Discuss what this suggests about the particular challenges facing Natural Language Processing technology.

It is clear, then, that NLP must be a complex technology if it enables computers to understand and interpret human language in a way that is similar to how humans comprehend it. It is considerably more than understanding words. How is this achieved? Three methods are adopted by NLP systems.

Part-of-speech tagging

Once a computer has been given a written sentence, the first thing it does is to tag the morphology of the words. Are they nouns, verbs, adjectives, prepositions etc.? This is typically achieved using AI machine learning algorithms.

Consider the sentence 'The cat chased the mouse'. Part-of-speech tagging would tell us that 'cat' is a noun (specifically, a subject), 'chased' is a verb and 'mouse' is another noun (this time, the object). The system would also attempt to attach meaning to these words. 'Cat' is fairly unambiguous, but 'mouse' can mean both a four-legged rodent and a device for controlling a computer. AI would consider the word in the context and note that when 'mouse' appears close to the word 'cat', it is most likely to be a reference to a rodent.

Parse trees

The second stage of the process is to consider the syntax of the sentence. The system would already know how English sentences are constructed (subject–verb–object as previously mentioned) and would break the sentence down into its component parts using a parse tree.

For example, the sentence 'The cat chased the mouse' would be broken down as shown in Figure 10.1.

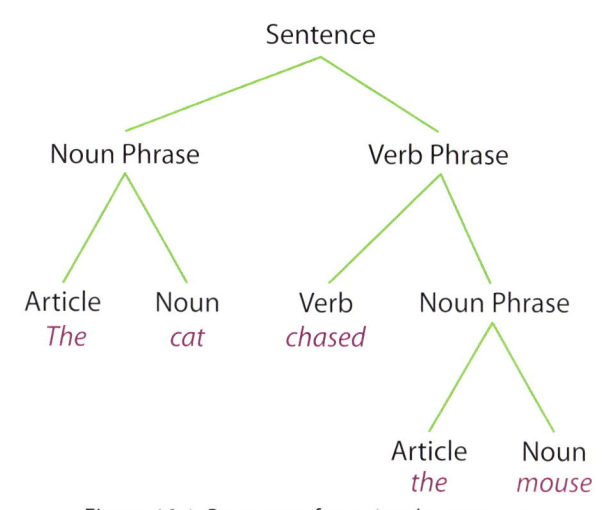

Figure 10.1: Parse tree for a simple sentence.

In this way, the system now understands that 'cat' is the subject, i.e. the thing carrying out the action, whereas 'mouse' is the object, i.e. the thing that the action is being done to. It is also aware that 'chased' is a verb.

The same process works for much more complex sentences, such as the ones you are reading now. The parse trees are more complex, but the end result is a structure of meaning.

Semantics

The final stage in the process is to look at the semantics of the sentence, now that they have been structured in this way, and derive meaning from them. For example, in our example the system can comprehend that the verb 'chased' placed between the subject ('cat') and the object ('mouse') means that the sentence is describing a cat chasing a mouse. It will also observe that the verb is in the past tense, so it will understand that the action took place in the past.

Semantics also involves further work to resolve ambiguity. This will often mean looking further away than the immediate sentence. For example, to understand the sentence 'It was completed by January', the AI will need to analyse the preceding sentences in order to determine what 'it' refers to. In a similar way, semantics requires an understanding of idioms, as previously discussed. For example, the sentence 'I dropped my son off at nine o'clock' means something quite different than the verb 'to drop' suggests when taken in isolation.

Of the three steps outlined above, semantics is the one that most requires further research. Most people can relate instances of a virtual assistant misunderstanding the meaning behind what they have said. This is because semantics involve such a breadth of understanding that achieving consistently reliable responses is a daunting task for software engineers.

10.3 Voice Recognition Systems

Voice recognition refers to the hardware and software that is used to convert spoken language into written text, and hence into commands that the computer can understand. The hardware is typically a microphone connected to a computer, or built into the device itself, such as in a smartphone. The analogue sound wave from the speech is converted, by an analogue to digital converter (ADC), into a digital signal representing the sound wave. The software then uses sophisticated algorithms to convert this into text format.

Once decoded, the software carries out whatever task the text represents. For example, if the device is a smartphone and the command is recognised as 'phone mum', the software will know to initiate a phone call to the contact listed as 'mum'. If the person is using a headset to dictate text into a text document, the software will add the text directly into the software.

The whole process can be summarised as shown in Figure 10.2.

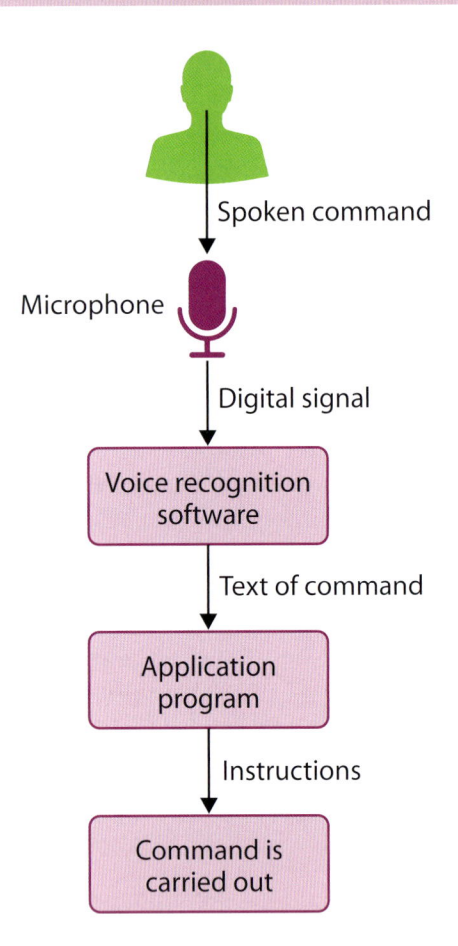

Figure 10.2: Flow chart of the process of controlling a device via voice recognition.

The process

Voice recognition software employs various techniques to accurately convert the digital signal from spoken language into text. These approaches leverage advancements in machine learning, signal processing and AI to achieve increasingly high levels of accuracy and reliability. Some of the technologies used are:

- **Pattern matching** involves comparing the incoming audio signal to a database of pre-recorded patterns representing different words and phrases. By identifying the closest match to the input signal, the software determines the corresponding transcription. Pattern matching is a straightforward method, but it may struggle with variations in speech patterns and different accents, since different people say the same word in different ways. They are typically used whenever the range of words expected is limited, for example automated call centres that invite people to read out numbers or answer yes/no questions.

- **Pattern and feature analysis** involves breaking down the audio input into smaller components, called phonemes, and analysing their characteristics, such as frequency, duration and amplitude. The phonemes can then be compared to a database of words and their phoneme representation. By this method, the software can identify speech across a wider range of speech patterns and accents.

Case Study

What are phonemes?

Phonemes represent the individual sounds that make up speech. There are many more phonemes than letters of the alphabet, as the same letters can be pronounced in different ways. For example, the letters 'th' are pronounced differently in the word 'the' than in the word 'thought'.

The phonemes of the word 'software' are represented like this: /ˈsɒftwɛː/

This may look strange, but it is simply a list of the following sounds:

- /s/: represents the 's' sound as in 'sit'.
- /ɒ/: Represents the 'o' sound as in 'hot'.
- /f/: Represents the 'f' sound as in 'fun'.
- /t/: Represents the 't' sound as in 'top'.
- /w/: Represents the 'w' sound as in 'way'.
- /ɛː/: Represents the 'air' sound as in 'fair'.

The same phonemes can be identified in a wide range of voice types and accents, so looking for these is more reliable than searching for whole words.

- **Statistical analysis** plays a crucial role in voice recognition, particularly in determining the likelihood of different word sequences in a given input audio signal. Statistical models are employed to calculate the probability of various word combinations and select the most probable transcription, based on the rules of grammar. For example, if the user says 'I buy ice cream' the computer might recognise the final two words as either 'ice cream' or 'I scream'. However, statistical models show that, following the rules of grammar, 'ice cream' is far the more likely phrase to appear after the words 'I buy' and it will make the selection on this basis. Statistical approaches are particularly useful in cases where the spoken text is not entirely clear, for example if the user is in a noisy environment.

- **Artificial neural networks** (such as those discussed in Chapter 8) are increasingly being used in voice recognition software to perform complex pattern recognition tasks. These networks are trained on large datasets of audio samples and corresponding transcriptions, learning to recognise patterns and relationships in the data. This leads to improved accuracy in voice recognition. This is an area of active research, and there have been significant advances in recent years.
- **Hybrid approaches**. Some voice recognition software may combine multiple methods to enhance performance. For example, hybrid systems may integrate rule-based algorithms with statistical models, or combine neural network-based classifiers with traditional pattern matching techniques. Often the best approach is a combination of more than one technology.

10.4 Evaluating Natural Language and Voice Recognition Systems

The use of natural language processing and voice recognition systems has significantly transformed human-computer interaction, especially in areas such as virtual assistants. These systems help us with many tasks, such as setting reminders, sending messages, conducting searches and controlling devices, allowing users to accomplish tasks more efficiently. However, as with all technology, they have both advantages and disadvantages.

It is important to remember that natural language processing and voice recognition are not the same thing. Voice recognition converts spoken language into text. Natural language processing aims to understand the meaning behind the language and implement it. When the two are combined, they can be very powerful, as shown in the following case study.

Case Study

Siri, Apple's virtual assistant, has revolutionised the way users interact with their devices through natural language processing and voice recognition software. It decodes spoken commands and then interprets the commands. Consider Sarah, who relies on *Siri* to assist her throughout the day. She uses it in a range of ways:

- *Setting reminders*: While doing the dishes, Sarah activates *Siri* and says 'Remind me to buy groceries tomorrow at 10 am'. *Siri*'s voice recognition software transcribes Sarah's command, recognises the specific task and time mentioned. *Siri* then creates a reminder in Sarah's calendar app, ensuring she does not forget to buy groceries.
- *Sending messages*: While driving, Sarah uses *Siri* to send a text message to her friend. She says, 'Send a message to Emily: I'll be there in 10 minutes'. Again, *Siri*'s voice recognition software captures Sarah's message and converts it into text. *Siri* then sends the text message to Emily, allowing Sarah to communicate safely without trying to type while driving, which is illegal.

- *Web searches*: Sarah is curious about the weather forecast for the weekend. She asks *Siri*, 'What's the weather forecast for Saturday?' *Siri* conducts a web search to retrieve the latest weather forecast for Saturday. *Siri* then provides Sarah with the relevant information, including temperature, precipitation and weather conditions.
- *Calculations*: That evening, Sarah needs to quickly calculate the total of three tickets she wants to buy. She asks *Siri*, 'What's three times nine point eight nine?' *Siri*'s voice recognition software transcribes Sarah's calculation request, converts it to numbers and then performs the calculation using built-in mathematical functions and provides Sarah with the answer: 29.67. This saves Sarah time and effort.

> **Task**
>
> In groups, discuss all the ways that you use voice recognition technology in everyday life. What is it useful for? What is it less useful for?

Advantages of natural language and voice recognition systems include the following:

- **Enhanced user experience**. Users can control devices more intuitively with natural language than they can by entering commands. As such, they require little if any training to use.
- **More efficiency**. The use of natural language speeds tasks up. For example, translating text into another language is much faster if the user can speak the words rather than having to type them.
- **Hands-free use**. Users can interact with devices and systems without the need for physical input devices such as keyboards or touchscreens. This hands-free operation is particularly beneficial in situations where manual input is impractical or unsafe, such as while driving, cooking or performing other tasks that require the user's hands to be free.
- **Accessibility**. People with physical disabilities that make it difficult for them to use traditional input devices may find voice recognition systems particularly useful.
- **More accurate input**. As the system converts a spoken word into text, the resulting text is less likely to contain spelling mistakes, as it is the computer that is spelling them.

Some disadvantages are as follows:

- **Ambiguity**. Natural language can be ambiguous and imprecise, so a natural language system may sometimes misinterpret what is being said. Allowance must be made for this eventuality, for example by asking for confirmation of commands that would make significant changes, such as deleting data, or allowing the user to use their voice to cancel an action.
- **Complexity**. A natural language control system is much more complex than, say, a text-based user interface. They are more expensive to implement.
- **Difficulty with a range of users**. Some voice recognition systems struggle when they have to work with users who have a wide range of voice types, intonation and accents.
- **Limited by environment**. Voice recognition systems are less useful in very noisy environments, such as building sites or music concerts, or in very quiet environments, such as a library, where speech would be disruptive to others.
- **Privacy concerns**. Some natural language systems upload the digital voice signal to a central server to be converted to text, which gives rise to privacy issues.

By combining natural language processing and voice recognition, systems like *Siri* offers great convenience and efficiency in how we interact with computers. Nevertheless, while they make many tasks easier, there are still challenges that limit their uses in some areas and which need further work.

Questions

1. Explain the difference between voice recognition and natural language processing.
2. Describe two uses of natural language processing.
3. Describe what is meant by each of the following terms in the context of natural language processing: syntax, semantics, phonology, morphology and pragmatics.
4. What are the three main methods adopted by natural language processing systems to understand and interpret human language?
5. How does part-of-speech tagging work in natural language processing?
6. What is the role of parse trees in understanding sentence structure?
7. What is voice recognition, and how does it convert spoken language into text?
8. What are phonemes, and why are they important in voice recognition?
9. Describe three processes by which computers can recognise speech. Give an advantage of each.

CHAPTER 10 – NATURAL LANGUAGE AND VOICE RECOGNITION

10. State three advantages and three disadvantages of natural language and voice recognition systems.

11. Explain the purpose of natural language processing.

12. Many mobile devices today use voice recognition. Explain how voice recognition is implemented, with reference to the technology required.

13. List three everyday scenarios where natural language and voice recognition systems could be used and describe the advantages of doing so.

CHAPTER 11
Robotics

By the end of this chapter students should be able to:

- describe the technology involved in the use of robotics;
- evaluate the use of robotics in a range of commercial situations.

11.1 Introduction

The term **robotics** refers to a combination of technology from mechanical engineering, electronics and computer science used to design, create and operate **robots**. A robot can be defined as a programmable machine that can perform actions autonomously in a way that mimics human actions. They are useful for tasks that require:

- more precision than a human would be capable of, such as assembling precision electronics;
- highly repetitive work that would be too boring for a human to do for extended periods;
- working in inaccessible locations, such as space or the deep ocean;
- working in dangerous situations, such as bomb disposal;
- working with toxic materials, such as spray paint or radioactive waste.

The term 'automation' refers to any device that can perform tasks without human intervention, such as a conveyor belt. Factories have made use of automation of one type or another since the Industrial Revolution in the eighteenth century.

Robotics, however, is a more specific type of automation which involves machines that can not only operate without human intervention, but which have additional features that distinguish them from more basic machines. There is no universally accepted definition of a robot. However, a robot typically has the following characteristics:

- **Hardware and software**: To be considered a robot, it must seamlessly combine mechanical components, electronics and software programs.
- **Sensing**: A robot must have the ability to perceive and interpret its environment through sensors, for example cameras, pressure sensors and microphones.
- **Programmability**: A robot must have the ability to be programmed and reprogrammed to carry out a range of different tasks.
- **Movement**: At minimum, a robot must be able to move some of its parts, such as an arm, in order to manipulate objects in its environment. Some robots have the ability to move themselves to other locations entirely, such as a robot exploring Mars.
- **Intelligence**: A robot must have the ability to make autonomous decisions based on sensor input and its internal programming. This can, but does not have to, involve artificial intelligence.
- **Power**: A robot needs to have a source of power. This can mean a direct electrical connection, a battery or another method of generating power, such as solar panels.

Some robots are designed to physically resemble human beings. Such robots are called 'humanoid'. However, most robots in the real world are not humanoid. They are generally referred to as 'industrial' robots. The key point is not their physical similarity to humans, but the fact that they can carry out tasks similar to what a human could carry out, such as applying paint, packing boxes or picking up rock samples.

11.2 Components of an Industrial Robot

As we have seen, an industrial robot is made up of mechanical, electrical and software components. We will examine each of these in more detail in this section.

Mechanical components

Mechanical components form the physical structure of a robot, providing support, mobility and manipulation capabilities. The most basic component is the robot's **chassis**, which provides the base for all the other mechanical and electronic components.

Most robots also feature one or more **arms**. The purpose of an arm is to move an **end effector** (see below) to the correct position in order to carry out work. Industrial robot arms typically have rigid frames with multiple joints, allowing precise movement and manipulation of objects, for example on assembly lines. To be most useful a robot arm should have three degrees of freedom (up/down, left/right, forward/back) which is typically achieved by having three joints. Greater flexibility can be obtained, however, by adding even more joints, as shown in Figure 10.1. This makes it easier for the arm to bend around obstacles and enter confined spaces.

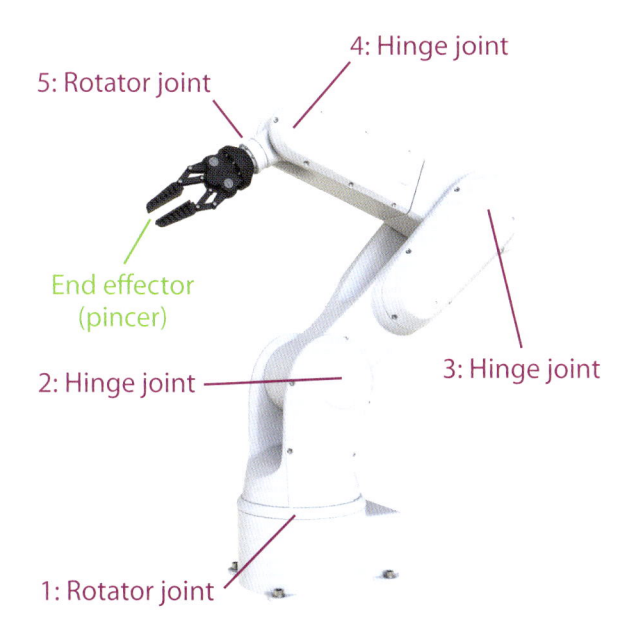

Figure 11.1: A robot arm with five degrees of freedom plus an end effector.

An **end effector** is a mechanical component attached to the end of a robot arm for interacting with its environment. For example, a vacuum gripper is an end effector that uses a suction pad to handle smooth, flat objects like glass or circuit boards. A paint spray nozzle is an end effector that allows the robot to direct a jet of paint to a precise location. Another example is a welding tool, which a robot can use to join metal sheets together. Often a robot will use more than one end effector using different arms. For example, a robot might hold a sheet of metal with one arm and weld it with another.

Electrical components

The role of the electrical components is to physically perform actions by manipulating the mechanical components. They are also used to monitor the robot's environment.

A key electrical component is an **actuator** (sometimes referred to as a **drive**). Actuators are what move the components of the robot. The most common type of actuator is an electric motor which can be used to provide many types of motion, such as moving arms or rotating wheels. Hydraulic and pneumatic actuators are also used in industrial robots and can provide large forces for heavy lifting. For instance, in automotive manufacturing, robots equipped with hydraulic actuators can move heavy car body panels with precision. Motors can also be used by a robot to turn wheels in devices which need to be able to move to a specific location to work, such as bomb disposal robots.

Another type of electrical component is the **sensor**. Sensors enable robots to perceive and interact with their environment. There are many types of sensors. Proximity sensors detect the presence or absence of objects in the robot's vicinity, enabling collision avoidance and object detection. Cameras capture visual information, allowing robots to recognise objects, navigate environments and perform tasks requiring visual feedback. Inertial sensors, such as accelerometers and gyroscopes, provide information about the robot's orientation and motion, aiding in navigation and stabilisation. Force sensors measure the interaction forces between the robot and its environment, enabling delicate manipulation tasks like object grasping and handling. Sensors can also be used to measure air pressure, radioactivity, temperature, moisture level and many other metrics.

The most critical electrical component of the robot is the **controller**. This is an electronic device that includes microcontrollers and computer memory. It stores the software that governs the robot's behaviour, processes the sensory input and executes commands to actuators to perform the programmed tasks. The controller serves as the 'brain' of the robot. Without it, the robot is simply a collection of electrical and mechanical components that cannot do anything useful.

Software components

The software components provide the intelligence and decision-making capabilities of robots, enabling them to perceive, plan and execute tasks autonomously or under limited human guidance.

Robots are designed to be reprogrammable. However, it would be arduous if the programmer had to think about the precise signals that needed to be sent to each arm every time the robot was to be reprogrammed. Therefore, an essential software component is the **robot operating system** (ROS), which provides tools and libraries for controlling the robot. The ROS provides a simple way for a programmer to write a program that can receive data from the sensors and send commands to the actuators. This allows developers to focus on higher-level tasks, without the need to program each movement from scratch.

Case Study

Roomba

Roomba is a robotic vacuum cleaner developed by iRobot Corporation. These autonomous cleaning devices are designed to navigate and clean floors in homes and offices without human intervention. Equipped with various sensors, such as bump sensors, cliff sensors (for detecting stairs) and dirt sensors, *Roomba* robots are capable of detecting obstacles, avoiding falls and identifying areas that require extra cleaning.

When placed in a new location, *Roomba* starts to move about, building a map of the area, including the type of flooring in different areas. It then autonomously generates a cleaning pattern to efficiently cover the entire floor area. *Roomba* vacuum cleaners can automatically adjust their cleaning behaviour based on the type of flooring and level of dirtiness, ensuring thorough cleaning across different surfaces.

With features like scheduling, Wi-Fi connectivity and smartphone app control, *Roomba* offers convenience and flexibility to users, allowing them to maintain clean floors with minimal effort. For example, *Roomba* can be scheduled to clean only when the owners are at work, or can be instructed remotely, for example if the owner suddenly invites a guest for dinner and they want the *Roomba* to clean before they return home.

11.3 Programming Robots

There are four main ways to program a robot.

1. **Online programming** involves entering commands in real-time through a computer interface, allowing immediate execution. For instance, a programmer might instruct the robot to 'Move actuator forward 10 cm' and then observe its response. It is user-friendly and suitable for tasks like programming a welding machine.

2. **Offline programming** involves using specialised software tools to create the program, without the need for the physical presence of the robot. Computer-aided design (CAD) models are used to simulate the movements of the robot, enabling repeated testing without needing to use the actual robot. This method is useful in cases where the robot arms are too powerful or the location is too dangerous for a human being to be in close proximity during training.

3. **Lead-through programming** involves the programmer physically guiding the robot through motions in real time using a manual input device such as a teach pendant or a joystick. This allows for immediate adjustments and corrections as the robot mimics the operator's movements. An example is a technician using lead-through programming to teach a robotic arm how to

perform a precise task such as painting a car component.

4. **Drive-through programming** involves the operator guiding the robot's end effector or manipulator through motions while the robot records the movements for later playback. During playback, the robot autonomously executes the recorded sequence of movements using its own arms or manipulators. If errors are detected during playback, the operator may need to re-record the sequence of movements to ensure accuracy. An example is a warehouse operator using drive-through programming to teach a robotic vehicle how to navigate a predetermined route for transporting goods.

When choosing a programming approach, programmers should consider factors such as the need for real-time adjustments to the program, the skill level of the operator carrying out the training, and the safety of the robot and its environment. Depending on each of these factors, different programming methods may be more suitable to particular situations.

Task

Consider each of the following robot programming tasks. Discuss which method of programming would be most appropriate. There may be more than one possibility.

- To teach a robot vehicle how to navigate a warehouse.
- To accurately weld the same part over and over again in a production line.
- Developing a robot for underwater exploration.
- Adjusting the positioning of a robotic arm for assembling small electronics.
- Teaching a robot to paint metal components in a car factory.
- To simulate the operation of a new production line before building it.
- To teach a robot to handle containers of molten iron.

11.4 Commercial Applications of Robotics

The CCEA specification requires you to evaluate the use of robotics in a range of commercial situations. We shall consider five applications in this section.

Car manufacturing

The use of robotics has revolutionised car manufacturing in recent decades. Robots are used extensively in tasks such as welding, painting, assembly and material handling, where they are particularly useful for repetitive and labour-intensive tasks. For example, when used in welding operations, robots ensure consistent weld quality, reducing the chances of defects. Similarly, on assembly lines, robots are used to automate tasks such as installing components or tightening bolts with a speed and efficiency much higher than humans can achieve. Cars can be moved along a conveyor belt where each robot can add a particular component, starting with the metal panels, then spraying paint, then adding wiring, trim, seats and wheels etc. until the car is completed. A modern robotic production line can produce a car from start to finish in less than 24 hours, whereas building a car by hand can take weeks.

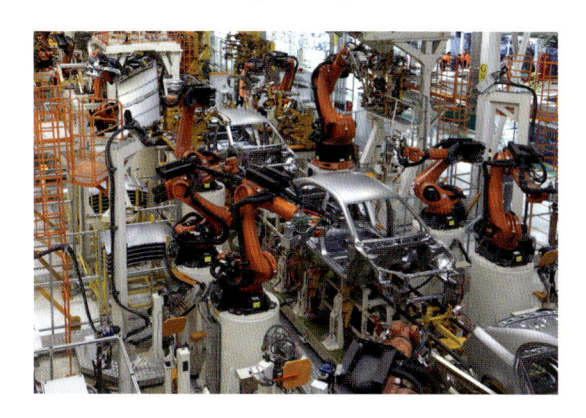

There are many advantages to using robots in car manufacturing. Firstly, they significantly increase productivity because they can work continuously, for 24 hours per day when necessary, leading to higher production capacity. Secondly, robots ensure consistency and uniformity in manufacturing. No matter how well a human works, there will always be minor differences every time a human carries out the same task, resulting in inconsistent quality and increasing the chances of a flaw. The precision and repeatability of a robot minimises such defects, contributing to cost savings and reducing waste. Thirdly, robots enhance workplace safety by carrying out hazardous tasks, thus reducing the risk of accidents for human workers.

Nevertheless, there are some issues around the use of robots in car manufacturing. Many jobs have been lost as human workers have been replaced with robots, raising ethical and social questions. While it is true that robots do not need to be paid a salary, they also require a large up-front investment, which means they are typically more useful for large companies that can afford the outlay. They also require regular maintenance and different sets of human skills to supervise them.

Overall, however, the huge increase in robotics in manufacturing demonstrates the value that industry places in them.

Space exploration

Given the enormous size and inhospitable nature of space, robotics has proven invaluable in space exploration, enabling the examination of celestial bodies throughout the solar system, leading to significant advancement in scientific knowledge. For example, NASA's Mars rovers, such as *Spirit*, *Opportunity* and *Curiosity*, have explored the Martian surface, conducting geological surveys, analysing soil samples and searching for signs of life. On Mars, in 2021, NASA flew *Ingenuity*, the first robotic helicopter to fly on another planet.

There are significant advantages of using robots in space exploration. Firstly, they can withstand harsh environments, extreme temperatures and radiation levels that would kill human explorers. Secondly, the use of robots eliminates the need for expensive life support systems, storage of food and oxygen and provision of living quarters. This hugely reduces mission costs and technological complexity. If the same mission that had been carried out by a single Mars rover had been carried out by human explorers, it would have required billions of pounds worth of technology, including a base with life support, oxygen generators and months of food supplies. Finally, robots can be programmed to operate autonomously, which is very useful in locations where the limitation of the speed of light means that they cannot be controlled in real time from the Earth. The time for a signal to get from Earth to Mars can be up to 20 minutes.

However, the use of robotics in space exploration is not without problems. As discussed, the limitations of the speed of light prevents real-time control at such large distances. While robots can perform programmed tasks autonomously, they still lack the intuition, creativity and problem-solving abilities of humans, which may limit their effectiveness in certain situations. Secondly, despite their technological complexity, missions can often fail due to problems that a human engineer could solve in a few minutes. For example, in 2024 the Japanese robotic Lunar lander *SLIM* fell onto its side upon landing on the moon, limiting its ability to generate electricity and carry out its scientific measurements. There was no way to solve this problem from Earth, even though a human astronaut could have easily lifted it back onto its legs. Missions can also fail due to pieces of grit getting stuck in moving parts or dust settling on solar panels, which are also issues that a human could resolve without difficulty. Nevertheless, despite these problems, the benefits of robots in space exploration are so significant that they will likely continue to be used for the majority of missions in the future.

Case Study

Perseverance

The *Perseverance* rover, part of NASA's Mars 2020 mission, was launched in July 2020 and landed on Mars on 18 February 2021. *Perseverance* is a state-of-the-art robotic rover whose primary mission was to search for signs of past microbial life on Mars, collect and cache Martian rock and soil samples, and pave the way for future human exploration of the planet.

The rover was almost three metres long and weighed just over one tonne. It was equipped with a suite of scientific instruments, including cameras, spectrometers and a drill for sample collection. It also carried the *Ingenuity* helicopter, an experiment, which was successful, designed to test powered flight in the thin Martian atmosphere.

Perseverance's robotic arm could manipulate objects, collect samples and conduct close-up imaging. The rover was equipped with autonomous navigation capabilities, allowing it to traverse the Martian terrain with precision and intelligently avoid obstacles. *Perseverance*'s data and findings were transmitted back to Earth for scientific analysis. It was still operating at the time of publication.

Surgery

Robots are employed in medical settings to assist surgeons in performing procedures. For example, robotic laparoscopic (keyhole) surgery allows surgeons to operate using smaller incisions than would be necessary with conventional surgery. One example is the *da Vinci Surgical System*, which provide surgeons with a range of advanced robotic tools. The surgeon sits at a computerised console while up to four robotic arms are used to carry out the operation itself. The surgeon has a screen with a 3D visualisation of the procedure, while the robot's arms are inserted through keyhole incisions into the patient's body. The end effectors on the arms include tools such as scalpels, scissors and graspers. The surgeon uses hand controls that mimic the tools inside the patient's body, giving the surgeon the sensation of operating directly.

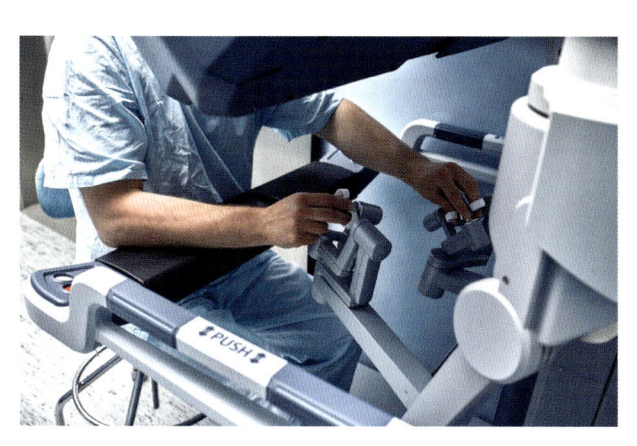

The use of robotics in surgery has a number of advantages. Firstly, it offers improved surgical precision and accuracy, reducing the risk of human error and therefore leading to better outcomes for patients. Secondly, robots enable surgeons to perform very precise surgery in confined spaces with greater ease and control. Finally, robotic systems reduce surgeon fatigue, because they can sit at a console and do not have to stand and strain to see into the body.

However, the use of robotics in surgery also has disadvantages. One limitation is that it takes a lot of time and training before a surgeon is sufficiently skilled to operate on a real patient. Secondly, the cost of buying and maintaining robotic surgical systems can be significant, which may limit access to these technologies, especially in poorer parts of the world. Finally, a reliance on robotic systems brings the potential risk of a system failure. It is absolutely vital that robotic surgery systems be equipped with fail-safes to prevent serious harm coming to a patient if a malfunction were to occur.

Task

Discuss the statement 'Robotic surgery should be standard in healthcare'. Do you agree? Why or why not?

Logistics and supply chains

Logistics and supply chains involves moving goods from one place to another. Robots are deployed in various roles across logistics operations, including warehouse automation, order fulfilment, inventory management and transportation. For example, autonomous mobile robots (AMRs) are used in warehouses to move goods between storage locations, increasing operational efficiency and reducing reliance on manual labour.

There are several advantages to using robots in logistics. Firstly, they improve efficiency by automating repetitive and labour-intensive tasks, allowing companies to handle higher volumes of orders and shipments with greater speed and accuracy. Robots can work continuously without breaks or fatigue, leading to increased operating hours. Secondly, robots enhance workplace safety by handling hazardous tasks, such as heavy lifting, reducing the risk of accidents for human workers. Finally, they can use complex algorithms and access very high shelving, which maximises storage space and hence efficiency in warehouses.

However, there are also disadvantages. As with other uses of robots, the initial investment required to buy and install robotic systems can be substantial, as can ongoing maintenance costs. Secondly, the integration of robotics into existing supply chain operations may not be straightforward. For example, it may require suppliers to send goods in a different format, one that the robotic systems can handle, and can require modifications to existing infrastructure. Finally, as is the case with car manufacturing, robotic supply chains raise ethical and social questions about the adverse impact of automation on human employment.

Agriculture

Robotics has revolutionised traditional farming practices, offering new ways for farmers to enhance efficiency, productivity and sustainability. Robots are deployed in a range of agricultural tasks, including planting, harvesting, weeding, spraying and crop monitoring. They can also be used to improve crop yields. For example, farmers can measure the nutritional level of soil at various points in their fields to create a map of which areas need the most fertiliser. Autonomous vehicles equipped with GPS can then spread fertiliser, automatically adjusting the quantity to what is actually needed at that spot, reducing waste and saving the farmer money. Once crops are grown, robotic harvesters and automated fruit and vegetable picking robots can be used to automate these labour-intensive tasks.

Robots offer many advantages in agriculture. Firstly, they offer increased operational efficiency by automating repetitive tasks and allowing farmers to accomplish more work in less time and with fewer resources. Secondly, they offer increased resource efficiency with products such as such as fertilisers and pesticides, minimising waste and pollution. Finally, they can improve crop quality and yield consistency by providing uniform treatment at all points in the growing cycle

However, the use of robotics in agriculture is not without problems. As before, the initial investment and ongoing maintenance costs are substantial, meaning that small-scale farmers or those in developing countries are unable to benefit. Secondly, because robotic systems work best with large fields, there have been controversies around some farmers removing hedgerows, which are important wildlife habitats, in order to use robotic systems more efficiently.

11.5 Evaluation of Robotics

In recent decades robotics have been increasingly integrated into many areas of life across a range of industries and applications. They have both advantages and disadvantages.

Some advantages of robotics are:

- **Enhanced productivity**. Unlike humans, robots can work continuously and autonomously enabling around-the-clock operation. This leads to higher output rates, which is particularly beneficial in profit-driven manufacturing and assembly processes.

- **Precision and accuracy**. Robots are capable of high precision and accuracy in performing tasks. They can execute complex commands with minimal error, making them ideal for applications requiring meticulous attention to detail, such as surgical procedures or intricate assembly in electronics.

- **Safety**. Robots can operate in environments that are hazardous or inaccessible to humans. They can be deployed in dangerous settings, such as handling toxic materials, working in extreme temperatures, conducting space exploration missions and lifting heavy objects, thereby reducing the risk of injury or harm to human workers.

- **Cost savings**. While the initial investment in robotics can be substantial, the long-term cost savings are significant. Robots can substantially reduce labour costs and minimise errors that lead to waste or rework. Over time, these savings can offset the initial setup and ongoing maintenance costs associated with robotic systems.

- **Flexibility**. Modern robotics systems are designed to be reprogrammed to perform a variety of tasks. This adaptability allows businesses to adjust quickly to changing market demands or production needs. Additionally, the versatility of robots means they can be used in multiple industries, from agriculture to healthcare.

CHAPTER 11 – ROBOTICS

Some disadvantages of robotics are:

- **High initial investment**. One of the primary barriers to the adoption of robotics is the significant initial investment required, both in terms of purchasing the robots themselves, and in terms of training staff to use them. This means that they are often only an option for large businesses.
- **Job displacement**. While robotics can increase efficiency and productivity, they can also lead to the reduction of jobs in certain sectors, particularly those involving repetitive or manual tasks, raising social and economic challenges related to unemployment and workforce re-skilling. The adoption of robotics typically reduces the need for low-skill roles and increases the need for high-skill roles, which can disadvantage those with fewer qualifications.
- **Maintenance complexity**. Robotics systems require regular maintenance, but their complexity means that specialised knowledge is often necessary to do so. If skilled technicians are not available, valuable time can be lost as the robot sits idle.

While robots offer many benefits in terms of efficiency, safety and the capacity to do jobs well beyond human limitations, they also have significant challenges related to cost, job displacement and maintenance. The skill in robotics comes from being able to balance these advantages and disadvantages to achieve an optimal solution.

Questions

1. Explain the term robotics.
2. Suggest some characteristics of a robot.
3. Outline the main components of an industrial robot.
4. Briefly describe two different ways to train a robot.
5. Describe two advantages and two disadvantages of using robotics in surgery.
6. Evaluate the role of robotics in space exploration.
7. Describe the benefits of robotics in the production of cars.
8. Evaluate the role of robotics in agriculture.
9. Explain how the problem of job displacement is associated with robotics.
10. Describe how robots can improve safety for factory workers.
11. Evaluate the impact of robotics on society, considering both its advantages and disadvantages.
12. How has the introduction of robotics transformed various aspects of car production processes, and what ethical and social considerations arise from the adoption of robotic systems?

CHAPTER 12
Mobile Technologies

> **By the end of this chapter students should be able to:**
> - describe how technology supports mobile phone communication: mobile phone masts, cells, handoffs, base station controller, mobile switching centre and public switched telephone network (PSTN) telephone system.

12.1 Introduction

Mobile technologies is the name given to a broad spectrum of wireless communication technologies that enable portable devices – such as mobile phones, tablet computers and laptops – to connect to networks and access information while on the move. They utilise radio signals to transmit content wirelessly, allowing users to stay connected regardless of their location. Originally designed to allow voice calls to be connected wirelessly to the traditional wire-based telephone network, today they are used more and more for internet access.

The first mobile phones (such as the one shown above) were heavy, due to the requirement for large batteries, and could only be used in places that had space to store them, such as in a car. The first hand-held mobile phone became available in 1973, but it was not until the 1990s that digital cellular networks were introduced. This led to the rapid adoption of the technology by the general public. Today, most people in the UK own at least one handheld mobile device, and more people now use mobile phones than traditional landline phones.

Since the millennium, mobile phones have become indispensable tools for both individuals and businesses, leading to much easier communication across vast distances. For individuals, mobile technologies allow people to keep in touch with each other when not at home, making it much easier to make or change plans at short notice. Being able to share experiences during a day enriches people's personal and social lives.

For commercial usage, mobile technologies help workers who have to travel, such as the emergency services, delivery drivers, salespeople and health visitors. Mobile technologies also allow businesses to interact with users directly, for example via banking apps and social media.

> **Task**
>
> Imagine you were no longer allowed to have a mobile phone. What impact would it have on your life? Describe as many things as possible that would be affected.

12.2 Cells and Mobile Phone Masts

The Public Switched Telephone Network (PSTN) is a global telecommunications infrastructure that facilitates the exchange of voice and data communications. The PSTN operates through a network of interconnected physical copper wires, fibre-optic cables and switches. When a user places a call using a landline, their landline telephone connects to a local exchange, where the call is routed through a series of switches and trunk lines to reach the destination telephone. However, this process is not possible for mobile devices since they do not have cable connections.

The main purpose of mobile technologies is to:
- allow mobile devices to wirelessly connect to other devices, and
- allow the devices to move around while in use, without being disconnected.

Imagine a person wishes to use a mobile phone to call another mobile phone. Mobile phones do contain radio transmitters, but these are not powerful enough

CHAPTER 12 – MOBILE TECHNOLOGIES

to transmit a signal more than a few kilometres (even less in built-up areas). So, they cannot call another mobile phone directly. Instead, they must be routed via a **mobile network**. This can be represented as shown in Figure 12.1.

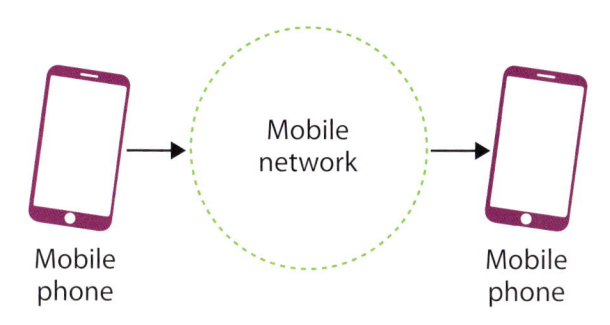

Figure 12.1: Basic operation of the mobile network.

But how do the mobile phones connect to the mobile network? Two key components of mobile architecture are mobile phone masts and cells.

Mobile phone masts (Figure 12.2) are tall structures equipped with antennae and transceivers that transmit and receive radio signals to and from mobile devices within their coverage area. Positioned strategically across the landscape, mobile phone masts ensure comprehensive coverage, enabling users to stay connected even while on the move. Each mobile phone mast is connected to the rest of the mobile network, as we shall see in the next section.

Figure 12.2: The top of a typical mobile phone mast. A box at the base of the mast houses the base station controller, discussed later in the chapter.

The whole landscape is divided into virtual **cells**, each of which is served by a dedicated mobile phone mast. Cells are typically hexagonal but vary in size depending on factors such as population density, terrain and network capacity requirements. In densely populated urban areas, cells may be smaller to accommodate the higher volume of users, while in rural areas, cells may be larger to cover expansive areas with fewer users, as shown in Figure 12.3. The boundaries of cells are not fixed and may overlap, allowing for seamless handoffs as mobile devices move between cells while maintaining continuous connectivity.

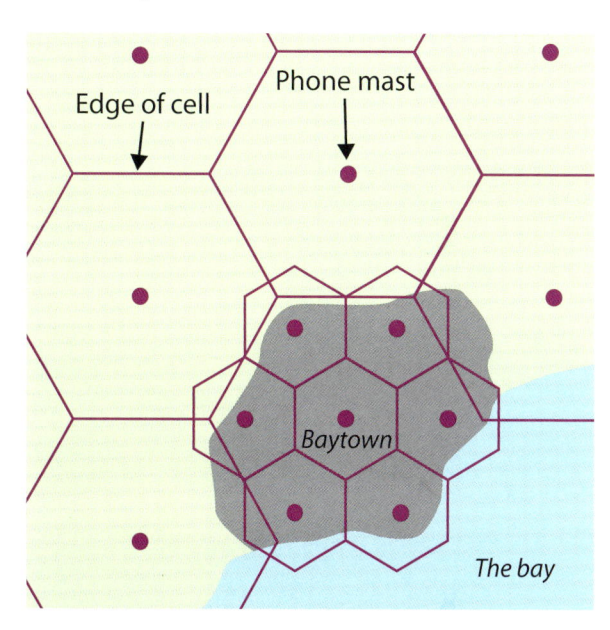

Figure 12.3: Mobile cells in a hypothetical landscape. Note that there is a greater number of small cells in the urban area, and fewer, larger cells in the rural area.

Mobile devices can experience poor connectivity if:

- they are too far from the mobile phone mast, so that the signal is weak;
- they are located where a natural feature such as a hill, or a structure such as a building, is blocking the signal to the mobile phone mast;
- there are too many devices trying to use the same mobile phone mast simultaneously;
- there is interference from other electronic devices or thunderstorms.

Case Study

Zinga Technologies have organised a staff evening out to a music concert at Belfast's Odyssey Arena. They are using electronic ticketing for entry, which each person can display on their mobile phone to gain entry. Customers are always advised to download the tickets to their phone before arriving at the venue because mobile phone coverage at events is often very poor. All but one employee has done so and gained access to the venue.

One employee attempts to download their ticket while in the entry queue but is unable to connect to the internet via their mobile phone. Why is this the case in a large urban area such as Belfast? The reason is that so many people have converged on such a small geographical area that the mobile phone mast for the cell at the Odyssey Arena is overwhelmed by all the phones attempting to connect to it. Coverage is therefore very slow, while some devices cannot connect at all.

Eventually the employee manages to download their ticket but gets to their seat late. The example illustrates how mobile technologies can struggle, even in well-connected cities, when thousands of users all try to use a single mast simultaneously.

To make a mobile phone call, the mobile device first uses its built-in radio transmitter to establish a connection to the mobile phone mast. The mobile phone mast then connects the call to the mobile network and, finally, another mobile phone mast transmits the signal to a radio transmitter in the receiving mobile phone. We can now see that the process of making a mobile phone call can be more accurately represented as shown in Figure 12.4 below.

12.3 The Mobile Network

How does the mobile phone mast direct a call on to the mobile network? This is achieved using the mast's **base station controller** and a **mobile switching centre**.

Base station controller

Each mobile phone mast has a **base station**. The base station serves as the connection between a high-capacity fibre-optic network, which connects it to the rest of the mobile network, and the radio transmitter and receiver mounted on one or more phone masts. The base station also contains various pieces of computer equipment that act as the **base station controller (BSC)**. This equipment is typically sited in a box at the base of a mast.

The purpose of the BSC is to:

- listen for mobile devices in the cell transmitting a message indicating that they wish to connect to the network;
- establish and maintain connections to each mobile device;
- establish links between the mobile devices and the rest of the mobile network, using its high-capacity fibre-optic connection;
- allocate resources and radio frequencies to ensure optimal usage of the base station's capacity;

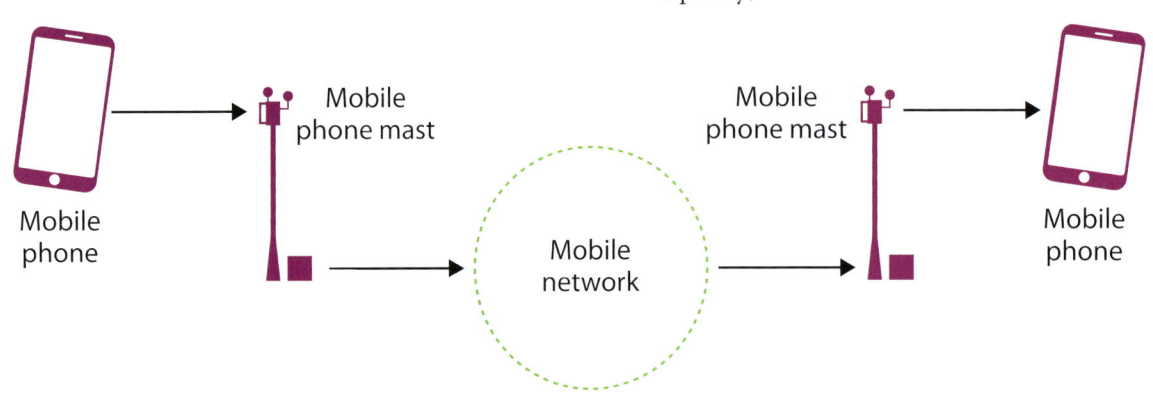

Figure 12.4: More detailed operation of the mobile network.

- terminate connections in a controlled way when required;
- check whether any devices are moving out of range of the mast, in which case the base station will collaborate with nearby cells to seamlessly hand over the connection.

Base station controllers have a high degree of automation and can carry out most operations autonomously. However, the base station provider can intervene remotely to make adjustments or solve technical problems. As base stations are unmanned, sometimes a visit by an engineer to the base station is required to make manual repairs.

Mobile switching centre

The base stations are themselves connected to a **mobile switching centre (MSC)**. Each network (for example O2 or EE) operates its own system of MSCs, which are located at strategic locations within the country. Each one is responsible for a large number of base stations and, together, they provide full coverage for the whole country.

The purpose of an MSC is to:

- connect calls from the BSC of the source mobile device to the BSC of the target mobile device;
- act as a central switching node, choosing the most efficient way to route phone calls through the core fibre-optic network;
- check the status of callers to ensure they have permission to use the network (for example, an EE subscriber would not be able to connect to the O2 network);
- keep track of the locations of all subscribers on the network when their devices are on but not making a call, so that incoming calls can be routed to them;
- coordinate the collaboration between BSCs when a moving device is to be handed over from one cell to another.

A call between two people on the same mobile network will be handled entirely by an MSC. However, there are cases when MSCs need to access other networks. Firstly, they provide connections to the networks of other mobile network operators so that, for example, a customer on the O2 network can call someone who is on the EE network. Secondly, they provide connections to the Public Switched Telephone Network (for landlines) so that a mobile customer can call a landline, or vice versa. Thirdly, they provide access to the internet generally, so that a mobile user can access data directly over the network. Finally, they provide connections to networks in other parts of the world so that a mobile customer can make a call to another country. All of the calls are tracked by the MSC, which can then be used to generate billing information to charge customers for the calls and data that they use.

This allows us to draw a more complete diagram of a mobile network, as shown in Figure 12.5.

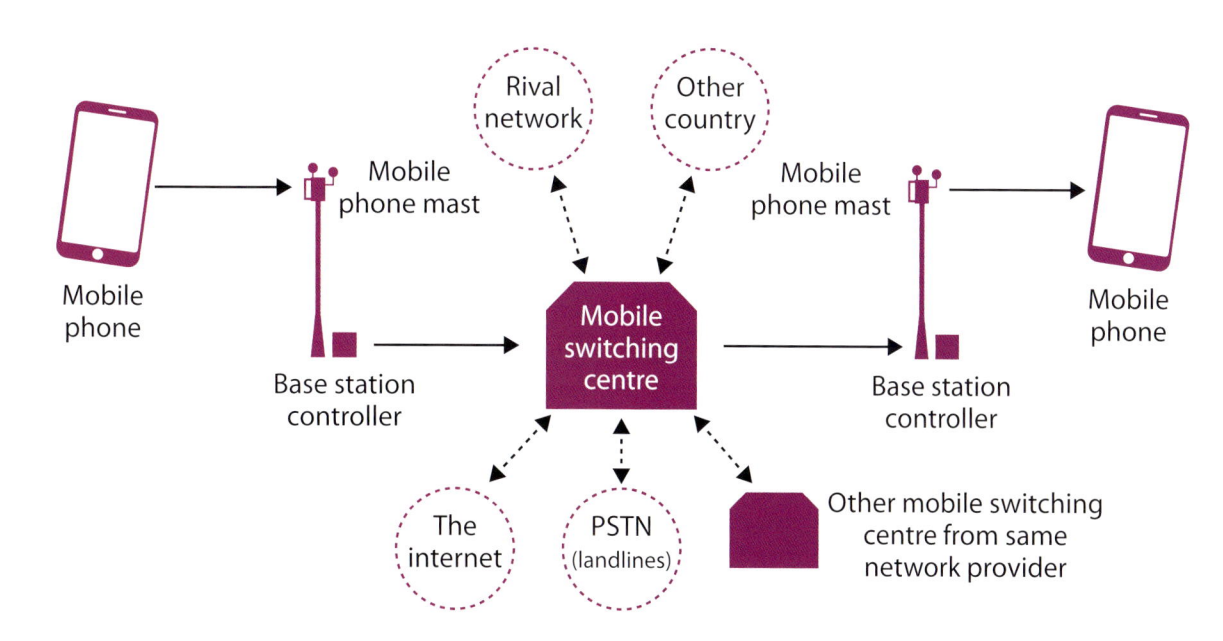

Figure 12.5: More detailed operation of the mobile network showing BSCs and an MSC.

12.4 Operation of Mobile Networks

Voice calls

Having considered the technology used for a mobile network, we will now consider the process of making a voice call using a mobile phone.

- When the mobile phone is first switched on, it listens for a periodic signal from the nearest phone mast, which indicates its presence. Each mast tags its signal with a system identification code (SIC) for the company that operates it. The phone knows which network it is subscribed to, so it will seek an SIC matching its home network. If it does not find one, it will display a 'no service' error.
- Once the phone has found a mast from its own network, it uses its internal radio transmitter to send a message to the mast stating that it wishes to connect to the network. The BSC for that mast then sends a message to the MSC so that the MSC knows that the device is connected and can keep track of where the device is located. The phone continues to send signals periodically to the BSC to stay in contact.
- When the user initiates a phone call, the phone sends a signal to the mast saying that it wants to establish a phone connection. The BSC for the mast allocates resources to the call, typically a particular frequency to use for the duration of the call, so that it does not interfere with other calls.
- The BSC then sends a message to the MSC telling it what phone number it wishes the call to be connected to. If it is another phone on the same network, the MSC will route it through a network of fibre-optic cables to the BSC of the mast nearest the destination. The destination BSC will then transmit a message to the target phone, causing it to ring and, when answered, complete the connection.
- If the call is on another network, or is a landline, the MSC will connect it to the MSC of the other mobile network, or route it through special connections to the PSTN landline network.
- For the duration of the call the MSC and BSCs work together to transmit the messages from source to destination and vice versa. The mobile phone's radio transmitter will transmit the voice of the user continuously during the call. As the transmitter uses power, the phone's battery will drain more quickly during a call than when the phone is idle.
- If the person making the phone call is moving, for example on a bus, then their location will change relative to the mobile phone mast it is connected to. The BSC continuously monitors the signal strength from each phone it is connected to. If it gets too weak, the BSC will ask the phone to search for another phone mast with a stronger signal. Once it has found one, the BSC will initiate a **handoff**.
- To carry out a handoff, the BSC coordinates resources with the BSC for the new mast that the call is to be transferred to, as well as the central MSC, to ensure that the call data is rerouted via the new mast. Once the new mast is ready, a signal is sent to the mobile phone telling it to switch to the new mast.
- Handoff is then carried out. It typically takes a fraction of a second so that the user does not notice any break. The new BSC is now in control of the call and the original BSC releases its resources ready for another call.
- If the mobile phone moves somewhere where it cannot establish a reliable connection with a mobile phone mast – either because there are no masts in the area, or because the signal has been blocked, say by passing through a tunnel – the signal strength will degrade to the point that the call quality will decline. If the signal gets too weak the connection is broken and the user will receive a 'call failed' error.

Accessing data

Phones can also be used to access data over a network, for example to browse the internet. In the context of mobile networks, the term 'data' refers to any digital content that is sent or received, whether it be a web page, music being streamed or video content. When accessing data, a permanent connection of the type used for a voice call is not made. Instead, the phone sends and receives data 'packets' to and from the nearest BSC. However, the principle of handoff is the same, so that a user accessing the internet while on the move can do so seamlessly.

The earliest generation of mobile phone networks only allowed voice calls to be made. The second generation added the ability to send text messages and some very basic data signals. Third generation (3G) networks were introduced to the UK in 2001 and were capable of transmitting data at speeds of a few hundred kilobits per second, which was sufficient to provide basic web connectivity.

Fourth generation (4G) networks were introduced in 2012 and offered much higher data speeds in the order of hundreds of megabits per second, sufficient for streaming video and for online gaming. These download speeds made app stores feasible, providing content that could realistically be downloaded over a 4G network.

Fifth generation (5G) networks, rolled out in the UK from 2019, offer speeds of several gigabits per second, allowing streaming of very high-definition video, virtual reality, augmented reality and immersive gaming experiences. Belfast was one of the first cities in the UK to get a 5G network. 5G brings other new technologies to enhance the performance of the mobile network. It is likely that technology will continue to evolve and that further enhancements will follow 5G as mobile technologies become more and more essential to everyday life.

Task

Apple's App Store allows users to download apps onto their mobile phones. It was launched in 2008 with 500 apps. The number of apps available passed one million in 2013 and two million in 2017. Discuss how these figures relate to the development of data access via the mobile phone network.

Questions

1. What is the main purpose of mobile technologies?
2. Explain the concept of cells in the context of mobile networks.
3. Explain the role of a mobile phone mast.
4. Why might mobile devices experience poor connectivity?
5. What is the role of the base station controller?
6. Outline the function of a mobile switching centre.
7. How does a mobile phone stay connected to a mobile network when not making a call?
8. Explain the process of cell handoff in a mobile network.
9. Differentiate between 3G, 4G and 5G networks in terms of capabilities.
10. Explain how communications technology enables an uninterrupted phone call to be made between two mobile phones.
11. Discuss the role of mobile switching centres (MSCs) in facilitating seamless communication across different mobile networks and between mobile and landline networks.

CHAPTER 13
Data Mining

> **By the end of this chapter students should be able to:**
> - explain what is meant by data mining;
> - describe how digital technology can be used in data mining to gather, store, process and analyse large volumes of data;
> - explain the importance of big data to the operation and competitiveness of organisations in the health, finance and retail sectors;
> - describe the threats to the privacy of the individual from the use of data mining.

13.1 Introduction

Data mining is the process of analysing large data sets with the aim of discovering patterns, trends and insights. More precisely, data mining aims to uncover hidden patterns and relationships that may not be immediately apparent through traditional analysis methods. Data mining typically involves a range of methods that can be a combination of statistical analysis, artificial intelligence and database systems.

The information uncovered from data mining can be used by organisations in the following ways:

- to identify trends and patterns in order to make future predictions;
- to summarise and interpret data in order to better understand it;
- to provide insights to support decision-making processes;
- to uncover previously unknown patterns and relationships that could suggest new routes for research or innovation.

In this chapter we will first introduce the concept of big data, before discussing how data mining works. We shall then consider how the use of big data benefits organisations specifically in the health, finance and retail sectors. We will conclude the discussion by briefly considering the privacy issues raised by use of the technology.

13.2 Big Data

Central to the concept of data mining is the idea of **big data**. The term 'big data' refers to vast and complex datasets that exceed the capabilities of traditional data processing methods. Big data has four features, commonly referred to as the 4Vs:

- **Volume:** Big data involves large volumes of data. While this is more a general reference to the quantity of data, rather than the amount of storage space it takes up, some big data can run to terabytes or even petabytes of size. Datasets this large can originate from various sources, but a common example is social media content.
- **Velocity:** Big data is generated at a rapid pace, with data usually being produced and collected in real time. The continuous arrival of new data requires storage and analysis methods that can cope with the rate. For example, in 2022 half a million Facebook posts and 500 hours of YouTube videos were being added to the internet every minute.
- **Variety:** Big data comes in a diverse range of formats, from structured data to unstructured data. Structured data is that which is already organised in some form, such as a database. Unstructured data is anything that is not broken down in a methodical way, such as text documents or videos.
- **Veracity:** The term 'veracity' means 'reliability'. Due to its sheer volume, and often dubious sources, big data will have a wide range of data quality, possibly containing inaccuracies, inconsistencies or incomplete information. For example, social media contains a large volume of fake news as well as posts generated by bots or spam accounts. However, the task of verifying the reliability of big data is difficult due to its sheer volume.

Task

Consider the data on a large social platform such as YouTube or Instagram. Discuss how each of the 4Vs relates to the material posted on these platforms.

13.3 The Process of Data Mining

The digital technology used in data mining can best be considered by the different stages in the process: gathering the data, storing the data, processing the data and analysing the data. Each is considered in turn below.

Data gathering

Data gathering is the first step in the process of data mining. It involves gathering relevant data from various sources to build a comprehensive dataset for analysis. As the amount of data being gathered is likely to be vast, great care must be taken to only gather data that is likely to be of relevance.

Many sources are possible. Internal sources are data already within the organisation, such as product databases, transaction data or CCTV feeds. External sources are outside the organisation and can include data from partner organisations, social media or market research.

Once the data sources are identified, they must be retrieved from these sources. Data collection methods vary hugely depending on the nature of the data source. They can include API access to social media platforms, transactional records from sales software, online surveys, direct feeds from commercial satellites, feeds from sensors located around (say) a factory, and even manual data entry. API (application programming interface) refers to tools that companies provide to allow trusted third-party programmers to access their systems in a controlled way. For example, Facebook provides API tools that allow programmers to download copies of posts directly from Facebook's database rather than through the normal graphical user interface.

It is very important that any data containing personal information be treated appropriately. Sensitive information can be entirely removed if desired, or generalised. For example, customers' exact addresses could be removed and instead grouped by postcode. Where sensitive data is required, the data mining system should be adequately protected from unauthorised access and should comply with the law (see Chapter 15).

Well-planned data gathering lays the groundwork for the rest of the process.

Data storage

Due to the volume of big data, data storage is a significant issue in data mining that needs careful planning. YouTube, for example, requires several thousand gigabytes of new storage space every minute just to store the new videos being uploaded. This means that a storage system is needed that can:

- store a large volume of data,
- cope with additional data being added at a high rate,
- retrieve data rapidly when requested.

Most organisations that use big data solve this problem with hyperscale computing.

There are two ways this can be set up. In the first approach, the company runs many thousands of individual servers, each of which has its own bank of direct-access storage (DAS) devices (Figure 13.1). These servers are often stored in large data warehouses but, with fast internet links, can be located anywhere in the world and do not all have to be in the same location. The main advantage of DAS devices is that they are highly responsive when data access is required. However, the addition of new storage does require new servers to be added, which makes them harder to scale.

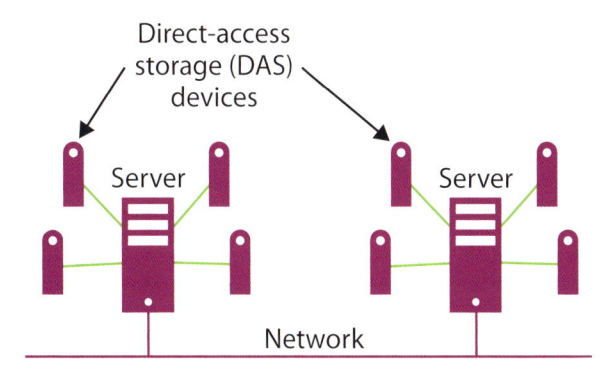

Figure 13.1: The direct-access storage architecture for hyperscale computing. Individual servers, each with their own dedicated storage devices, are connected to the network.

An alternative approach is to use network-access storage (NAS) devices (Figure 13.2). These are storage devices that are directly connected to a network, without needing to be connected to a server. Systems like this are more scalable as it is more straightforward to add new NAS devices to a network. However, they can sometimes be less responsive as they are more limited by network bandwidth, depending on how the network has been designed.

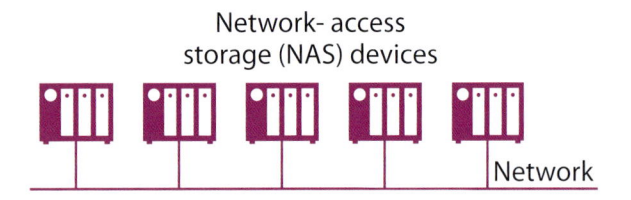

Figure 13.2: The network-access storage architecture for hyperscale computing. Network-enabled storage devices are connected directly to the network.

Examples of hyperscale environments that are available to the public are *Amazon Web Services* and *Google Cloud Platform*, though many organisations run their own private systems, such as those behind social media apps such as Facebook or Instagram.

Once the storage architecture has been selected, a decision needs to be taken on how data will be stored so that it can be retrieved quickly. One method for achieving this is to spread the data across the whole system so that one single part does not become a 'hot spot' for data access, slowing down access for everyone. This is often achieved by partitioning the data across multiple storage nodes and/or replicating the same data in more than one location. This not only ensures faster data access times, but also protects against data loss in the event of a power failure in one location, or a hardware fault in one server.

To find the data at a later date it is necessary to know where it was stored. This is often done by maintaining an index that matches a specific set of data (for example all social media posts that were posted during a given minute) to a specific server where it can be found.

Another method, which enables faster access, is to allocate the storage location using a hashing algorithm to generate a number calculated from the data itself. The number generated is used to identify the specific server where the data is actually stored. For example, for a system storing text documents, a simple hashing algorithm could add up the ASCII codes of the characters of the filename of the document and use this to identify the server where that document will be stored. The system does not need to look up an index to know where to find the data – it simply has to use the same hashing algorithm to go straight to the server needed. Many different hashing algorithms exist and can be employed to ensure optimal performance.

At all times, the data storage system must be protected from unauthorised access, as it may contain sensitive personal information.

Data processing

Once gathered and stored, the data is not yet ready because it first needs to be pre-processed for analysis. This refers to the process of checking the data for errors (and removing them if possible) transforming the data into better formats for analysis and reducing the complexity of data where possible.

Error checking includes tasks such as removing duplicate records, standardising data formats (such as times given in different time zones) and detecting any obvious errors in data, such as a postcode that does not exist. It can also involve looking for missing values and, if possible, filling them in. For example, a missing age can be calculated if the person's date of birth is known. If missing data cannot be reconstructed, it can be replaced with (for example) a known average value, so that it does not impact the data analysis.

Data transformation involves collating data in different formats and/or from different sources and ensuring they are in the same format. For example, a system might collect sales data from point-of-sale terminals in physical shops, from a server hosting the company's website and from a spreadsheet sent over by a distributor. The system needs to convert all this data into the same format so that it can then be analysed as a unit.

Finally, data complexity can be reduced, provided that doing so does not compromise the desired result of the data mining exercise. This can not only save storage space, but also a lot of processing time. For example, a medical data mining system may be designed to look for patterns in patients suffering from heart disease. The system may be given each patient's entire medical record, but not all this information will be relevant. Information such as the name of the patient's GP is not needed and can be discarded. Another example is a system that takes input from a camera to monitor the number of cars entering and leaving a tunnel. These images may be in colour, but this information is not necessary, so the colour data can be discarded, making the images both smaller and simpler to analyse.

Data analysis

Once gathered, stored and processed, the system is ready to perform the analysis that forms the core of data mining. Some of the methods used are as follows:

- **Classification** is a technique used to categorise data into predefined classes or categories. Algorithms are first taught using data that has already been labelled by a human in order to learn how to classify new, unseen data. An example is Gmail's junk mail filter, which analyses millions of emails every minute and attempts to identify spam.
- **Clustering** is used to group similar data points together based on their characteristics or attributes. Unlike classification, clustering does not require training on existing data. Instead, it uses mathematical equations to try to find structures in the data. An example is a supermarket chain that tries to identify groups of customers who have similar buying habits.
- **Association rule mining** is used to identify patterns in financial datasets. It is most commonly used to identify products that are frequently purchased together. This allows retailers to identify products that could be grouped in some way. Customers browsing on Amazon, for example, are usually shown lists of other items often purchased with the one being viewed.
- **Regression analysis** is a statistical technique used to identify the relationship between two sets of data. For example, a retailer might use this method to try to discern the link between sales and certain types of advertising.
- **Anomaly detection** is used to identify patterns in the data that deviate significantly from the norm. Anomalies may indicate possible fraud, data errors or abnormal activity, all of which require further investigation. Banks routinely use this method to analyse credit card transactions and flag anything unusual. For example, if a customer who usually makes purchases in County Fermanagh suddenly makes a series of transactions in Hong Kong, the data mining system will flag this as possible fraud.
- **Dimensionality reduction** is used to reduce the complexity of a dataset while preserving its essential information. An example is a system in an airport that attempts to detect suspicious packages in live footage from CCTV cameras. A system that warns of a suspicious package several hours later will not be useful to the airport, so it is essential that the analysis be carried out in real time. To achieve this, such a system will often simplify the images in order to speed up further analysis. This is not as straightforward as reducing the resolution, as important information must be retained, and many algorithms can be employed to achieve this.

Depending on the nature of the data being used, and the specific needs of the organisation carrying out the data mining, a combination of techniques may be applied to the same data. Whatever method is chosen, the output will be useful information that can be applied by the organisation in whatever ways are useful to it, as we shall see in the next section.

13.4 Importance of Big Data to Organisations

The CCEA specification requires you to be able to describe the importance of big data to the operation and competitiveness of organisations in three different sectors – health, finance and retail. We shall consider each in turn.

Health

Health organisations primarily use big data and data mining to improve patient treatments and to make healthcare operations more efficient.

At the highest level, health organisations can monitor the health of entire societies by analysing data from across the healthcare system, such as hospitals, GP practices, research studies and surveys. Data mining can reveal emerging trends, such as an increase in certain diseases or a deterioration in mental health in certain groups of people. This allows managers to target interventions in a timely manner.

For example, healthcare professionals in Northern Ireland used monitoring of this type to observe a small number of cases of measles in children in early 2024, which prompted rapid action to encourage immunisation and reduce the risk of a more widespread outbreak. On a more global scale, data mining is routinely used to search for viruses that have the potential to become an epidemic or even a pandemic, such as the coronavirus that caused the pandemic of 2020–21.

Health organisations can also use data mining techniques to identify patterns in health data that may otherwise have gone unnoticed. For example, many rare health disorders occur spontaneously. However, if a rare disorder was identified in a number of patients living in a single geographical area, or among people who worked in the same location, this would raise an alert that further investigation is needed. Individual doctors may only see a single patient with the condition and may not make the link to other cases that data mining can identify.

Similar techniques can also be used to predict those at risk of future health conditions. For example, this can be achieved by analysing a large number of patient records and cross-referencing them with lifestyle factors, such as diet and exercise habits, and even genomic sequencing data. This can identify individuals at higher risk of developing certain genetic conditions, or of developing certain types of cancer. These can then be used to offer screening to those at higher risk, which can catch illnesses earlier than otherwise.

On an individual level, many people now have wearable devices such as smartphones or watches that continuously monitor a person's health, using metrics such as steps, heart rate and amount/quality of sleep. This data can already be shared and, in the years to come, such devices could – with the patient's permission – feed data continuously into a system that would allow GPs or even AI systems to alert patients of any concerning changes, such as increased blood pressure or poor-quality sleep.

Data mining has an important role in personalising medicine for patients. While doctors routinely use guidelines, such as those issued by NICE (National Institute for Health and Care Excellence), to treat specific conditions, data mining techniques could create a bespoke treatment plan for every individual that would tailor interventions, such as exact drug doses, to a degree that a doctor would have neither the time nor knowledge to do themselves, since it would be based on lifestyle data and continuous data feeds from sensors on the patient's own body.

Finally, medical professionals can use data mining to look back over past treatments and assess their effectiveness. For example, some conditions have more than one possible treatment. Data mining can look back over patients who received each treatment and look at how their health changed in the years after treatment to try to see which treatment gave the better outcome, and whether this applied uniformly to all patients, or to specific patients. For example, one treatment might have led to better outcomes in men, while a different treatment might have been better for women with the condition.

Finance

Financial organisations have come to rely heavily on big data and data mining techniques in recent years. One reason for this is the sheer number of transactions that take place each day, and the impossibility of human staff being able to monitor them all. Since money is inherently valuable, financial transactions are particularly susceptible to fraud and therefore banking organisations are primarily interested in protecting both themselves and their customers from fraudulent and illegal activity.

Banks continuously monitor transactions taking place in real time and use data mining techniques to detect unusual or concerning activity. This could include transactions that are unusual for a given customer or larger than normal amounts being transferred. Some people have had the experience of being abroad and their credit card being blocked by their own bank. This will have been triggered automatically by a data mining system concerned by transactions suddenly occurring in a part of the world different from normal. The customer can usually resolve the matter by telephoning the bank's call centre to reassure them that the transactions are legitimate.

Banks also use big data to ensure that they are complying with the law. The law around financial transactions is now so complicated that banks can only meet the requirements with computer assistance. This can range from the routine, such as verifying a customer's identity, to the more complex, such as legal limits on certain types of cash transfer, to those related to geopolitics, for example when a government applies economic sanctions to certain foreign states or organisations.

Banks even use data mining to improve how they interact with customers. For example, data analysis might show customers making a lot of mistakes trying to do a money transfer. This would suggest that the design of the money transfer web page might need to be examined. Or they might notice certain types of customer closing their accounts, presumably to move elsewhere. Data mining can help managers work out what is driving the loss of custom and hence take steps to address the problem.

In the area of investment banking, big data is absolutely essential. Customers investing money in the stock market want fund managers who can maximise their returns. Stock prices can change on a minute-by-minute basis and only those who can respond rapidly will be able to maximise gains and minimise losses. Data mining techniques are used to quickly identify new trends and analyse the past to predict future trends. Even events such as election results in foreign countries or accidents at oil refineries are fed into the systems as input, such is the range of factors that can impact prices on the stock market.

At the other end of the scale, data mining is used by banks to judge the creditworthiness of individual customers. Every time a customer carries out a transaction, buys something on credit, takes out a loan or applies for a mortgage, the information is logged as big data. At a later date a bank can apply data mining on all this big data to assess the risk level of an individual, often in the form of a credit score.

Case Study

Zinga Technologies has a new customer who wants to buy several thousand pounds' worth of computer equipment on credit. Giving a customer credit always involves risk, as the customer might not be able to pay at the later date. But often the risk is worth it to gain the sale. How does Zinga Technologies make the decision?

Their financial director logs into their online business banking and runs a 'credit check' on the customer. This system uses big data that the bank has acquired to look back at the customer's financial history. Do they pay invoices on time? Have they ever defaulted on a loan? Have they ever been convicted of fraud? Do they have a credit card and, if so, do they pay on time? Do they have a good level of assets in the bank?

For privacy reasons, Zinga's financial director cannot see the answers to these questions, but the bank can, and it uses them to provide a percentage credit score that represents their estimate of the customer's risk. The higher the score, the lower the risk. Fortunately, in this case, the customer comes back with a high credit score and the financial director feels comfortable giving the customer the requested credit.

Retail

The retail sector uses big data in all aspects of operation, including how to market their products, planning what products to stock and the logistics around getting goods to stores.

A supermarket chain will constantly monitor society, often though social media, to identify the mood of the buying public. They will notice trends, such as a surge in interest in organic foods, or a trend for barbequing, and this will inform managers planning what products to bring out. They will also look for negative comments from customers. For example, data mining might detect people posting complaints about queues in stores, which managers could respond to by acting to reduce the problem.

Data mining systems can also help the stores predict future demand by looking at external factors, such as world events and the weather. For example, a major football tournament might trigger a surge in sales for snack foods. A forecast heatwave will trigger demand for ice cream and soft drinks. The system will predict these in advance and place additional orders with suppliers to ensure that the snack food and ice cream are actually on the shelves when people start looking for it. In some cases, the response may need to be more localised. For example, if a major football tournament had Scotland in the final, then forecast demand for match day is likely to be higher in Scotland than in the rest of the UK.

The systems that place orders with suppliers are often automated, with managers overseeing them, rather than making the individual choices. The computers are often better at making these decisions as they ensure that stock arrives 'just in time', to minimise food wasted by being stored too long. However, humans are still needed as even the best systems can still fall foul of inadequacies in their programming.

Case Study

Irish Moles?

B&Q is a large chain of DIY stores that operates across the UK and Ireland. In 2014 a sonic mole-repellent product for gardeners was put on sale by the retail giant. The automated computer system allocated stock to each store and the items were sent and displayed on the shelves.

However, this included stores in Northern Ireland. While moles are found throughout Great Britain, they do not live in Ireland. After some humorous news coverage, B&Q withdrew the product from stores in Northern Ireland.

This is a good demonstration of a how a computer system is only as good as the information it is given. In this case, the geographic distribution of moles was unknown to the computer!

Retailers use big data to create highly personalised advertising campaigns. Most supermarkets operate loyalty cards, where points are earned. For the supermarket, the most useful aspect of this is that it allows them to match sales to individual people and hence target marketing. Many people will have the experience of receiving discount vouchers, highly tailored to the types of food they usually buy. There is no point in advertising wine to a customer who never buys alcoholic beverages. But a customer who buys large quantities of children's breakfast cereal is likely to receive offers for other children's products.

13.5 Privacy Concerns

While data mining offers numerous benefits, it also presents significant challenges and risks to individual privacy. Some specific concerns are as follows.

- **Data breaches.** Big data often contains sensitive personal information that can be compromised by unauthorised access, for example via a cyberattack. Once stolen, the data can be misused for purposes such as identity theft and financial fraud.

- **Profiling and targeted advertising.** As we have seen, data mining enables the creation of detailed profiles of individuals based on their online activities and purchases. While useful for marketing, it can result in intrusive and manipulative advertising practices that cross ethical boundaries of a person's right to privacy.

- **Discrimination.** Data mining algorithms may inadvertently perpetuate discrimination against certain groups based on race, gender, age or other demographic factors. For example, an algorithm may notice that a particular area of high crime is also home to people from a certain ethnic background and conclude that this demographic is more likely to commit crime. In fact, it may be that people from this demographic are on lower incomes and thus only able to afford to live in high crime areas.

- **Loss of anonymity.** Sometimes data that has been anonymised can still be used to identify private information. For example, data that has been grouped by postcode is effective at anonymising data in dense urban areas, but in a rural area it may be sufficient to narrow it down to a small number of households.

- **Government surveillance.** The widespread collection of personal data through data mining technologies could enable mass surveillance by governments and police. This would infringe on an individual's right to privacy and threaten free society.
- **Lack of consent.** Individuals may not be fully aware of the extent to which their personal data is being collected and used, often because they have approved terms and conditions that most people are unlikely to read because they are lengthy and use legal jargon. This can not only threaten privacy, but breed distrust in technology in general.

Task

A person says 'I don't use social media at all because I don't want to risk my privacy'. Is this a reasonable position to take? Why or why not? To what extent are you concerned about your own data privacy?

Each of these concerns can be related to the three specific sectors discussed in the previous section. For example, in the banking sector, customers could face financial discrimination through data mining, or suffer in the event of financial data being exposed in a data breach.

In the healthcare system, patients may not realise the extent to which professionals have access to their personal data. Some may be concerned that their personal data could potentially be accessed by government agencies in the future, for example by identifying people who have been treated for drug abuse.

In the retail sector, marketing may become overly intrusive, for example by showing adverts that are so specific to an individual's browsing history that it feels creepy or even sinister. People may also not realise how widely their personal data is shared between organisations.

Questions

1. What is data mining, and what is its primary goal?
2. What are the four features of big data (the four Vs)?
3. What are the main stages involved in the use of digital technology in data mining?
4. How is data gathering carried out?
5. Describe two storage architectures commonly used in data mining.
6. Explain the process of data processing in the context of data mining.
7. What are some of the methods used in data analysis during data mining?
8. Describe how data mining can benefit marketing by the retail sector.
9. What are some of the privacy concerns associated with the use of data mining technologies?
10. Describe how the health sector can make use of big data.
11. Describe two ways in which the banking sector uses big data.

CHAPTER 14
Cloud Computing

By the end of this chapter students should be able to:

- explain what is meant by cloud computing;
- explain the terms virtualisation, hosted instances, hosted solutions and clustering;
- describe how cloud computing provides services, such as: data storage; email; virtualised software; backup; and remotely hosted applications;
- evaluate the use of cloud computing in terms of business benefits and security issues.

14.1 Introduction

Cloud computing refers to the delivery of computing services such as data storage and software applications over the internet, without the user needing to have the physical or software resources on their own computer or local area network. Instead, data is stored in large server farms that may be located anywhere in the world. The user of a cloud service is typically unaware of the location of the server farm and, indeed, it is largely irrelevant to them because they are interested solely in the fact that they can access and use the resources when required.

Cloud computing is normally provided by **cloud service providers**, large companies that operate the server farms that contain banks of networked file servers. They then sell computing resources to customers for a fee, typically in the form of a subscription. Many different customers share the same resources, but the cloud system is set up in such a way that each user cannot access, and indeed is unaware of, other customers' data.

Three levels of service are made available by cloud service providers:

- **Infrastructure as a Service** (IaaS) provides raw computing resources, such as data storage, to which users can then add their own software. An example is Amazon Web Services, which provides raw computing power for customers.
- **Platform as a Service** (PaaS) is a step up from IaaS, providing a pre-made platform for software development, such as a database, that can be customised and used without worrying about details such as installation or operating systems. An example is Heroku, which allows users to program applications in several programming languages and make them available online to their own customers.
- **Software as a Service** (SaaS) is a higher level still, where users access the software via a web interface and do not need to know anything about how the software operates. An example is Microsoft *Office 365*, which provides a suite of web-based applications including web versions of *Word*, *Excel* and *PowerPoint*.

Many cloud service providers offer their services as a **public cloud**, meaning the resources are connected to the public internet and are hence accessible to anybody with a web connection and the correct security credentials.

Clients who are particularly concerned about security may instead opt for a **private cloud**, which is hosted solely for a single company. Security is greater to begin with, and the fact that servers are not shared makes them even more secure. Private clouds are best suited to companies with sensitive data, such as those in the banking or defence industries.

Task

Based on the text above, list as many cloud computing services as you can that you either use or are aware of. Then, once you have progressed through the chapter, decide if they really are examples of cloud computing.

14.2 Core Concepts of Cloud Computing

Cloud computing is based on a number of core concepts, which we shall explore in this section. The most important concept for understanding cloud computing is virtualisation.

Virtualisation is the idea that a single, physical server can be divided into several **virtual** servers. The software on each virtual server 'believes' that it is actually operating on its own physical server, but in fact the system is invisibly sharing the resources between several virtual servers. Each virtual server has its own operating system, which can be different to the others. Each one also has its own virtual storage, which, again, is actually being invisibly shared with other virtual servers on the same physical server.

In a cloud computing system, the service provider has a server farm consisting of multiple physical servers. Each server then uses virtualisation to create multiple hosted instances on each server. Figure 14.2 illustrates the basic architecture of cloud computing.

Case Study

Virtualisation

Parallels Desktop for Mac (*PDfM*, Figure 14.1) is an example of virtualisation software that is available to the general public. Users of *PDfM* can create as many 'virtual machines' as they wish. Although the software is run on a Mac, each virtual machine emulates a typical PC hardware architecture, including virtual hard disks, virtual RAM and a virtual processor.

A user of *PDfM* can use the software to simultaneously run different PC operating systems on the same computer.

PDfM has many advantages. Firstly, because a user can use several different operating systems at the same time, it is useful for running older software that only works on an older operating system. Secondly, software developers can test software in a virtual machine without risking corrupting their own computer. Finally, a user can use a single physical machine to host several different operating systems, without having to purchase several computers.

Figure 14.1 shows *PDfM* which has been used to create five different virtual machines. Two of them are open – one running *Windows 7* and one running *Windows 11*. Each operating system 'believes' that it is running on its own, dedicated hardware.

Note: *Parallels Desktop* is not an example of cloud computing. It is an example of virtualisation, a concept that is then used in cloud computing.

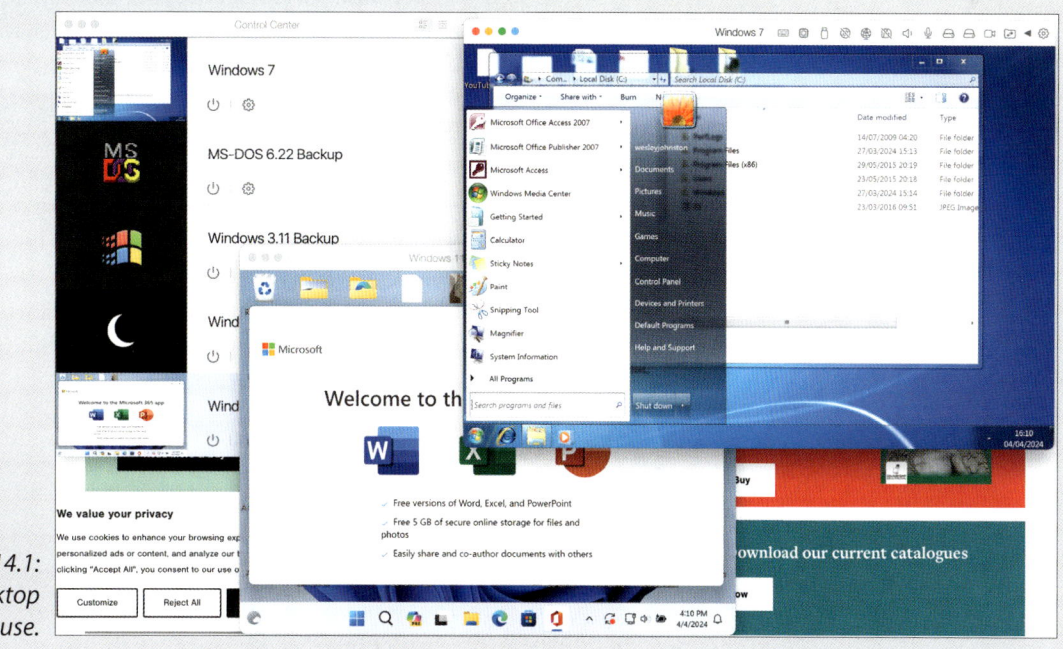

Figure 14.1: Parallels Desktop in use.

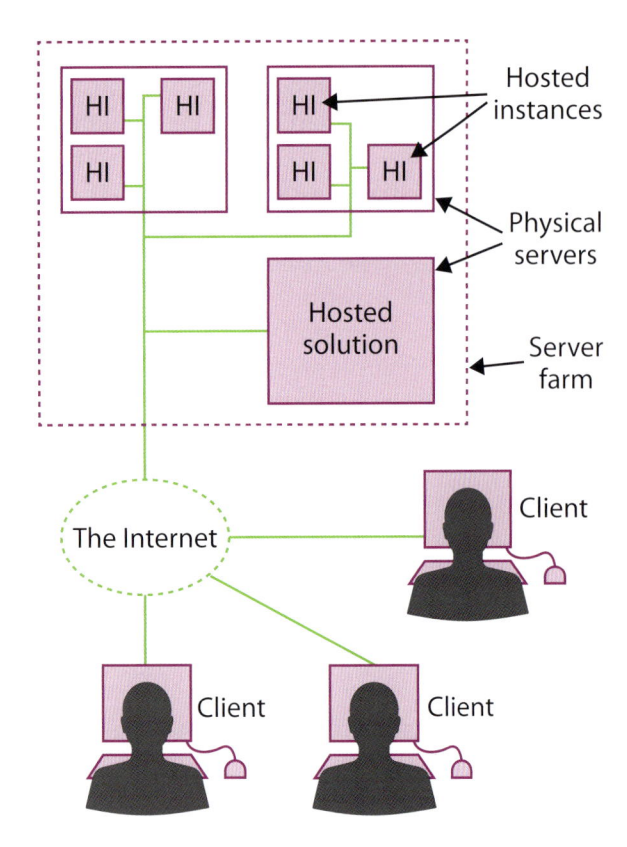

Figure 14.2: The basic architecture of cloud computing, featuring a server farm with three servers. Two are providing multiple hosted instances, while one is set up as a hosted solution, as discussed in the text.

A **hosted instance** (sometimes called a cloud instance) is a virtual server that is sharing a physical server. As thousands of hosed instances are needed in a typical server farm, different groups of hosted instances are located on different physical servers within the server farm. However, all of them are connected to the computer network within the farm and ultimately to the wider internet.

When a user first purchases (subscribes to) a hosted instance, they specify the desired computing resources such as CPU, memory, storage and operating system. However, the actual physical resources are not assigned to the user's hosted instance until the user actually logs in to use the resources. At that point, the service provider allocates the necessary disk space and computing power to the user. When the user stops using the hosted instance, the cloud provider reduces resource allocation, either by pausing the hosted instance or closing it entirely.

This model gives the service provider the flexibility to dynamically allocate resources between different users as demand rises and falls, meaning they are using their physical resources more efficiently. From the user's point of view, they save money because they only pay for the resources they need and – depending on the subscription model – might not need to pay at all for periods when they are not using the hosted instance. The user also benefits from rapid scalability – if they find that their resources are no longer adequate, they can pay for additional resources, which are then dynamically allocated by the cloud system.

For some users, however, a hosted instance is not a sufficient solution. For example, if a client wants their server to be operating continuously, or if their software cannot cope with the processor speed rising and falling as other users share the physical server, they can pay for their own dedicated hardware and software resources. This is known as a **hosted solution** (see Figure 14.2). With a hosted solution, the cloud provider guarantees to allocate the resources to the client for their exclusive use. The advantages are guaranteed performance and availability of resources without the need to physically manage a server on the client's own premises. The disadvantages are the higher cost associated with hosted solutions, and the greater difficulty in scaling up resources if the hosted solution becomes inadequate.

Within the server farm, dedicated software continuously manages the distribution of resources and hosted instances across the physical servers. This is known as **clustering** and its aim is to ensure maximum performance. For example, the system will seek to distribute active hosted instances in such a way that no single server becomes overloaded. If a particular cloud service – for example *Office 365* – has many thousands of users, the clustering system will create multiple hosted instances for the same cloud service, so that each one only has to handle a certain number of connections at once. This also improves reliability: if one hosted solution were to suffer a software failure and need to be restarted, clients can be switched seamlessly to a different instance while the problem is corrected.

14.3 Services Offered by Cloud Computing

Cloud services have become widespread in recent years and provide a huge range of services. In this section we shall consider five specific services.

Note: The CCEA specification explicitly mentions all five of these, so you should be able to explain how cloud computing can provide each service.

Data storage

Cloud computing can provide data storage on a remote server so that users do not need to store the data on their own devices. There are different ways in which this can happen. For example, the cloud might provide a database that users then interact with to store and update records. Some financial accounts software now offers cloud storage so that the data files themselves are stored 'in the cloud' and then accessed via software on the user's machine. Other services such as *Dropbox* offer a classic file storage system, which resembles a hard disk, except that it is being accessed remotely.

There are several advantages of providing a data storage service in the cloud:

- **Increased access to data**: A user can access the same data from multiple devices, located in multiple locations. They do not need to save it to flash drives or other removable storage in order to use it in different places.
- **Increased data durability**: As it is stored in remote locations, it is unaffected by localised issues such as a fire in the business premises.
- **Increased data security**: Encryption and password protection ensure that data is secure both as it is stored and as it is transferred to and from the cloud.
- **Automated backups**: Software can be configured to automatically back up data from a local computer to the cloud. For many enterprises, this has eliminated the need to make manual backups and physically store them off site.

Case Study

iCloud

iCloud is a cloud storage service provided by Apple. Its purpose is to securely store and synchronise data across Apple devices, including *iPhone*, *iPad*, *Mac* computers and Apple *Watch*.

Users typically have a variety of data types on their devices, such as photos, videos, documents, music, contacts and calendars. *iCloud* acts as a centralised repository for this digital content, making it accessible from any Apple device with an internet connection that is logged into that *iCloud* account.

For example, a user may take a photograph with their *iPhone* and, a few minutes later, the same picture will appear in the Photos app on their *iPad*.

iCloud can also be configured to automatically back up users' devices to the cloud so that, in the event of a hardware or software fault, all their data can be recovered safely.

At the time of writing, Apple offers a free account with up to 5 GB of storage space. Users can then take out a monthly subscription to increase this by various amounts, up to 2 TB, depending on the service level chosen.

Email

At its core, an email service relies on servers to send, receive, store and manage email messages. With a cloud service, these servers are located on the cloud, rather than requiring hardware or software within an organisation's premises. The cloud provides the mail server to send and receive email, as well as storage to keep the email data long term.

A well-known example is *Gmail*, which provides email services in the cloud that can be accessed in different ways. The simplest way is to log in to the service using a web browser and use the web interface directly. Another way is to connect an email client such as Microsoft *Outlook* to the *Gmail* server, which then uses the cloud service in the background, while the user can enjoy the specific features of the *Outlook* software.

Cloud-based email systems have a number of advantages:

- **Reliability**: Cloud-based email systems rarely go 'down' because they are hosted by service providers who have thousands of servers that can come online in the event of a fault.
- **Accessibility**: A cloud-based email system can be accessed from any device with a web browser and, because the emails themselves are stored remotely, users can see their previously sent and received mail from anywhere in the world.
- **Ease of use**: A company can set up a cloud-based email solution without needing specialist IT managers or setting up dedicated servers.

Virtualised software

Software virtualisation occurs when software is run on a virtual computer (a hosted instance) located in the cloud, rather than on a local device. Virtualisation was discussed earlier in this chapter: as we saw, the virtual computer runs an operating system that supports the software that needs to be run. The user connects to the virtual computer using a program on their local computer that simply acts as a gateway – it sends keyboard and mouse input to the virtual computer and receives back the screen image to display to the user. To the user it feels as if they are using a traditional desktop computer.

In some organisations, such as the NHS, when a staff member logs in to their computer what they are actually accessing is a virtual computer (the hosted instance) located in the cloud. Because the applications are also run in the operating system on the virtual computer, the user can run applications that may not even be able to run on their own computer. So, for example, a user using an old computer with an outdated version of *Windows* can use it to log into a virtual computer running the most recent operating system.

There are several advantages to virtualised software:

- **Ease of management**: Organisations do not need to manually install software on every computer in the enterprise or keep every computer fully up to date. Software can be installed in the cloud much more easily and then replicated to every hosted instance.
- **Instant updates**: Software updates, for example a new version of Microsoft *Word*, can be installed and made instantly available to all users.
- **Flexible working**: Organisations can set up 'hot desks' – computers that are used by different people at different times – with ease, as nobody's files are stored on the computer itself, so it can be treated as a generic console.
- **Security**: As nobody's files are stored locally, the data is more secure. A potential data thief would gain nothing from stealing the physical computer.

Backup

A backup is simply a copy of data made to guard against the risk of data loss. Cloud computing, with its remote storage, is ideal for backup services as it ensures that the copies are stored far from the organisations' premises. In addition, the amount of storage available is effectively unlimited as it can be increased as required.

A backup service requires some software on the local network that can communicate with the cloud service to manage the process. Backups can be automated to take place at regular intervals, for example during the night when there is less data traffic on the network, or continuously, where files are constantly uploaded to the cloud as they are modified. In both cases, historic copies of data are kept, as well as the most recent version. So if, for example, the organisation discovered that a file had been corrupted ten days previously, the cloud service could retrieve the last uncorrupted version from an earlier backup. The service will determine the exact backup policy and for how long files are kept.

There are several advantages to a cloud-based backup. In addition to the advantages offered by generic cloud storage discussed earlier in this section, these are:

- **Offsite storage**: Backups made by a business are often stored on the premises, which makes them vulnerable to destructive events, such as fire or earthquake. Cloud backups are always located offsite.

- **Automation**: Once set up, the backup system typically runs with no further human input required. It is, of course, worth checking periodically that the backups are still being made properly.
- **Ease of management**: Cloud backup systems have user-friendly interfaces meaning that even non-experts can set them up successfully.

Remotely hosted applications

Remotely hosted applications have some similarities with virtualised software, except that, instead of providing an entire virtual machine for the user, the remote server provides the user with direct access to the software. The user only sees the software itself, rather than the environment it is running in. This is an example of Software as a Service.

We have already seen the example of *Office 365*, Microsoft's remotely hosted application service. Subscribers can access cloud versions of Microsoft *Word*, *Excel*, *PowerPoint* etc., which they can use via a web browser. Users log in and use the applications directly, without needing to interact with a virtualised remote operating system.

Another example is Google *Workspace*, which is a web-based remotely hosted application service. In addition to providing access to the *Gmail* email system, users can access various applications including a word processor, a calendar, a chat system, as well as Google *Meet*, software that facilitates remote meetings. None of this software has to be installed on a person's own computer.

There are a number of advantages to remotely hosted applications:

- **Compatibility**: There are no issues with software being incompatible with different operating systems. The software can be used on any device that has an up-to-date web browser.
- **Collaboration**: Cloud-based applications make it easy for different users to work on the same files from different locations.
- **Integration**: Because cloud-based services typically offer a suite of software that is mutually compatible, it is easy to move data from one application to another, such as from a calendar to a meeting app or from a spreadsheet program to an email app.

14.4 Business Benefits of Cloud Computing

In the previous section we discussed the particular benefits of specific types of cloud service. In this section we shall consider the benefits of cloud computing to business in a more general sense.

Firstly, it means businesses do not have to invest in expensive hardware that has to be stored on their premises. Such hardware could end up being insufficient or, alternatively, be under-utilised and hence wasted. Instead, businesses can use cloud services, paying only for the resources they use. The up-front cost is minimal, while the ongoing expenditure can be scaled depending on need, and within the limits of the cloud subscription model. This means that future expenditure is more predictable for management, since it will more closely correlate with the level of business activity.

Secondly, cloud computing offers scalability, because it means that businesses can scale resources up or down at short notice. For example, if the company suddenly wins a new job or experiences a surge in website visitors, and they rapidly need more infrastructure, this can be done in hours rather than weeks. Conversely, if there is a sudden downturn in activity, such as occurred during the 2020 Covid-19 pandemic and lockdown, resources can be released to save money, albeit within the terms of the subscription service. With cloud services there is effectively no limit to the scalability of the service being used by a business.

Thirdly, cloud computing reduces the need for businesses to employ IT specialists to maintain their servers and network. Such specialists will still be needed in larger enterprises, but the cloud providers take care of much of the background work such as maintaining the servers, running backups and installing software updates.

Fourthly, cloud computing promotes innovation for businesses because a business can hire a server, on which to try out new software or a new product offering, at a lower cost than hosting it themselves. This can get the product to market more rapidly, potentially beating competitors. This method also reduces risk because, in the event of the new product being a failure, the costs incurred are lower. This would encourage business owners to be more innovative.

Fifthly, cloud computing allows businesses to benefit from a wider range of services than would be possible with their own in-house server. The business could subscribe to a range of servers with different architectures and operating systems, or different software services such as databases, without having to operate a separate physical machine for each one. A company could use several cloud service types for the same cost as a single in-house service.

Finally, cloud computing allows even small businesses to use high-quality server infrastructure, because they can subscribe to the services from a cloud provider, rather than having to invest in equipment that might be too expensive for a start-up. Cloud services can, therefore, act as an incubator to allow news businesses to get established.

Task

Two entrepreneurs, Declan and Suzanne, are considering starting a new, small IT business. Assess the pros and cons of using cloud computing for their infrastructure needs. (If helpful, you can choose what type of IT services they will offer.)

14.5 Security Issues in Cloud Computing

Cloud computing is not without problems, and the principal one is security. In this section we shall discuss some of the security issues raised by this technology.

Firstly, the security of data itself is an important issue. Because cloud computing involves storing and processing data on remote servers operated by third-party providers, there is always the risk of unauthorised access or data loss. Cloud providers mitigate this problem by using security measures, such as encryption, for data in transit and when stored, strict controls over who can access the data, and constant vigilance against cyber-attacks. Customers of cloud services must reinforce this by co-operating with the security measures, for example by limiting which employees have access to data and ensuring proper use of password protection.

Secondly, cloud computing raises concerns about the privacy of sensitive or personal information stored in the cloud. Cloud providers and their customers must adhere to local data protection laws to ensure privacy. This goes beyond simply securing the data. There are laws about whether it is even legal to store certain types of personal data, and for what purpose. In addition, there are laws about where data can be sent in the world. The European Union, for example, has laws limiting what personal data can be transferred outside the EU. This means that, in some cases, it *does* matter where in the world a server farm is located.

Thirdly, many businesses – such as those in the banking and arms industries – are regulated in ways that go further than the general laws that apply to everyone. Cloud providers must be able to certify that they comply with any specific regulations that might apply to sensitive military data and valuable financial information. This does not remove the responsibility from businesses, who must also ensure that they are aware of such regulations and ensure they comply with them themselves.

Finally, businesses that rely on cloud services may become concerned about vendor 'lock-in'. Once a business has established a relationship with a cloud provider, their own systems may become so closely tied to the cloud provider that it would be very difficult to switch providers. This is bad for business, because it could encourage the cloud provider to raise prices, since they know that the business would face significant costs to transfer even to a cheaper provider. Larger businesses can mitigate this risk by choosing to subscribe to more than one cloud provider at once, effectively setting up competition between the providers and thus establishing an incentive for the cloud providers to continue to provide the best service.

Task

An airline decides to store all its data in the cloud. Assess this decision, with a particular focus on data security.

CHAPTER 14 – CLOUD COMPUTING

Case Study

As Zinga Technologies grew, managers eventually faced a critical decision about their infrastructure investment. Their expanding portfolio of projects and need for development resources meant that the company needed additional resources. The company had to choose between investing in a dedicated server for their software development or leveraging a cloud service.

Deirdre, the IT manager, carried out a detailed study into the pros and cons of both solutions. With a dedicated server the company would have complete control over the server and could customise it exactly to their needs. They would also be able to predict the (high) setup costs exactly, and the ongoing costs would be lower than a cloud solution. They would also be able to better ensure data privacy, since no data would have to leave the building.

On the other hand, she also recognised that a dedicated server would take a lot of work and skill to set up and maintain, and that the company would be wholly responsible for ensuring the software was kept up to date, making the company more vulnerable to a cyber-attack and less able to recover in the event of data loss.

Deirdre then considered the cloud solution. She noted that there would be minimal setup costs and the Zinga staff would not need to spend time configuring the server. While ongoing costs were higher with a subscription to a cloud service, the bills were predictable and would mirror the amount of work the business had. The cloud service would also be more scalable, meaning that she could pay for additional server resources quickly if the need arose. Finally, she was drawn to the fact that the cloud company would take care of backups and the security of the data on the cloud server.

After careful consideration, Zinga Technologies decided to opt for a cloud solution for their software development needs. By choosing a cloud solution, Zinga Technologies gained the agility, scalability and cost-effectiveness needed to support their growing software development initiatives with high standards of data security and reliability.

Questions

1. What is meant by cloud computing?
2. What is the difference between a public cloud and a private cloud?
3. Define the concept of virtualisation in the context of cloud computing.
4. What is a hosted instance in cloud computing?
5. Explain what is meant by the term 'hosted solution'.
6. How does clustering contribute to the efficiency and reliability of cloud services?
7. Briefly explain the advantages of using *iCloud* for data storage.
8. Describe how cloud computing can provide an email service.
9. Describe two advantages and one disadvantage of using cloud computing for data storage.
10. Describe how cloud computing can provide remotely hosted applications.
11. Explain how cloud computing can provide a backup service and assess the business benefits of doing so.
12. Discuss the security concerns associated with cloud computing and some ways these concerns can be addressed.

CHAPTER 15
Legislation

> **By the end of this chapter students should be able to:**
> - describe the main features of the following legislation:
>   – the Data Protection Act;
>   – the Copyright, Designs and Patents Act; and
>   – the Computer Misuse Act;
> - understand and apply how each piece of legislation may impact on organisations, their employees and members of the public.

15.1 Introduction

This chapter provides an overview of the key legal frameworks in the digital technology sector. We will explore three significant pieces of legislation: the Data Protection Act, the Copyright, Designs and Patents Act and the Computer Misuse Act. The discussion covers the content of each piece of legislation, as well as how these legislative frameworks impact organisations, employees and members of the public.

15.2 The Data Protection Act

The Data Protection Act (DPA) is a comprehensive piece of UK legislation that is intended to protect the personal data of individuals. Prompted by the rapid growth of the internet and increasing levels of processing of digital data, it established legal requirements for organisations on how they collect, process, store and share personal information.

> **Note:** The DPA applies only to personal data, that is, data that relates to an individual person. It does not apply to non-personal data, such as data about a company as a whole or generalised information such as its annual accounts.

The DPA was first passed into law in 1984. However, it has been revised and updated several times since then, most recently in 2018 to incorporate changes introduced by the European Union's General Data Protection Regulation.

Principles

The DPA defines eight principles that organisations must comply with. These are:

1. **Fair and lawful processing**: Personal data must be processed in a way that is both fair and lawful, and individuals must be informed about how their data will be used. For example, a company that collects the email addresses of customers in order to send them a newsletter cannot use the same data for targeted advertising without the customers' expressed permission.

2. **Purpose limitation**: Personal data should only be collected for specified and legitimate purposes and not be further processed in a manner incompatible with those purposes. For example, a healthcare company that collects data on patients cannot sell this data on to a pharmaceutical company without the patients' consent.

3. **Data minimisation**: Organisations should only collect personal data that is adequate, relevant and limited to what is necessary for the purposes for which it is processed. For example, a company should not collect customers' home addresses if they are only planning to communicate by email.

4. **Accuracy**: Personal data should be accurate and kept up to date. Inaccurate data should be rectified or erased without delay. For example, if a customer lets a company know of a change of address, the company must update their records as quickly as possible. Failure to do so might result in personal data being seen by third parties.

5. **Storage limitation**: Personal data should not be kept for longer than is necessary for the purposes for which it is processed. For example, an online retailer must not store customers' credit card details after the payment has been processed.

6. **Integrity and confidentiality**: Personal data should be processed in a manner that ensures appropriate security, including protection against unauthorised processing and accidental destruction. For example, a company should protect customers' personal data with passwords and other security to prevent unauthorised access.

7. **Accountability**: Organisations are responsible for complying with the data protection principles and must be able to demonstrate compliance. For example, every organisation should have policies in place to comply with the legislation.

8. **Lawful basis for processing**: Organisations must have a lawful basis for processing personal data. For example, an organisation should not store data about employees' use of the internet without having a sound, business reason for doing so or having sought explicit permission from the employees.

Key roles

In addition to these eight principles, the DPA also defines four key roles. These are:

- **Data subject**: This refers to anyone whose personal data is being stored. This can include a customer, patient, employee or website user. Data subjects are granted rights under the DPA, such as the right to see a copy of the data held about them, the right to have errors corrected and (in some cases) to have data deleted.

- **Information Commissioner's Office**: This refers to an independent regulatory organisation that is responsible for ensuring that companies comply with the DPA, that people understand their rights and responsibilities under the law, and attempts to resolve disputes.

- **Data controller**: This refers to the person or organisation that holds the personal data and decides what to do with it. This could be a sole trader, an organisation or a government department. Data controllers are responsible for complying with the DPA and for registering with the Information Commissioner's Office.

- **Data processor**: This refers to any person or organisation that processes personal data. This role is wider than a data controller and can include other organisations such as a cloud service provider or a company that processes staff payrolls on behalf of a company. Data processors must only use data for the purposes defined by the data controller and must take adequate steps to protect data security.

Impact

For organisations, compliance with the DPA is mandatory, ensuring that personal data is processed lawfully, fairly and transparently. They must obtain a lawful basis for processing data, implement robust data security measures and respect individuals' rights under the legislation. Organisations are accountable for their data processing activities and are required to maintain records of their processing activities, conduct data protection impact assessments where necessary, and, in certain cases, appoint a data protection officer (DPO).

Because they are often the ones processing data, employees play a crucial role in ensuring compliance with the DPA. Employees need to be made aware of their organisation's data protection policies and procedures and receive adequate training on handling personal data responsibly. Employees must also uphold confidentiality obligations when handling personal data as part of their job roles and must comply with their organisation's policies under the DPA. For example, NHS staff often have access to patients' records, but are only permitted to do so for a clinical purpose. A staff member who accesses a patient's record without a good healthcare reason can be disciplined and even prosecuted.

For members of the public, the DPA grants rights and protections regarding their personal data. Individuals have the right to have their personal data processed fairly and lawfully, to be informed about how their data is used, and to exercise control over their data. They can make a request to access any personal data held by organisations, as well as request corrections or deletions if the data is inaccurate or no longer necessary.

Additionally, the DPA gives individuals the

right to be notified if their personal data has been compromised in a data breach that poses a risk to their rights and freedoms, enabling them to take appropriate measures to protect themselves. If an individual is unhappy with how an organisation is using with their personal data, they can make a complaint to the Information Commissioner's Office, which not only has the authority to investigate complaints, but to enforce compliance with the DPA.

> **Task**
>
> Search recent news stories and find a case of data being compromised due to a data breach. What happened after the breach? Was any organistion other than the organisation that was using the data involved?

The General Data Protection Regulation

> **Note:** The CCEA specification does not explicitly require you to have knowledge of the General Data Protection Regulation (GDPR), as it came into existence after the CCEA specification was written. However, it is discussed briefly here because it had a significant impact on the DPA. You can refer to it when asked to discuss data protection legislation generally.

The GDPR is a piece of legislation passed by the European Parliament in 2018. It applies in the EU and the European Economic Area. It also applies to organisations outside the EU that use data of individuals from the EU. When the UK left the European Union in 2020 its provisions remained in UK law.

Its aim was to harmonise data protection laws across the EU and increase the rights for individuals. Its main impact was on the DPA, which was updated to take GDPR into account. The main impacts on the DPA were the following:

1. **Strengthening data protection standards**: GDPR introduced stricter data protection standards and requirements compared to the DPA, including giving individuals enhanced rights regarding their personal data, such as the right to access, correct and erase their data, as well as 'the right to be forgotten'.

2. **Increased accountability and compliance requirements:** GDPR requires organisations to more clearly demonstrate compliance with data protection principles and regulations. This includes establishing comprehensive data protection policies, procedures and documentation.

3. **Enhanced enforcement and penalties**: GDPR significantly increased the penalties for failure to comply with data protection regulations. Organisations found in breach of GDPR may face fines of up to €20 million or 4% of their global annual turnover, whichever is higher.

4. **Enhanced data breach notification requirements**: GDPR requires organisations to report certain types of data breaches to the relevant supervisory authority within 72 hours of becoming aware of the breach.

All four of these enhancements were included in the 2018 revision of the DPA. Members of the public will have noticed these changes primarily in an increased number of requests for consent to use data, for example on websites and the need to explicitly 'opt in' to receiving marketing communications, rather than having to consciously 'opt out'.

15.3 The Copyright, Designs and Patents Act

For centuries, the law has recognised people's right to personal property and to be protected from theft. However, the advent of digital technology has focused greater attention on the concept of 'intellectual property' (IP), namely people's original ideas, and the principle that creators should be able to benefit from their creations and be protected from those who want to unfairly gain by copying them.

Traditional examples of IP are paintings, novels, poems and inventions. More recently, digital material such as movies, eBooks and computer software has been added to the list.

Consider if an obscure author wrote a novel, but a large book publisher they took the novel without permission and published it verbatim under a different name and sold thousands of copies. Most people would agree that is this would be unfair because the publisher was profiting from someone else's creation. The novel was the author's intellectual property and should be protected. The same principle applies to those who create computer software or any other type of IP.

Intellectual copyright theft, as it is known, not only has a negative impact on creators, but also discourages innovation as companies will not spend time and money producing products if they think people are going to copy them without paying for them. An educational book publisher would not produce school textbooks if schools were photocopying them in their entirety to avoid paying for them.

The Copyright, Designs and Patents Act (CDPA) is a piece of UK legislation designed to address this problem. It was first passed in 1988 but has been updated several times since then.

Principles

The CDPA establishes a number of key principles in the area of intellectual property. Some of the main principles are as follows:

- **Copyright**: The CDPA provides legal protection for original literary, artistic, musical, movie and dramatic works. Copyright automatically applies to eligible works upon creation, though many will include a copyright notice anyway, such as the one that appears at the start of this book. It gives creators the exclusive right to control how their works are used.
- **Moral rights**: The CDPA grants moral rights to creators, including the right to be identified as the author of a work, the right to object to unfairly critical treatment of their work, and the right not to have their work falsely attributed to someone else.
- **Duration of copyright**: The CDPA specifies the duration of copyright protection for different types of works. Generally, copyright lasts for the lifetime of the creator plus an additional 70 years after their death. For some government publications, such as Ordnance Survey maps, copyright expires after 50 years.
- **Exceptions and fair dealing**: The CDPA provides certain exceptions and limitations to copyright, allowing for fair dealing with copyrighted works. For example, a person can copy a certain amount of a book for research or quote short extracts in a review. Examination bodies such as CCEA can use copyrighted material in an examination paper without seeking permission, because the act of seeking copyright clearance might reveal the content of the paper ahead of time.
- **Performers' rights**: The CDPA grants performers certain rights, such the right to control the recording, copying and distribution of their performances.
- **Patents**: The CDPA grants inventors patents, namely the exclusive rights to their inventions for a limited period. For example, if someone invented and patented the perfect mousetrap, other companies could not copy the design. Perhaps one of the most well-known patents is that for the Tetra Pak's *Tetra Brik* packaging, which is used for distributing drinks.

- **International treaties**: The CDPA implements obligations arising from international treaties and agreements related to intellectual property between nations. Some countries have more relaxed intellectual property laws than others, which can create issues with companies whose products are produced or sold across the world.

Impact

Compliance with the CDPA is not only essential for organisations but is ultimately in their interests as it protects their own intellectual property and prevents expensive litigation. Organisations must ensure adherence to its provisions when dealing with copyrighted works, designs and patents. For example, a book publisher must obtain the rights to a work from the author. They must also seek copyright permission for any images or text quoted in the book that were not produced by the author. Failure to do so could result in legal action and loss of reputation.

Organisations also need to manage their own IP, which can include acting against individuals or organisations who breach the legislation. The CDPA encourages innovation and creativity because creators know that their ideas will have legal protection. This encourages organisations to invest in research and new product development to gain a competitive advantage.

One of the most significant areas that the CDPA applies to in organisations is computer software. Copying software without permission and without paying for it – commonly called **piracy** – is illegal and, in legal terms, amounts to theft. The CDPA gives software publishers the same protection as authors and composers. Companies must, therefore, ensure that all software they use has been legitimately obtained, paid for and properly licensed. Organisations must also take steps to protect software to ensure that it is not stolen by unscrupulous employees. Individuals and companies can be prosecuted if found to be engaging in software piracy.

Employees need to understand the organisation's policies and procedures regarding IP rights and comply with the requirements of the CDPA. This may involve education about copyright, design and patent laws, as well as their responsibilities and obligations. Employees should also be aware of their rights and obligations regarding IP created in the course of their employment, including rules governing ownership. For example, copyright in a work created as part of one's employment typically lies with the employer. Employees who create works need to be clear what their contract says on such matters. Some companies may reward employees who innovate by giving them a share of the IP rights.

Members of the public benefit from the CDPA because it grants them consumer rights and legal redress in the event of a legal breach. The limitations of the Act also gives reassurance to people in ambiguous situations, such as people seeking to reprint historical works that are out of copyright or wishing to quote a work as part of a book review or news article. A member of the public who creates a work has the same copyright protection as a large corporation.

Case Study

Zinga Technologies and the CDPA

Zinga Technologies' legal team conducted an internal audit to assess the company's adherence to the CDPA. They identified potential areas of concern regarding the unauthorised use of third-party code snippets and libraries in some of Zinga's software products. While the developers responsible for integrating these components had acted with good intentions to speed up software development, it raised significant legal implications.

Recognising the urgency of the matter, Zinga's management convened a team comprising legal experts, software engineers and project managers to address the compliance issue. Under the guidance of the legal department, the team meticulously reviewed each software component, documenting its origin, licensing terms and usage within Zinga's products.

In parallel with this job, Zinga initiated communication with the original creators and licensors of the identified third-party code to rectify any licensing discrepancies and obtain formal permissions where necessary.

Zinga then implemented stringent protocols and quality assurance measures to prevent similar compliance lapses happening in the future. They held employee training sessions on copyright law and software licensing practices, emphasising the importance of conducting due diligence and seeking appropriate permissions before integrating external code into proprietary software projects.

As a result of Zinga's proactive efforts, the issues were identified and rectified before they resulted in expensive legal action and public embarrassment.

15.4 The Computer Misuse Act

The Computer Misuse Act (CMA) is a piece of UK legislation first passed in 1990 and subsequently amended. While the previous two pieces of legislation were largely intended to guide legitimate uses of data, the CMA explicitly addresses computer-related crimes and unauthorised access and misuse of computer systems.

Principles

The CMA created three new criminal offences. These are as follows:

- **Unauthorised access**: The CMA makes it an offence to access a computer system or its data without permission or lawful authority. This can mean bypassing security measures, using stolen credentials or exploiting software vulnerabilities. The maximum penalty is a fine and/or up to two years in jail.

- **Unauthorised access with intent to commit or facilitate further offences**: This builds upon the offence of unauthorised access, by making it a more serious offence to gain unauthorised access with the intent to commit or facilitate further offences, such as theft, fraud, extortion or the creation and distribution of malware. This reflects the greater harm and financial risk that could come from malicious access. The maximum penalty is a fine and/or up to five years in jail.

- **Unauthorised acts with intent to impair the operation of a computer**: The CMA makes it an offence to carry out an unauthorised act that has the intent to impair the operation of a computer, either its system or the data. Examples of acts covered include launching denial-of-service attacks, introducing malware or viruses, disrupting network communication or altering or deleting critical system files. The maximum penalty is a fine and/or up to ten years in jail.

The CMA allows UK citizens to be prosecuted if they commit the offence outside the UK, provided it impacts a UK individual or causes significant effects in the UK.

The law does allow for unauthorised computer access in some cases. For example, in certain circumstances, law enforcement officers are permitted to access computer systems without permission.

Impact

The CMA focuses on the importance of cybersecurity, compliance and ethical conduct in the digital age.

Organisations must implement robust security measures to protect their computer systems, networks and data from unauthorised access and misuse. However, the focus of the CMA is the crime rather than protection from the crime. This means that an organisation must ensure that it is not breaking the law itself. For example, a company trying to break into a competitor's computer network to steal data would be committing a serious offence. Similarly, the act of breaking into a computer network in order to unlawfully encrypt data with the intention of extorting a payment (called a ransom attack) is illegal. However, offences committed under CMA are difficult to enforce when they originate outside UK jurisdiction.

Employees should adhere to ethical standards and professional conduct when using computer systems and accessing data, respecting privacy rights and refraining from activities that could compromise cybersecurity or violate the law. There may be a temptation for an employee to misuse data. For example, if an employee is leaving a job and moving to a competitor, they may be tempted to copy some of their employer's data to take with them. This would be unauthorised, as it would not have their employer's permission, and hence be a criminal offence.

Members of the public can take precautions to protect themselves from cyber threats, such as using strong passwords, keeping software up to date, being cautious of 'phishing' attempts, and avoiding sharing sensitive information online. In the event of becoming victims of unauthorised access to their computer systems or data, members of the public have legal remedies under the CMA. This gives police more powers to investigate such events.

Task

'My boss got me to hack into a competitor's computer network. But I didn't do anything wrong because he's my boss and I have to do what he says.' Do you agree with this statement? Why or why not?

Questions

1. What is the primary purpose of the Data Protection Act?

2. Describe four principles of the Data Protection Act.

3. Describe what is meant by the following key roles defined by the Data Protection Act: data subject, information commissioner, data controller.

4. How did the General Data Protection Regulation impact the Data Protection Act?

5. What is meant by the term 'intellectual property'?

6. What are some of the key principles established by the Copyright, Designs and Patents Act?

7. Give an example of an exception to copyright allowed for by the Copyright, Designs and Patents Act.

8. What is the primary purpose of the Computer Misuse Act?

9. What are the three criminal offences defined by the Computer Misuse Act?

10. Describe how the Copyright, Designs and Patents Act protects the rights of creators.

11. Discuss the impact of the Data Protection Act on a bank.

CHAPTER 16
Ethical Considerations

> **By the end of this chapter students should be able to:**
>
> - explain the ethical considerations around:
>   – automated decision making;
>   – online censorship;
>   – monitoring of personal behaviour;
>   – artificial intelligence; and
>   – the capture, storage, and analysis of personal information.

16.1 Introduction

Ethics relates to the question of what is right and wrong, and how people should act in situations involving the concept of right and wrong. Some ethical questions are easy to answer – whether it is right or wrong to murder someone, for example. However, many ethical questions are more nuanced than this. For example:

- A friend tells you something in confidence, but you know the information could harm another friend. Should you respect the first friend's privacy, or pass on the information to the second friend?
- Is it OK to take £10,000 from your employer without permission? What about a box of blank paper? What about a piece of Blu Tak?

- A supplier fulfils an order but forgets to send you an invoice. Do you tell them?
- A friend asks you to repair their computer. You notice that all their private files are on the computer. Is it OK to look at them? What if you do, and then discover they have been doing something illegal? Do you respect their privacy or the law?

Task

Discuss each of the four examples above with another person. Do you agree or disagree with each other's points of view? Collate views from the whole class. Does everyone agree to the answer to each question?

The point is that there are no absolute answers to questions like this – different people will have different responses. In many cases ethical dilemmas are not governed by legislation and must instead be decided by the person using their own worldview and their concept of right and wrong.

Those who work in digital technology face ethical questions of different types on virtually a daily basis, so it is vital for you to understand not only that you will do so, but to consider the various ways you have of responding to them. In some cases, there is a consensus in the industry – for example, that you should not look at someone's personal files without permission. In other cases, the industry has yet to reach a consensus – for example, the right way to use images generated by artificial intelligence (AI). And in some specific cases you will have to decide yourself. It is important, therefore, for you to spend time thinking about your own ethics and principles before you take up employment, and as technology continues to develop.

The CCEA specification requires you to consider the ethical issues around five distinct areas of digital technology. We shall consider these in this chapter. However, these are only some examples of ethical issues, and you should be aware that there are many others.

16.2 Automated Decision Making

Systems that are capable of automated decision making are often – though not necessarily – driven by AI. Examples of automated decision making include recommendations algorithms for platforms such as Spotify and Amazon, self-driving cars, just-in-time ordering systems in supermarkets, and spam filtering algorithms. All these systems can make decisions that impact humans to various degrees – from the mundane (such as what music to recommend) to the irritating (such as putting genuine emails in the junk folder) to matters of life-and-death (such as how to drive an automated car in fast-moving traffic). Systems that can make decisions autonomously raise a range of ethical issues, some of which are:

- **Transparency**: Unlike human decision-makers, AI algorithms often use neural nets that a human cannot 'read', making it challenging to understand how they are arriving at their conclusions. This lack of transparency raises questions about fairness and the potential for biases to be encoded within the algorithms, leading to discriminatory outcomes. If historical data used to train an algorithm reflects existing societal biases, the algorithm may perpetuate or even exacerbate inequalities.

  For example, a company may develop an AI to screen job applications, trained on the recruitment process that was followed for existing employees. If the company has historically had more male than female employees, the system may, by using this training data, develop an unfair bias against female applicants.

- **Mistakes**: While algorithms can process vast amounts of data at impressive speeds, and may even be more reliable than a human, this does not mean that they are infallible. In critical domains such as healthcare, these errors can have serious consequences for individuals' lives. If a healthcare AI led to improved outcomes for nine patients but a worse outcome for one patient, would this be ethically acceptable? The tenth patient would have had a better outcome if the AI had not been used, but is this outweighed by the better outcome for the other nine?

- **Accountability**: Who should be held accountable when an algorithm produces a harmful outcome? Should it be the developers who designed the algorithm, the individuals or organisations that are using it, or the algorithm itself? Is it even possible for an algorithm to be held responsible for its actions? In the UK, it has now been established that responsibility for crashes involving self-driving cars will lie with the car manufacturer, but there are many other similar dilemmas to be resolved.

- **Employment**: Human beings typically earn a living through work. Companies can use automated technology to do jobs that previously required a computer. Doing so often costs the company less, improving profitability and potentially making products better and more affordable. Yet doing so can also reduce jobs for humans and lead to increased unemployment. Is this 'just one of those things', such as when textile factories destroyed the home weaving industry, or do we have an ethical duty to put the needs of human beings ahead of business considerations? And if the latter, how ca that be done in practice?

Case Study

Automated decision making in war

Recent wars, such as that between Russia and Ukraine that intensified in 2022, have involved the intensive use of un-manned drones fitted with explosives. These drones are typically controlled by humans. However, several states are developing autonomous drones that can hover over enemy territory and select targets and strike using algorithms, without a human being involved in making the decision. This raises the prospect of AI-controlled drones autonomously deciding to kill people.

This triggers significant ethical questions. Is there is an ethical difference between (1) a soldier shooting an enemy soldier with a gun (2) a solder sitting in a base ten miles from the front line killing an enemy soldier with a drone (3) an AI-controlled drone deciding to kill an enemy soldier using only its internal algorithms? As a computer programmer, would you be comfortable developing technology such as this?

Moral issues like this are likely to increase as AI increasingly becomes a tool for the military.

16.3 Online Censorship

Censorship refers to the practice of banning or suppressing certain types of information, normally to suit a particular cultural or political agenda. These come with varying degrees of ethical acceptability. For example, at one end of the spectrum, a social media site deciding to ban material that celebrates violent crime would have broad support in society. At the other end of the scale, if a government decided to ban all online activity by a rival political party, this would be seen in a poor light in most Western countries. Censorship, therefore, can be done for both good and bad reasons: ethical dilemmas usually arise when there is disagreement about whether the reasons are sufficient to justify the censorship. For example:

- **Freedom of speech**: This term refers to the freedom to express one's opinions and ideas without being restrained or censored by government. This principle protects not only popular viewpoints, but also unpopular viewpoints, and is generally regarded as one of the key components of a successful democracy. In practice, all democracies ban people from expressing certain viewpoints – for example encouraging terrorism – so there is always a balance to be struck. Online censorship becomes an issue for digital technology when IT companies, such as social media, attempt the practice. For example, should social media firms attempt to suppress viewpoints that (1) promote far-right views, (2) support capital punishment, (3) attempt to influence elections in foreign countries, (4) oppose same-sex marriage, (5) discuss graphic details of the Holocaust on a site designed for primary-school aged children? There is no limit to the number of questions that will arise, so it is important for you to have a well-developed worldview and framework of ethics to help you deal with questions like this.

Task

Discuss each of five examples of types of viewpoints that a social media company might attempt to suppress. In each case decide whether it should be suppressed or not. If you have different answers to each of the five, think about why you decided differently.

Case Study

Zinga and Censorship

Zinga Technologies runs websites for various companies. These companies must comply with the local laws in the countries they operate in. Two dilemmas they faced were as follows:

1. One company that allows people to post opinions on their site asked Zinga to write code to suppress posts by right-wing political parties and promote posts by left-wing political parties. This is censorship, but it is also the company's own decision to do this. Do they agree to write the code?

2. A second company operates in a country with a repressive government. There are widespread reports of ethnic cleansing in that country. The company said it wanted all posts about that topic to be deleted, otherwise the government would block the site in their country.

These were tough questions for Zinga. They decided to gather opinions from their own employees. The general view was that they should agree to the first request, but not the second. Management agreed to the first request, but was less sure about the second request, as it would mean a substantial loss of income. In the end management agreed to the request, on the grounds that their client would just get another company to do the work, so nothing would be gained by refusing.

Do you agree with their decisions? Why or why not?

- **Bias**: The decision on what to censor always informed by a certain set of underlying assumptions and beliefs about what is right and wrong. Therefore, all censorship promotes one worldview over another. Who gets to decide what that worldview is? News agencies are often accused by both the Left and Right of being biased against them. How does a social media website, for example, decide which political opinions cross the line into justifying censorship, and which do not?
- **Overreach**: Freedom of speech primarily protects people against government actions. Individual companies have more room to choose their own policies. However, if a particular company is large enough – for example, a social media giant – then their actions can have a significant impact on society. An ethical problem can arise if one company becomes so powerful that it can start censoring material to a degree that has a significant impact on society, politics, or even the course of wars. If companies are not clear exactly how they decide to censor material, this can raise issues of transparency and accountability.
- **Cultural sensitivity**: Something that is offensive in one culture may not be offensive in another. For example, publishing a caricature of the Prophet Muhammad is seen as highly offensive in Islamic countries and would likely be censored there, but would generally not be censored in the West. A Western computer scientist who was not well-versed in the social norms in other parts of the world might not even realise that it would be seen as offensive in other countries.

In Western countries such as the UK and Ireland, a great deal of value is placed on freedom of speech; therefore the bar for censorship must be set very high. However, some form of censorship is appropriate in certain cases, for example to protect children, or to prevent the spread of views that promote violence. The ethical dilemmas that we face in this area often derive from the tension that exists between these two needs.

16.4 Monitoring of Personal Behaviour

Every day both governments and private companies collect huge amounts of data about what we do in our everyday lives. Our phones typically record all the places we have been during the day and when this happened. Other people's phones may be doing the same thing. This means that someone who had access to all this information could, in theory, build a database of everyone in the country and who their friends were. Analysis of text messages and emails could add information about what you talk about, revealing your political and religious viewpoints and your plans for the future.

Such a terrifying level of digital monitoring might please an authoritarian regime but would be quite unacceptable in a Western democracy.

The ethical issues arise, then, from how we balance the potential benefits of technology with the right of individuals to their private lives. For example:

- **Privacy**: The Universal Declaration of Human Rights states that nobody can be 'subjected to arbitrary interference with [their] privacy, family, home or correspondence'. This means that states cannot monitor people's private lives without a very good reason. So, for example, police accessing someone's email if they have good reason to think the person is planning to carry out a terrorist act would likely be acceptable, but monitoring someone's movements purely to create a database of everyone's activity would be unacceptable. Just because digital technology can be used to do something does not mean that it should be used to do it. IT workers need to be aware not only of their own ethics, but also what the law says (see Chapter 15).
- **Humiliation**: Some companies monitor what their staff are doing to ensure productivity and spot potential issues. This is allowed, provided employees have been told and have consented to the monitoring. Problems can arise when companies monitor employees to a degree that may cause embarrassment or humiliation. For example, a company may decide to record how long employees take to go to the bathroom. A disabled employee may feel humiliated if then forced to explain why they take longer than other staff to do so.

Similarly, employees may be allowed to use the internet during their lunch breaks. It is generally considered inappropriate for a company to monitor what websites their staff visit in their own time, even if it is done on a work computer. This is because it may reveal private information that the employer has no business knowing. For example, an employee may be observed visiting sites to research personal matters such as a health issue or a marriage problem. Digital technology may allow monitoring at this level of detail, but when dealing with human beings, it may not be appropriate to do so.

Case Study

Amazon and monitoring staff

Starting in 2023, workers in Amazon's French warehouses had to wear a smart device on their wrists. The device tracked their movements in order to decide which task they could most efficiently be given next. It also flagged potential errors in scanning goods. The wristband was introduced to improve the efficiency of the warehouses. However, the device also tracked how long employees were spending on their breaks, and flagged alerts if they lasted more than a predefined period. The data was kept for up to a month.

In January 2024, a court in France ruled that the monitoring was 'excessive' and fined the company €32m (£27m) because some of the monitoring breached the General Data Protection Regulations (GDPR; see Chapter 15). Amazon disagreed with the ruling and said that they planned to appeal.

The British government has raised concerns, on a more general basis, that employee surveillance to this degree would lead to distrust between employees and managers, and that it would cause unnecessary stress to employees. This is an example of how technology can be used to improve businesses, but that it is necessary to find a balance with privacy.

Task

Do you think the level of monitoring Amazon engaged in in their French warehouses was reasonable? Why or why not?

- **Data security**: Personal data is, by its nature, personal and therefore unscrupulous people could use the data to their own advantage. It is therefore vital that personal data be kept as secure as possible. This was highlighted in Northern Ireland in August 2023 when the Police Service of Northern Ireland (PSNI) accidentally released a document containing the personal details (surnames, initials, rank, location, and department) of over 9000 employees. As PSNI officers are sometimes targeted by paramilitaries, the leak was later described as 'the most significant data breach that has ever occurred in the history of UK policing'. This is an example of the serious consequences that can arise from the inadequate security of personal data.

- **Informed consent**: At a minimum, ethical monitoring of personal behaviour requires the informed consent of those whose data is to be collected. In practice, however, many software companies have lengthy and complex user agreements that many users do not read and would not understand even if they did. It is important, therefore, that IT companies ensure that they are informed of what is going to happen in a way that they are likely to understand. It is also important that people know their rights in terms of withdrawing consent.

16.5 Artificial Intelligence

AI raises significant ethical issues that humanity is already debating. Some of these issues are:

- **Fake images:** One significant ethical concern with AI revolves around the creation and dissemination of fake images or 'deepfakes'. AI can generate highly realistic images or videos, often indistinguishable from authentic content. This technology raises concerns about identity theft, misinformation, and potential misuse in various fields. Notable instances include deepfake videos impersonating public figures for malicious purposes, making it increasingly difficult to trust visual media.

- **Fake news:** AI technologies, particularly natural language processing, can be employed to generate and spread fake news and disinformation on social media. Chatbots and automated content creation tools can be programmed to produce misleading narratives, influencing public opinion, and potentially undermining democratic processes. Large amounts of such information can be produced in minutes, leading to multiple reports of the same fictitious event – lending it credibility – before human reporters have time to independently verify whether it even happened.

- **Copyright:** The use of AI in content generation and creative works raises complex ethical questions related to copyright and intellectual property. For example, if a chatbot has been trained on the contents of copyrighted works, is this a breach of copyright? AI algorithms can autonomously create art, music, or written content, leading to challenges in determining ownership and proper attribution. Currently UK law states that only human beings can benefit from copyright protection, but this is a position that is likely to be challenged.

- **Bias and fairness:** AI systems, particularly those involved in decision-making processes, may inherit and perpetuate biases present in the data upon which they are trained. This can result in discriminatory outcomes, reinforcing existing societal inequalities. For instance, facial recognition algorithms have demonstrated biases against darker skin, leading to concerns about racial profiling and unjust treatment. Similarly, since AI must be trained by human beings, an AI can be trained to have any desired worldview. To demonstrate this point, a computer scientist in 2023 created a far-right chatbot that expressed xenophobic and racist views. The same problem occurred in February 2024 when Google launched their new *Gemini* chatbot. However, it was immediately criticised for being excessively inclusive, for example by generating images of ethnically diverse Nazis and insisting that mis-gendering someone was always wrong, even if doing so would be the only way to prevent a nuclear apocalypse.

- **Privacy:** AI applications often involve the collection and analysis of vast amounts of personal data, raising privacy concerns. Examples include surveillance technologies, predictive policing algorithms, and targeted advertising systems. Striking a balance between harnessing the benefits of AI and safeguarding individual privacy requires robust regulations, transparent data practices, and informed consent mechanisms.

- **Autonomous weapons:** As discussed earlier, the development of autonomous weapons and lethal AI systems introduces ethical dilemmas related to accountability, decision making, and the potential for misuse. Delegating life-and-death decisions to machines raises fundamental moral questions. Establishing international norms and regulations to govern the ethical use of AI in military contexts is an ongoing challenge.

Anyone seeking to harness the power of AI must also appreciate the ethical dimensions to the field. As AI advances, ethical considerations surrounding privacy, bias, and accountability will continue to take centre stage. Addressing challenges from deepfakes to autonomous weapons requires a commitment to transparency, fairness, and minimising biases.

16.6 The Capture, Storage, and Analysis of Personal Information

Many organisations – including businesses, government, and health services – collect, store, and analyse personal data (see Chapter 13 on data mining). This process raises a number of ethical questions. All of these have been considered in relation to the topics already discussed in this chapter, but include the following:

- **Privacy**: An organisation, such as a supermarket, collects a lot of personal information about customers. This includes not only names and addresses, but also sales data, which can be used to identify buying habits, the presence of children in the home, and so forth. The law is clear about how this information can be used, that the customer must consent to its collection, and how the customer can obtain copies of the data. The law also requires the organisation to only use the data for legitimate purposes. IT professionals must be aware of these laws and ensure software respects them. Some developers may even be able to access personal data while developing software. It is vital that the developers respect the privacy of individuals and their data in the course of their work.

- **Data security**: Once again, organisations must take adequate precautions to protect data from unauthorised access. An ethical company must take this risk seriously, since the consequences of a data release could be severe and long-lasting.

- **Intrusive marketing**: Companies are able to use data mining techniques to analyse personal information to generate highly bespoke marketing campaigns, tailored to each individual customer. However, excessively tailored campaigns can be unwelcome and even threatening. For example, people sometimes have the experience of searching for a particular product, and then a few days later they start to see adverts on other websites for the same product. While this may be intended to be useful, it can be intimidating if it makes the user feel that they are being monitored. People generally value their ability to live their private lives without other people knowing the details of what they are doing.

- **Bias and discrimination**: As before, the way personal information is analysed can lead to inadvertent bias. This can happen if algorithms are trained on biased data or have biased assumptions. It is important that IT professionals are aware of such possibilities and work to ensure that, as much as possible, software does not risk such biases.

16.7 Summary

Ethics permeates every area of digital technology. In this chapter we have considered ethics in a range of contexts, such as the ethical implications of automated decision-making systems, which can lack transparency and accountability. Online censorship brings ethical questions regarding the balance between regulating harmful content and preserving freedom of speech. The monitoring of personal behaviour raises concerns about privacy, data security, and the potential for intrusive surveillance. Artificial intelligence introduces ethical challenges related to bias, fairness, and accountability, particularly in the context of fake content generation, facial recognition technologies, and autonomous weapons systems. Finally, the capture, storage, and analysis of personal information requires ethical considerations in the areas of privacy, data security, informed consent, and the risk of bias and discrimination in data analysis.

The IT professional will regularly encounter ethical issues and must be clear about their own view of right and wrong, and how they should deal with the many ethical questions they will encounter. The questions are often complex, lacking an obvious answer. Navigating these ethical complexities requires a conscientious approach rooted in clear principles.

Questions

1. Define ethics and explain its relevance to digital technology.
2. How does the lack of transparency in AI algorithms contribute to ethical concerns?
3. Why is freedom of speech considered to be a crucial ethical principle in online censorship debates?
4. State three ethical concerns around artificial intelligence.
5. What is meant by 'informed consent' and how does it relate to ethical data gathering?
6. Why is accountability a challenging issue in the context of AI decision making?
7. State three ethical concerns around the monitoring of personal behaviour.

8. Explain the ethical significance of data security in the capture, storage, and analysis of personal information.

9. Describe the main ethical problems that could arise from automated decision making.

10. Assess the problem of deepfakes from an ethical perspective, and the implications it has for the IT industry.

11. 'It is OK for a programmer to read personal information held in a computer system as long as they don't use it'. Assess this statement from an ethical perspective.